DENYING DEATH

This volume is the first to showcase the interdisciplinary nature of terror management theory, providing a detailed overview of how rich and diverse the field has become since the late 1980s, and where it is going in the future. It offers perspectives from psychology, political science, communication, health, sociology, business, marketing, and cultural studies, among others, and in the process reveals how our existential ponderings permeate our behavior in almost every area of our lives. It will interest a wide range of upper-level students and researchers who want an overview of past and current TMT research and how it may be applied to their own research interests.

Lindsey A. Harvell received her Ph.D. from the University of Oklahoma in Social Influence and Political Communication in 2012. She is an assistant professor in the School of Communication Studies and an affiliate faculty member in the Department of Psychology at James Madison University. Dr. Harvell's research focuses on the extension of terror management theory (TMT) and using existential awareness in persuasive message design. Her research also focuses on political advertising messages and studying the effects of existential awareness on these messages.

Gwendelyn S. Nisbett received her Ph.D. from the University of Oklahoma in Social Influence and Political Communication in 2011. She is an assistant professor of strategic communication in the Mayborn School of Journalism at the University of North Texas. Dr. Nisbett's research examines the intersection of mediated social influence, political communication, and popular culture. Her research incorporates a multimethods approach to understanding the influence of fandom and celebrity in political and civic engagement.

DENYING DEATH

An Interdisciplinary Approach
to Terror Management Theory

*Edited by Lindsey A. Harvell
and Gwendelyn S. Nisbett*

Routledge
Taylor & Francis Group

NEW YORK AND LONDON

First published 2016
by Routledge
711 Third Avenue, New York, NY 10017

and by Routledge
2 Park Square, Milton Park, Abingdon, Oxon, OX14 4RN

Routledge is an imprint of the Taylor & Francis Group, an informa business

© 2016 Taylor & Francis

Library of Congress Cataloging-in-Publication Data
Denying death : an interdisciplinary approach to terror management
  theory / edited by Lindsey A. Harvell and Gwendelyn S. Nisbett.
    pages cm
  Includes bibliographical references and index.
  ISBN 978-1-138-84313-4 (hbk : alk. paper)—ISBN 978-1-138-84314-1
(pbk : alk. paper)—ISBN 978-1-315-64139-3 (ebk)
  1. Risk—Sociological aspects.   2. Death—Psychological aspects.
3. Terror—Psychological aspects.   I. Harvell, Lindsey, editor.
II. Nisbett, Gwendelyn S., editor.
  HM1101.D46 2016
  155.9'37—dc23
  2015034067

ISBN: 978-1-138-84313-4 (hbk)
ISBN: 978-1-138-84314-1 (pbk)
ISBN: 978-1-315-64139-3 (ebk)

Typeset in Bembo
by Apex CoVantage, LLC

Printed and bound in the United States of America by Publishers Graphics, LLC on sustainably sourced paper.

Lindsey dedicates this book to her mother, Cindi Reding, who always taught her anything was possible if you just put your mind to it and put your faith in God.

Gwendelyn dedicates this book to her parents, Patricia and Lindel, for their enduring support.

This book is also dedicated to our late adviser, Michael W. Pfau, Ph.D., who taught us that "theory is everything." Thank you for teaching us that being theory focused is the key to a successful program of research. We miss you every day. This one's for you.

CONTENTS

FIGURES AND TABLES

Figures

Table

PREFACE

For the past couple of decades, terror management theory (TMT) has taken a theoretical journey through psychology. During this journey, other disciplines began to take interest in TMT. The existential ponderings, while housed in psychology, penetrate our behaviors in almost every area of our life. Therefore, it makes sense that disciplines such as communication, business, culture, and law, to name a few, would take interest in this theory. As I was finishing my dissertation at the University of Oklahoma, I began thinking about how wonderful it is that TMT is emerging in all these other disciplines, giving the theory new life and breadth. Once this idea marinated for a while, the idea for the book occurred. There is yet to be a text explaining the interdisciplinary nature of TMT, until now. Collaborating with the top TMT scholars in the field, as well as up-and-coming TMT scholars, this book explores TMT in different disciplines with both overview chapters and original research chapters. These chapters provide an amazing snapshot into where TMT is today and where it will be going in the future.

—Lindsey A. Harvell, Ph.D.

ACKNOWLEDGMENTS

I would first like to thank my mother. After I finished my doctoral program, she said the next step was to write a book. I said, right, I'm a little young for that, don't you think? But alas, I ended up starting a book project. Thank you for always believing in me and never allowing me to give up. You are truly an inspiration. Thank you for teaching me that working hard always pays off in the end. I also want to thank Trent Bowman. Thank you for always listening to me lovingly during the final stages of the book and always understanding when plans needed to be changed in order to finish certain projects within the book. Next, I would like to thank my late adviser Michael W. Pfau for teaching me that theory is everything. Without the knowledge I gained from you at the beginning of my career, this book never would have happened. Thank you to my editor, Paul Dukes, for being amazing through this entire process and believing in the project. I would also like to thank all of the contributors to this volume. Without you, this book would not be possible. I am truly humbled to have you as a part of this project. I have enjoyed getting to know each and every one of you and look forward to future collaborations. Last, but not least, I know none of this would be possible without the peace and grace that the Lord provides. Thank you for giving me strength and peace of mind even when things were not going according to plan.

—Lindsey A. Harvell, Ph.D.

Thank you to my family for their support, my friends for always messaging me back, and a special thank you to the "Team" for providing a much needed distraction.

—Gwendelyn S. Nisbett, Ph.D.

1

TERROR MANAGEMENT THEORY

Exploring the Role of Death in Life

Alex Darrell and Tom Pyszczynski

Prior to the emergence of terror management theory (TMT; Greenberg, Pyszc-zynski, & Solomon, 1986) in the mid-1980s, empirically oriented psychologists devoted little attention to the possibility that the problem of death might play an important role in everyday life. When TMT was initially introduced, the idea that awareness of death might affect diverse aspects of human behavior that bear little obvious connection to human mortality seemed highly unlikely, if not patently absurd. Perusing the social psychological literature of the time, one might surmise the problem of death was of little, if any, consequence to people. As the ideas and research presented in this volume show, this turned out to be a serious oversight. Over the past 30 years, TMT has been used to shed light on a multitude of issues of longstanding interest both within the subdiscipline of social psychology and beyond. As this volume shows, it has also had a substan-tial impact on thinking outside of psychology, and touches on many issues of considerable practical and social significance (for a recent overview of TMT and discussion of how it relates to diverse aspects of life, see Solomon, Greenberg, & Pyszczynski, 2015). In this chapter, we provide a brief overview of TMT and the initial waves of research bearing on its fundamental propositions. We start with a brief consideration of the intellectual roots of the theory.

Intellectual Forefathers of Terror Management Theory

A human being is a synthesis of the infinite and the finite
—*Søren Kierkegaard (1983; p.13)*

Man is on the "cutting edge" of evolution; he is the animal whose develop-ment is not prefigured by instincts, and so he is open to becoming what he can
—*Ernest Becker (1975; p.34)*

The problem of death has likely troubled human beings ever since awareness of its inevitability first emerged among our early ancestors. Evidence of ritualized funerary practices, which predate the emergence of agriculture and written language, demonstrate that death was an early concern, dating back at least 20,000 years; there are even some hints of the possibility of ritual burial among Neanderthals 100,000 years ago, but this evidence is less clear (Mithen, 1996). Thus it is not surprising that history is full of musings about death from diverse cultural perspectives. Cultural mythologies portray death, or awareness of it, entering the world as a result of human caprice or divine punishment. In the Judeo-Christian tradition, eating from the tree of knowledge bestowed Adam and Eve with the awareness of mortality; in the Greek account, opening Pandora's Box released death and suffering into the world; and for the Chiricahua Apache, the Coyote tricked humankind into acknowledging death. Philosophers and theologians have continued to discuss the role that death plays in life ever since Gilgamesh, the first epic hero, sought immortality after the death of his close friend Enkidu at the hands of fickle gods. For all of Gilgamesh's legendary strength and bravery, it was the singular knowledge of death that terrified him. Cultural anthropologist Ernest Becker synthesized ideas about the role that death plays in life from various prominent thinkers, including Søren Kierkegaard, Otto Rank, Sigmund Freud, William James, Charles Darwin, Gregory Zilboorg, Norman Brown, Eric Fromm, and Robert Jay Lifton, in his Pulitzer Prize winning book, *The Denial of Death*, which was the primary inspiration for TMT.

Becker observed the human preoccupation with death and concluded that it stemmed from an inherent paradox unique to our species. The cognitive developments of language, future-oriented thinking, and self-awareness provide distinct adaptive advantages, increasing the flexibility of human behavior and therefore the likelihood of survival and procreation. Humans are able to use abstraction, which is manifested in the manipulation of symbols as well as long-term planning such as setting goals and imagining possible future situations in the absence of direct experience. These increased cognitive capabilities rendered our ancestors able to imagine the end of their individual existence, and thus aware of the inevitability of death. Awareness of certain mortality in an organism with a strong desire for life is the paradox at the core of our existence. According to Becker, this awareness creates the potential for an ever-present fear of death that must be continually repressed to make productive functioning in the world possible.

Becker theorized that one way of addressing the problem of death was through culture. According to Becker all societies and cultures are manifestations of the belief that human existence is meaningful, significant, and unending. By living up to the standards of value that our cultures provide, our existence, matters. As Becker put it, "Society itself is a codified hero system, which means that society everywhere is a living myth of the significance of human life, a defiant creation of meaning" (Becker, 1973; p. 31). It is the shared illusion of permanence and immortality among members of all cultures that gives the societal myth its power.

In the 1980s Sheldon Solomon, Jeff Greenberg, and Tom Pyszczynski, encountered Becker's ideas and thought they provided a useful framework for understanding a wide array of social psychological findings. Together they produced terror management theory (Greenberg et al., 1986) using Becker's work as their point of departure. TMT integrated Becker's ideas with ideas from contemporary experimental social psychology to establish a base from which to generate empirically testable hypotheses. This chapter provides an introduction to the theory and research assessing its fundamental propositions.

Terror Management Theory

Although the problem of death is at the heart of TMT, the theory was originally put forward as an explanation of what self-esteem is, how it is maintained, and, most importantly, why it is needed. Before TMT, a large body of research had demonstrated how low self-esteem led to a wide array of problems and led people to distort their perceptions of reality in order to defend against threats; the idea that the need for self-esteem was a driving force behind much human behavior was also widely discussed. However, a functional account of why the need for self-esteem existed and how it emerged did not exist.

Becker was fond of the term *hero*, which he used as an archetype of potential human greatness. The hero was one who set a moral example, who lived without fear of death, and in some instances, was able to conquer it. For Becker, a hero was a symbolic ideal, an amalgam of cultural values condensed into the ideal form of humanity. Societies constructed such exemplars as a means of expressing shared values, beliefs, mores, and traditions, which in turn allowed individuals within each culture to measure themselves against these symbolic standards. By this account, culture gave meaning to experience and established the standards that valuable individuals must meet. Living up to such standards provides self-esteem, and thus emotional security, while failing to do so leaves one vulnerable to fear, anxiety, and terror. This was the initial reasoning behind TMT.

According to TMT, in order to provide existential protection, cultural worldviews provide a shared lens for viewing life and reality that (a) gives life meaning and significance, (b) is perceived as permanent and enduring over time, (c) establishes the standards of value for individuals within the culture to live up to, and (d) provides some hope of immortality. Cultural worldviews provide the hope for two kinds of immortality: literal and symbolic. *Literal immortality* consists of continued existence after biological death; usually this takes the form of a prescribed religious afterlife (e.g., reincarnation, heaven, Elysium, Valhalla, etc.). *Symbolic immortality* entails being part of something greater than oneself that endures long after one's own physical death. It involves making meaningful and valuable contributions to something greater than oneself and thereby remaining relevant and remembered after one's biological death. For example, although Gilgamesh failed to obtain the secret of literal immortality, his story is still recounted and his name remembered many thousands of years after his purported death.

Once awareness of morality emerged, it could not be sealed back in Pandora's Box. However, death awareness did not occur in a vacuum, but rather alongside many otherwise highly adaptive cognitive capacities (e.g., symbol creation/use, forethought). TMT posits the same cognitive adaptations that led to awareness of the inevitability of death also enabled a partial solution to the terrifying problem it posed: Humans invented ritual, which allocated a sense of control over the vast unpredictability of the natural world and simultaneously allowed for moderate security in the face of inevitable terror. Anthropologists view ritual practice and thought as techniques for increasing the good in life while avoiding the bad. Rituals were used for increasing one's power (e.g., taking a scalp, eating the heart of an animal), increasing resources (e.g., crops, rainfall, game), and even in the formulation of one's self. Becker asserts the latter is what is expressed through "rites of passage," which constitute various symbolic practices at momentous occasions in life (i.e., birth, marriage, death) that metaphorically annihilate and re-create an individual. Regardless of its efficacy, ritualistic thought and practice allowed for beliefs to form around what was important to individuals and the group, and were transmitted orally until they solidified in the form of fixed cultural knowledge, where their efficacy was consensually validated by agreement from others rather than objectively scrutinized.

As cognitive evolution continued, human life became increasingly dependent on cultural symbol use. For example, if bad crops, natural disasters, disease, and so on, were not understood symbolically, then individuals would have to stand naked before the vast indifference of nature; however, cultural symbols allowed for explanation and an accompanying semblance of control. People did not get sick and die arbitrarily; they offended deities or forces and were punished. Occasionally a transgression was so egregious that the whole group suffered. The beliefs that were more psychologically protective for early humans were propagated over generations, and gradually our species moved away from hunter-gatherer bands concerned with immediate circumstances, to *cultural animals* that lived in rich symbolic landscapes of their own design, full of intangible entities and abstract values, which were created to assuage their ultimate fears.

Cultural worldviews are symbolic constructions that are by definition abstractions of observable reality, and therefore cannot be directly observed. For example, a dove is widely used as a symbol of peace; however, one does not ever observe peace, but rather understands the concept metaphorically as qualitatively similar to a dove, such as tranquil, fragile, beautiful, and so on. Additionally, certain components of a cultural worldview may contradict observable reality. If two armies each receive omens of victory, one will invariably have to admit that they "misread" the signs. Due to the ephemeral nature of cultural worldviews, confidence in them requires others who share one's beliefs to continually validate them. Sharing a belief system lends credibility to its claims, and the more individuals that share and consequently reinforce a cultural worldview, the more valid it appears. However, cultural worldviews vary (sometimes dramatically) over place and time. Therefore, becoming aware of a differing construction of reality calls into question the legitimacy of both perspectives. This conception is central to TMT. Indeed a good deal of the initial empirical support for the theory came from findings of increased bias, derogation, and aggression toward those who do not support, and subsequently threaten, an individual's cultural worldview.

Although cultural worldviews are shared constructions, people construct their own individualized worldviews by abstracting the diverse experiences and ideas to which they are exposed over their early years of life, which continue to evolve for most people over the course of life. Clearly we do not begin life with an understanding of death; we do not even begin life with a fundamental understanding of ourselves. This lack of understanding about ourselves leads to the question of how death awareness and the anxiety-buffering capacities of cultural worldview and self-esteem develop in an individual. TMT has drawn heavily from attachment theory (Bowlby, 1982) to answer this question.

Newborns are incapable of fending for themselves and rely entirely on their primary caregivers for comfort and sustenance. This caring behavior supports strong bonds between primary caregivers, usually parents, and developing children, who come to associate parental affection with security. As children develop, their primary caregivers gradually stop showing unconditional affection, but rather favor increasingly complex and culturally desirable behaviors (e.g., crawling, walking, verbalization, etc.), while withdrawing affection for incorrect conduct (e.g., biting, hitting, tantrums, etc.). Consequently, children shift their center of security to living up to their parents' standards. Parents are presumably already instilled with a cultural worldview and thus their responses to the child reflect what is valued by their culture. As children develop further, they not only become aware of themselves as individuals, but become aware of their parents' limitations. Since parents inevitably fall short of the godlike security they initially project, a broader base of security is necessary. Children begin attending school and religious services, and in so doing, learn about their national and spiritual heritage. A shared history of values, beliefs, mores, and ethics is revealed to them, which contain the basis of their cultural worldview. With increasing exposure to these ideas, children gradually shift their sense of security away from their parents and toward their culture. However, the attachment bond remains active as a source of emotional security throughout the lifespan (Mikulincer & Shaver, 2003). Indeed, close relationships have been proposed as a third component of the anxiety-buffering system, along with worldviews and self-esteem (Mikulincer, Florian, & Hirschberer, 2004). Empirical evidence for this third pillar will be elaborated on later in the chapter and discussed in more detail throughout this volume.

At its heart, TMT posits that people are consistently, and unconsciously, motivated to maintain faith in their cultural worldviews, self-esteem, and close relationships to protect themselves from the anxiety produced by awareness that death is inescapable. However, as previously mentioned, cultural worldviews are symbolic, and even if they are supported by others, they remain ultimately unstable. Their fragile construction means that a modicum of vigilance is always necessary, especially during social interactions. Social interactions pose the largest potential threat, as one's worldview can always be challenged by others; however, these interactions are also essential for consensual validation of the anxiety buffer to occur. We turn now to a brief overview of the empirical support for the central propositions of TMT.

Evidence for the Fundamental Propositions

Researchers have been testing hypotheses derived from TMT for over 30 years. Hundreds of experiments testing distinct hypotheses across diverse cultures have yielded support for the theory and its core propositions. To date this literature consists of over 500 experiments conducted in over 30 different countries the world over. In the following paragraphs we provide a very brief overview of the major lines of evidence relevant to the theory. For more thorough recent reviews, see Greenberg, Vail, and Pyszczynski (in press), or Solomon et al., (2015).

Mortality-Salience Hypothesis

The first empirical support for TMT came from studies testing what has become known as *the mortality-salience hypothesis*, which states that if cultural worldviews provide protection from the ever-present fear of nonexistence (i.e., death), then explicitly reminding people of death (morality salience, MS) should increase defense of their worldviews, self-esteem, and attachments. To test this hypothesis Rosenblatt, Greenberg, Solomon, Pyszczynski, and Lyon (1989) asked municipal court judges to review a case and recommend a bond amount for a woman accused of prostitution. Judges are typically thought of as stewards of social order who are tasked with safeguarding law and order in society; prostitution violates moral values and state laws and was therefore considered to be a violation of the judges' cultural worldviews. Therefore, it was hypothesized that if MS increased the need to defend one's worldview, judges who thought about their own death would render harsher judgments (i.e., set higher bonds). The MS manipulation, which is still commonly used, is described as a type of novel personality assessment and takes the form of two open-ended questions: (a) Please briefly describe the emotions that the thought of your own death arouses in you, and (b) jot down, as specifically as you can, what you think will happen to *you* as you physically die and once *you* are physically dead. Judges reminded of their mortality levied significantly harsher penalties against the prostitute than those who did not receive these reminders ($455 and $50, respectively; Rosenblatt et al., 1989).

Follow-up studies using undergraduates helped expand our understanding of responses to MS. The initial MS results could lead some to reasonably wonder if the observed response might be due to some general type of negative affect, or physical arousal. Because thinking about death is unpleasant and bound to put one in a bad mood, perhaps the effects are not due to fear of death, per se, but rather due to the arousing and unpleasant nature of the questions. The first follow-up studies indicated that MS effects are not mediated by affect and do not result in general negative affect. But they do largely depend on previously established beliefs and values: MS leads to harsher judgments of prostitutes only for those who view prostitution as wrong (Study 2; Rosenblatt et al., 1989). Importantly, responses to MS are not categorically negative: Individuals who are perceived to uphold societal values are rated as significantly as deserving of a greater monetary reward under MS compared to the control condition (Study 3; $3,476 and $1,112, respectively). Additionally, MS effects are different from those produced by self-awareness and negative mood (Study 4), do not increase and are not mediated by physiological arousal (Study 5), and can be induced in multiple ways (Study 6). The initial battery of experiments provided compelling evidence that thinking about death produced a unique pattern of results directed at bolstering one's worldview.

In a complementary set of studies, Greenberg et al. (1990) examined how MS affects responses to ingroup and outgroup members and to people and ideas that either directly support or challenge one's worldview. Because people require consensual validation of their worldviews, TMT suggests that reminders of death would lead to more positive evaluations of those who share one's worldview and more negative evaluations of those who hold worldviews different from one's own. To test this idea, Christian participants were given either the previously described MS induction or a parallel set of neutral questions and then asked to indicate their impressions of either a fellow Christian or a Jew (Study 1; Greenberg et al., 1990). As predicted, MS increased ingroup bias, leading to more positive evaluations of the fellow Christian and more negative evaluations of the Jewish student. Many other studies have shown that MS increases positive reactions to those who explicitly praise one's worldview and more negative reactions toward those who criticize one's worldview (e.g., Greenberg et al. 1990, Study 3; Heine, Harihara, & Niiya, 2002).

H. McGregor et al. (1998) investigated whether these effects would extend to actual physical aggression. Participants with strong and clear political attitudes were randomly assigned to MS or aversive thought control conditions, and then received an essay ostensibly written by a fellow student that was highly critical of either liberals or conservatives, and thus either supported or challenged participants' own political ideologies. They then participated in a bogus "food preference" study, in which their task was to measure out and administer a painfully mouth-burning hot sauce to their politically similar or dissimilar fellow participant. MS increased the amount of hot sauce given to the politically dissimilar other, but decreased the amount given to the politically similar other participant. Later studies showed that MS increased support for the use of violence in international conflicts. Americans, Israelis, Koreans, Palestinians, and Iranians have all been found to be more supportive of extreme military tactics, or suicide terrorism, when reminded of their mortality (for a review, see Motyl & Pyszczynski, 2010).

Other research has shown that thinking about death increases people's striving to maintain self-esteem. In one of the first studies to document this effect, individuals who tied a significant portion of their self-worth to their driving abilities engaged in more risky driving behavior on a driving simulator after MS. However, this MS-enhanced risky driving was eliminated if participants were given positive feedback about their driving before using the simulator (Taubman-Ben-Ari, Florian, & Mikulincer, 1999). In a related vein, Peters, Greenberg, Williams, and Schneider (2005) found that MS increased the grip strength of people who value physical strength as a source of self-esteem, and Goldenberg, McCoy, Pyszczynski, Greenberg, and Solomon (2000) found that MS increased identification with one's body and sexual desire among individuals who place a high value on physical appearance as a source of self-esteem. Mikulincer and Florian (2002) provided further evidence of the terror management function of self-esteem by showing that MS increases self-serving attributional biases.

Additionally, research has demonstrated that MS increases the desirability of close romantic relationships among securely attached individuals. Mikulincer and Florian (2000; Study 5) demonstrated that following the typical MS induction, securely attached participants scored significantly higher on a measure of desired intimacy following MS compared to a control condition. A battery of studies by Taubman-Ben-Ari, Findler, and Mikulincer (2002) also demonstrated that MS increases willingness to initiate social interaction, increases perceived interpersonal skills, and decreases sensitivity to social rejection. Taken together these studies suggest that close relationships can be sources of existential security and that individual differences in attachment moderate these tendencies.

Together these studies provide general support for the *MS hypothesis*: that the psychological structures of cultural worldview, self-esteem, and close relationships buffer against the awareness of death, as explicit reminders of mortality increase the activation of, striving, and reliance on these structures.

Death-Thought Accessibility Hypothesis

It follows from TMT that if cultural worldviews, self-esteem, and close attachments protect against the anxiety produced by awareness of death, then challenges to these structures should increase the accessibility of death-related thoughts. Most of these studies use a word completion task to measure death-thought accessibility (DTA) in which participants are asked to complete a set of word stems, which can be completed with either a neutral or death-related word (e.g., COFF_ _; COFFEE/COFFIN). Completing more words with death refer-ents is interpreted as having easier access to mortality concerns.

In a battery of studies, Schimel, Hayes, Williams, and Jahrig (2007) demon-strated that threatening one's culture, in this case Canada, produced an increased accessibility of death-related thoughts as measured by the word completion task. This effect was also observed when a lexical decision task was used as a primary dependent measure (Study 3; Schimel et al., 2007). Following a worldview threat, participants responded faster to death-related words than to neutral or negative words (e.g., suffer, fail, etc.). Finding that these threats increased the accessibility of words related to death, but not other negative words, shows that these effects are specific to death and do not reflect a general increase in the accessibility of negative or aversive concepts. Research has also shown that these effects extend to worldview threats other than criticisms of one's nation. For example, Schimel et al. (2007) found that reading an article critical of creationism increased DTA among individuals committed to a creationist, but not an evolutionary account of human existence.

Research has shown that threats to other aspects of the anxiety buffer also increase DTA. Hayes, Schimel, Faucher, and Williams (2008) demonstrated that threats to self-esteem, in the form of negative feedback on a supposed intelligence test, increased DTA on a lexical decision task. Only participants who received negative feedback on the test responded to death-related words significantly faster than neutral or negative words. This same pattern of results was demonstrated when participants were led to believe that their personal-ity was not suitable for their desired career (Study 2; Hayes et al., 2008), and when participants believed they were not prepared to give a public speech (Study 3).

Mikulincer, Florian, Birnbaum, and Malishkevich (2002) demonstrated that thinking about an unspecified separation from, or death of, a close relationship partner increased DTA on a word-stem completion measure (Study 1). Addition-ally, separation from a relationship partner increased DTA more than perceived academic failure (Study 2) and the length of the perceived separation (e.g., never see again, long term, and short term) positively correlated with increases in DTA (Study 3). Importantly, all results were significantly qualified by attachment anxiety. As attachment style became more anxious, then perceived separation from a close other led to significantly higher DTA (Mikulincer et al., 2002). This pattern of results was not demonstrated among avoidant individuals, or indi-viduals scoring low on attachment anxiety. In another study, Cox et al. (2008) showed that, following MS, thinking about a positive experience with one's primary attachment figure (i.e., mother) decreased DTA on a word-stem com-pletion measure (Study 1). This pattern of results was not demonstrated when thinking about a negative experience with one's mother, a neutral experience with an acquaintance, or a positive experience with an acquaintance.

Taken together these findings show that various threats to cultural worldview, self-esteem, and close attachments increase DTA. This reinforces the initial theoretical proposition that these systems function to protect against the existential anxiety produced by the awareness of death.

Anxiety-Buffer Hypothesis

Finally, there is the *anxiety-buffer hypothesis*, which states that if there are psychological structures that protect against the anxiety of death, then strengthening such structures should make individuals less susceptible to existential anxieties and anxiety in general. Greenberg, Solomon, et al. (1992) provided the first empirical support that self-esteem could function as an anxiety buffer. Participants' self-esteem was either elevated, through positive feedback on a supposed personality assessment, or not (i.e., neutral personality assessment). Participants then viewed graphic death scenes from the documentary film *Faces of Death* before taking a measure of state-anxiety. Results indicated that although the disturbing film increased anxiety in the control condition, this effect was eliminated by the boost to self-esteem (Study 1). Temporarily bolstering self-esteem also reduced physiological arousal, measured by skin conductance, when anticipating painful electric shock (Studies 2 and 3).

Harmon-Jones, Simon, Greenberg, Pyszczynski, Solomon, and McGregor, H. (1997) demonstrated that both experimentally boosted (Study 1) and high dispositional (Study 2) self-esteem eliminated the defensive response to those who criticize one's cultural worldview following MS. Similar results have been demonstrated by Schmeichel and Martens (2005), who showed that affirming of a self-important value following MS reduced derogation to a worldview threatening others. Importantly, this study also demonstrated that affirming a self-important value before MS significantly reduced DTA (Schmeichel & Martens, 2005; Study 2). Additionally, Cox et al. (2008) showed that priming participants to think about a parent, or close friend, not only reduced the severity of punishment to a perceived moral transgressor following MS (Study 2), but increased self-esteem as measured through an implicit associations test (IAT; Study 3).

Taken together these studies show that adherence to cultural values, high self-esteem, and close relationships are capable of reducing both existentially related anxiety, as well as anxiety in general.

Combining the Hypotheses

At this point you are hopefully beginning to see that the main empirical pillars of TMT share a great deal of conceptual overlap. In the previous section, examples of how boosts to cultural worldview, self-esteem, and close relationships eliminate MS effects on worldview defense and self-esteem striving were presented. If one part of the anxiety-buffer system can be bolstered to compensate for weaknesses or threats to other components, then it would appear that all three components are capable of working together.

From a TMT perspective this makes intuitive sense. Since cultural worldviews are fragile, and social interactions can produce a diffuse number of threats, protective processes should be capable of compensatory operations at a multitude of levels. For example, H. McGregor et al. (1998) found that, following MS, when participants were exposed to political rhetoric that derogated their own views, they demonstrated increased aggression toward the outgroup target (i.e., increased volume of hot sauce). However, following MS, if participants were given the opportunity to derogate the threatening other, their aggressive response was eliminated (Study 2), and conversely, if they were able to be aggress by administering hot sauce, their derogation was eliminated (Study 3). Similarly, Cox et al. (2008; Study 6) found that following MS, participants with secure attachment styles demonstrated increased preference for a close romantic partner, while participants with insecure attachment styles increased their relative preference for a more primary attachment figure (i.e., parent).

These examples highlight some important concepts: (a) People vary in which aspects of their cultural worldviews, self-esteem, and close relationships they use for protection against existential fear; (b) there are multiple potentially effective responses to any perceived threat; and (c) once a potentially anxiety producing threat is addressed, there is no further need of additional existential defense. The following section will elaborate on these concepts and help to clarify what has become known as the dual-process model of terror management.

Psychological Processes Through Which Thoughts of Death Affect Attitudes and Behavior

As research testing basic TMT processes accumulated, it became clear that a more detailed analysis of the cognitive and motivational processes through which death-related thoughts affect attitudes and behavior was needed. Research was showing that, unlike most other psychological effects, weaker death reminders produced stronger worldview defense effects than stronger ones. It also soon became apparent that the effects of MS on worldview defense emerged more consistently when the MS induction and worldview defense assessment was separated by a delay and distraction. In response to these findings, Pyszczynski, Greenberg, and Solomon (1999) proposed that people employ very different defensive processes to cope with thoughts of death when they are in current conscious attention and when they are on the fringes of consciousness.

Proximal defenses deal with the problem of death in a direct and seemingly rational manner. When confronted with the inevitability of one's own death, typically the first thing a person tries to do is push this thought out of direct awareness. For instance, you (i.e., the reader) may have read the last sentence (or probably any page in this volume) and become fleetingly aware that you are not exempt from this fate; however, if you stop to acknowledge this for a moment then the subsequent series of thoughts will likely consist of some sort of temporal distancing (i.e., I know I am going to die, but that's a long time from now). This is a superficially reasonable way of addressing the awareness of your own mortality that consequently allows you to stop thinking about it. This is a proximal response. Proximal defenses take forms such as distraction, a focus on meaning (e.g., I'll go when it's my time), denial of risk (e.g., I don't smoke so I'll live longer), or focusing attention toward life promoting activities (e.g., I'm quitting smoking and starting daily exercise). While the forms are varied, the primary function of proximal defenses is to push the awareness of death out of conscious focus; therefore, these defenses occur immediately following MS and subsequently cease to be utilized.

Distal defenses, on the other hand, have no logical or semantic connection to the problem of death. Rather, they enable people to view themselves as valuable contributors to a meaningful and significant reality. These are the defenses posited by the original version of TMT. They are especially intriguing because of their lack of obvious connection to the problem of mortality. Distal defenses may be described as irrational and symbolic, and become triggered when death is no longer in direct awareness but while the concept remains highly accessible. The first evidence that distal defenses required a delay came from Greenberg et al. (1994), who demonstrated that keeping death in focal awareness did not increase worldview defense. In a more direct examination of this temporal sequence, Greenberg, Arndt, Simon, Pyszczynski, & Solomon (2000) showed that proximal defenses only occurred immediately after contemplating death, while distal defenses only occurred following a delay.

Following MS, death thoughts are elevated until proximal defenses are engaged; after which DTA drops, but following a brief distraction the accessibility of death-related thoughts increases once again. TMT posits that while proximal defenses are well suited for removing death concerns from our immediate awareness, they ultimately do nothing to change knowledge of the inevitability of death. After an individual has developed awareness of the certainty of death, it can never be erased, and while most people only rarely consciously think about this fact, the information remains inseparable from oneself. It was one of Becker's central arguments that the terror of death remained ever present no matter how elaborately it was repressed. TMT concurs and posits that death thoughts remain in a state of deep activation (Wegner & Smart, 1997) following MS and a delay, in which they are no longer consciously experienced yet remain capable of producing measurable changes in attitude and behavior, or distal defenses. Distal defenses are symbolic belief sets that allow people to derive self-worth as significant contributors to a meaningful world, which in turn push death thoughts further from consciousness. Distal defenses are therefore the foundation of the anxiety-buffer system that developed to keep awareness of our mortality out of consciousness by decreasing accessibility of death-related thoughts at the unconscious level.

Summary and Conclusion

TMT, and the research that it inspired, shows that awareness of death plays an important role in diverse aspects of life. Whereas proximal defenses deal with the problem of death in a seemingly rational manner, by distracting us from the problem or denying our vulnerability, distal defenses promote behavior that has no obvious logical or semantic connection to the problem of death, but enables us to view ourselves as valuable contributors to a meaningful and eternal universe. The chapters to follow illustrate the diverse and multifaceted ways that awareness of death affects life.

References

Becker, E. (1973). *The denial of death.* New York: Free Press.

Becker, E. (1975). *Escape from evil.* New York: Free Press.

Bowlby, J. (1982). *Attachment and loss: Vol. 1. Attachment.* (2nd ed.). New York: Basic Books.

Cox, C. R., Arndt, J., Pyszczynski, T., Greenberg, J., Abdollahi, A., & Solomon, S. (2008). Terror management and adults' attachment to their parents: The safe haven remains. *Journal of Personality and Social Psychology, 94,* 696–717. doi:10.1037/0022–3514.94.4.696

Goldenberg, J. L., McCoy, S. K., Pyszczynski, T., Greenberg, J., & Solomon, S. (2000). The body as a source of self-esteem: The effect of mortality salience on identification with one's body, interest in sex, and appearance monitoring. *Journal of Personality and Social Psychology, 79*(1), 118–130. doi:10.1037//0022–3514.79.1.118

Greenberg, J., Arndt, J., Simon, L., Pyszczynski, T., & Solomon, S. (2000). Proximal and distal defenses in response to reminders of one's mortality: Evidence of a temporal sequence. *Personality and Social Psychology Bulletin, 26*(1), 91–99. doi:10.1177/0146167200261009

Greenberg, J., Pyszczynski, T., & Solomon, S. (1986). The causes and consequences of a need for self-esteem: A terror management theory. In R. F. Baumeister (Ed.), *Public Self and Private Self* (pp. 189–212). New York: Springer-Verlag. doi:10.1007/978–1–4613–9564–5_10

Greenberg, J., Pyszczynski, T., Solomon, S., Rosenblatt, A., Veeder, M., Kirkland, S., & Lyon, D. (1990). Evidence for terror management theory II: The effects of mortality salience on reactions to those who threaten or bolster the cultural worldview. *Journal of Personality and Social Psychology, 58*(2), 308–318. doi:10.1037/0022–3514.58.2.308

Greenberg, J., Pyszczynski, T., Solomon, S., Simon, L., & Breus, M. (1994). Role of consciousness and accessibility of death-related thoughts in mortality salience effects. *Journal of Personality and Social Psychology, 67*(4), 627–637. doi:10.1037/0022–3514.67.4.627

Greenberg, J., Solomon, S., Pyszczynski, T., Rosenblatt, A., Burling, J., Lyon, D., & Pinel, E. (1992). Why do people need self-esteem? Converging evidence that self-esteem serves an anxiety-buffering function. *Journal of Personality and Social Psychology, 63*(6), 913–922. doi:10.1037/0022–3514.63.6.913

Greenberg, J., Vail, K. E., & Pyszczynski, T. (in-press). *Terror management theory and research: How the desire for death transcendence drives our strivings for meaning and significance.*

Harmon-Jones, E., Simon, L., Greenberg, J., Pyszczynski, T., Solomon, S., & McGregor, H. (1997). Terror management theory and self-esteem: Evidence that increased self-esteem reduced mortality salience effects. *Journal of Personality and Social Psychology, 72*(1), 24–36. doi:10.1037/0022–3514.72.1.24

Hayes, J., Schimel, J., Faucher, E. H., & Williams, T. J. (2008). Evidence for the DTA hypothesis II: Threatening self-esteem increases death-thought accessibility. *Journal of Experimental Social Psychology, 44*(3), 600–613. doi:10.1016/j.jesp.2008.01.004

Heine, S. J., Harihara, M., & Niiya, Y. (2002). Terror management in Japan. *Asian Journal of Social Psychology, 5*(3), 187–196. doi:10.1111/1467–839x.00103

Kierkegaard, S. (1983/1849). *Sickness unto Death.* New York: Start Publishing LLC.

McGregor, H. A., Lieberman, J. D., Greenberg, J., Solomon, S., Arndt, J., Simon, L., & Pyszczynski, T. (1998). Terror management and aggression: Evidence that mortality salience motivates aggression against worldview-threatening others. *Journal of Personality and Social Psychology, 74*(3), 590–605. doi:10.1037/0022–3514.74.3.590

Mikulincer, M., & Florian, V. (2000). Exploring individual differences in reactions to mortality salience: Does attachment style regulate terror management mechanisms? *Journal of Personality and Social Psychology, 79*(2), 260–273. doi:10.1037/0022–3514.79.2.260

Mikulincer, M., & Florian, V. (2002). The effects of mortality salience on self-serving attributions-evidence for the function of self-esteem as a terror management mechanism. *Basic and Applied Social Psychology, 24*(4), 261–271. doi:10.1207/s15324834basp2404_2

Mikulincer, M., Florian, V., Birnbaum, G., & Malishkevich, S. (2002). The death-anxiety buffering function of close relationships: Exploring the effects of separation reminders on death-thought accessibility. *Personality and Social Psychology Bulletin, 28*(3), 287–299. doi:10.1177/0146167202286001

Mikulincer, M., Florian, V., & Hirschberger, G. (2004). The terror of death and the quest for love: An existential perspective on close relationships. In J. Greenberg, S. L. Koole & T. Pyszczynski (Eds.), *Handbook of Experimental Existential Psychology* (pp. 287–304). New York: Guilford Press.

Mikulincer, M., & Shaver, P. R. (2003). The attachment behavioral system in adulthood: Activation, psychodynamics, and interpersonal processes. In M. P. Zanna (Ed.), *Advances in Experimental Social Psychology* (pp. 53–152). New York: Wiley. doi:10.1016/s0065–2601(03)01002–5

Mithen, S. (1996). *The prehistory of the mind: A search for the origins of art, religion and science.* London: Thames and Hudson.

Motyl, M., & Pyszczynski, T. (2010). The existential underpinnings of the cycle of terrorist and counterterrorist violence and pathways to peaceful resolutions. *Revue Internationale de Psychologie Sociale, 22*(3), 267–291.

Peters, H. J., Greenberg, J., Williams, J. M., & Schneider, N. R. (2005). Applying terror management theory to performance: Can reminding individuals of their mortality increase strength output. *Journal of Sport & Exercise Psychology, 27*(1), 111–116.

Pyszczynski, T., Greenberg, J., & Solomon, S. (1999). A dual-process model of defense against conscious and unconscious death-related thoughts: An extension of terror management theory. *Psychological Review, 106*(4), 835–845. doi:10.1037/0033–295x.106.4.835

Rosenblatt, A., Greenberg, J., Solomon, S., Pyszczynski, T., & Lyon, D. (1989). Evidence for terror management theory I.: The effects of mortality salience on reactions to those who violate or uphold cultural values. *Journal of Personality and Social Psychology,* 57(4), 681–690. doi:10.1037/0022–3514.57.4.681

Schimel, J., Hayes, J., Williams, T., & Jahrig, J. (2007). Is death really the worm at the core? Converging evidence that worldview threat increases death-thought accessibility. *Journal of Personality and Social Psychology, 92*(5), 789–803. doi:10.1037/0022–3514.92.5.789

Schmeichel, B. J., & Martens, A. (2005). Self-affirmation and mortality salience: Affirming values reduces worldview defense and death-thought accessibility. *Personality and Social Psychology Bulletin, 31*(5), 658–667. doi:10.1177/0146167204271567

Solomon, S., Greenberg, J., & Pyszczynski, T. (2015). *The worm at the core: The role of death in life.* New York: Random House.

Taubman-Ben-Ari, O., Findler, L., & Mikulincer, M. (2002). The effects of mortality salience on relationship strivings and beliefs: The moderating role of attachment style. *British Journal of Social Psychology, 41*, 419–441. doi:10.1348/014466602760344296

Taubman-Ben-Ari, O., Florian, V., & Mikulincer, M. (1999). The impact of mortality salience on reckless driving: A test of terror management mechanisms. *Journal of Personality and Social Psychology, 76*(1), 35–45. doi:10.1037/0022–3514.76.1.35

Wegner, D. M., & Smart, L. (1997). Deep cognitive activation: A new approach to the unconscious. *Journal of Consulting and Clinical Psychology, 65*(6), 984–995. doi:10.1037//0022–006x.65.6.984

2

COMMUNICATING ABOUT DEATH

A Look Inside Terror Management Theory and the Field of Communication

Gwendelyn S. Nisbett and Lindsey A. Harvell

In its very nature, terror management theory (TMT) is about how people interpret culture and communicate about culture. Through communication, people come to understand their place in society, understand cultural values, and understand how their actions reify those cultural values. Examining TMT in tandem with communication theory is both fruitful and important, though it has only been limitedly applied in communication research. These studies have primarily examined the theory in conjunction with social influence and political communication.

This chapter will explore further potential for TMT in communication research. In terms of interpersonal, the chapter will examine the interplay of TMT, self-esteem, cultural obligation, and the way in which we communicate on an individual level. In organizational communication, TMT will be examined in terms of organizational responses to crisis. An increasingly important research area for personal well-being, health communication and TMT is explored. Building on research regarding TMT and ideological tolerance, this chapter will further examine TMT in intercultural communication. TMT has limitedly been examined in political communication in terms of ideology, advertising, and decision making; these applications are examined further. Lastly, TMT will be applied to mass communication with emphasis on the potentially prolific context of social media.

Moreover, this chapter will explore an interesting aspect of TMT that is particularly relevant to communication—social death salience. Building on traditional TMT research utilizing physical death salience, social death salience examines the ability to create existential anxiety stemming from a loss of social connection. Social death is particularly interesting in all aspects of communication research because social death anxiety is generated almost entirely by social interaction.

Theoretical Overview

TMT grew out of a desire to understand the role existential anxiety plays in our everyday lives (Solomon, Greenberg, & Pyszczynski, 1998). It includes the primary components of mortality salience, cultural worldview, self-esteem, and close relationships. Driven in part by evolutionary biology and in part by the very philosophical nature of the human condition, TMT incorporates important communication elements. This section will explore the foundations of the theory and how communication may help us understand them better.

TMT was originally developed as an examination of self-esteem within a socially constructed culture. Our meaning in this world is partially derived from a biological need, driving us forward to survive and prosper. Unlike our animal counterparts, however, we are blessed and burdened with a detached self-awareness and an understanding of our place in the natural order. Humans have the ability to project themselves into the future and understand themselves as conscious beings within the spectrum of our shared past, present, and future (Solomon et al., 2004).

It is in our nature to seek immortality. Our spiritual life prevails beyond our finite timelines and biological circumstances. We also build a sense of immortality through our cultural collective consciousness. Communication is the essential element of life that allows us to create and share meaning.

When we are pressed to consider death, existential anxiety is generated; TMT scholars have labeled this *mortality salience*. Mortality salience is uncomfortable, prompting a diversionary defense mechanism. People tend not to dwell on their own demise, instead opting to think of the importance of their lives or avoiding death thoughts altogether (Koole, Greenberg, & Pyszczynski, 2006).

The basic tenants of TMT argue people use self-esteem, cultural worldview, and close relationships to deflect and diminish existential anxiety. These are known as distal defenses; a person is not fully aware of their death salience, but a wary unease still persists and thus people attempt to abate the discomfort of mortality salience (Arndt, Cook, & Routledge, 2004). Each of these elements is socially constructed and communication dependent.

When presented with death, it is in our nature to seek immortality. In some ways we desire to live longer and longer. We have children partially as homage to our ancestors' memories and partially to ensure our own legacy. Perhaps the most powerful immortality, however, is created through communication— we seek immortality in the culture that we have collectively formed.

Our every belief and value creates a cultural gestalt—an abstract yet powerful grounding in our lives. Our very essence and meaning have been intricately crafted through our social interactions. TMT scholars call this our cultural worldview (CWV; Solomon, Greenberg, & Pyszczynski, 2000). Each person's CWV is unique, influenced by an individual's sense of self and their sense of culture. Through every facet of communication, a CWV is socially constructed of elements important to a person and the people around him or her. We use interpersonal communication in our close relationships and group communication in our families. We use organizational communication in our religious organizations and political institutions. We use mass communication to inform, persuade, and entertain on a large scale. Communication allows us to understand, collaborate, and craft culture; it is also essential for understanding death, loss, and isolation.

TMT in Communication Research

TMT has only been limitedly investigated in communication research. Given the important communication aspects at the heart of TMT, it is important to see how the theory has been applied and explore the potential for future research.

Interpersonal Communication

At the most basic level, TMT processes are interpersonal in nature. Specifically, as you start to act out the defenses to your existential anxiety (i.e., CWV defenses), it is often done so through talking (verbal communication) or not talking (nonverbal communication) to people. However, most TMT research to date focuses on the psychological processing of the awareness of death. Communication scholars would be interested in the interpersonal interaction that takes place *because* of death anxiety.

The main TMT interpersonal communication research area concerns the anxiety-buffering aspects of close relationships first introduced by Florian, Mikulincer, and Hirschberger (2002). Both self-esteem and close relationships interplay with CWV and are very communication dependent. Self-esteem is rooted in our ability to place ourselves as a valued member of our culture (Pyszczynski, Greenberg, & Solomon, 1997). Moreover, seeking a way out of the darkness of a life empty of meaning and connection, we rely heavily on personal connections. Close relationships function as an anxiety buffer (Florian, Mikulincer, & Hirschberger, 2002; Smieja, Kalaska, & Adamczyk, 2006).

The very idea that contemplating problems in a romantic relationship will lead to a higher accessibility of death thoughts when compared to a neutral theme suggests interpersonal communication does play a role in TMT, but couched from a psychological perspective (Florian et al., 2002; Mikulincer, Florian, & Hirschberger, 2003; Miller, 2003). Therefore, it is no surprise that imagining the death of a loved one produced the same TMT effects (Miller, 2003).

After the initial TMT literature on close relationships developed, Smieja, Kalaska, and Adamczyk (2006) continued work in the context, finding close relationships can serve as an anxiety buffer, especially for those individuals that can be described as low-anxiety and low-avoidance individuals (i.e., securely attached people). However, Smieja et al. (2006) found only avoidance played a role in the process. Therefore, you do not necessarily have to be low anxiety, rather one can only be nonavoidant for it to be sufficient (Smieja et al., 2006). Interestingly, this study examined direct behavioral manifestations, whereas the other studies used self-report in hypothetical situations (Smieja et al., 2006).

Recently, TMT literature has begun to examine aspects of close relationships. For instance, Van Tongeren et al. (2013) examined how TMT can guide us in our thinking about forgiveness in close relationships. In less committed relationships, mortality salience elicited less forgiveness; however, in more committed relationships, mortality salience elicited more forgiveness (Van Tongeren et al., 2013). This relationship is mediated by empathy; when individuals do not really care about the person, death reminders further this feeling (Van Tongeren et al., 2013). When the person is not like you, forgiveness does not provide existential security, but when they are like you, it helps to reestablish an emotional bond that, in turn, increases existential security (Van Tongeren et al., 2013). All in all, death increases preexisting feelings, but other factors such as religious similarity can also affect forgiveness decisions (Van Tongeren et al., 2013). This study was the first to measure actual relationships instead of hypothetical situations.

Communication scholars can offer much to the world of TMT literature and close relationships. The current literature examines the psychological effects of close relationships. What communication scholars can bring to the table now is how existential awareness actually affects relationships (e.g., type and communication). By looking at how existential awareness affects things like relational communication, we can delve further into the psychological constructs of close relationships as an existential buffer. Furthermore, it can help guide talks about improving communication with people struggling with existential issues.

Organizational Communication

Currently, TMT has not infiltrated organizational communication directly. However, the TMT literature on crisis management after terrorism events does examine some of the same structures that organizational scholars are interested in. For instance, Christensen, Laegreid, and Rykkja (2013) examined challenges that faced political and police leadership following the July 2011 terrorist attacks in Norway. While this study does not use TMT as its theoretical framework, it would fit quite well. Specifically, TMT could be used to examine how organizational members process crisis events and help with crisis management. By understanding how people process these types of death salient events (e.g., natural disasters, mass shootings, terrorism, etc.), we can better inform crisis management plans to aid first responders and communities.

Additionally, it would be interesting to investigate death salience in extremist and terrorist organizations. While it would be difficult to gain access to these populations, it would be worthwhile to investigate what role death anxiety plays in terrorist plots that utilize tactics like suicide bombers. The idea of religious radicals and death is an interesting intersection to examine for both psychology and communication scholars.

Health Communication

TMT is slowly infiltrating health communication research. While there is a large amount of health communication literature examining existential subjects (e.g., cancer, end-of-life care, etc.), most have moved away from using noncommunication theories (e.g., heavy reliance on the extended parallel process model) mainly due to pressure from within the discipline to focus on communication-based message theories. This is doing a great disservice to the field of health communication. To ignore the psychological processes that are the framework for developing communication messages has the potential to severely limit the scope of the discipline.

One health communication article to date has examined TMT through the terror management health model (TMHM; Goldenberg & Arndt, 2008). This model is explained more in depth in Chapter 4. However, the most basic premise of the model is awareness of one's mortality can affect health decisions one makes. Therefore, it is possible mortality salience could affect how one talks about those health decisions. A recent study preliminarily incorporated TMT into antismoking health message design. The study found both negative physical and social impacts of smoking were effective in message design, but impacts were dependent on self-esteem and how much a CWV involved the importance of smoking (Wong, Nisbett, & Harvell, 2015).

Intercultural Communication

Intercultural aspects of TMT can be categorized into two main areas: the impact of mortality salience on cultural intolerance and culturally specific beliefs about death. Communication is essential for both.

In terms of cultural intolerance, much of the research focuses on CWV bolstering and levels of tolerance. An early study investigating the different mortality-salience manipulations and their effects on cultural worldviews found both subliminal and standard mortality-salience manipulations led to more favorable views of people who agreed with their CWV and less favorable views about those who challenged their worldview when compared with controls (Arndt et al., 1997). It is important to note that only death stimuli produced these effects (Arndt et al., 1997), and based on the Arndt et al. (1997) findings, the death stimuli do not necessarily need to be subliminal.

Death reminders produce an exaggerated need for the anxiety-buffering properties of CWVs (Solomon, Greenberg, & Pyszczynski, 2004). In turn, CWVs have the potential to be bolstered when presented with threatening (anything not part of their CWV) people or behaviors (Solomon et al., 2004). In other words, when mortality is made salient, people have the potential to turn to their CWV for guidance on how to react to those individuals who are not part of their culture.

Overall, the existence of people with differing beliefs threatens an individual's primary basis of psychological security (Solomon et al., 2000). When alternative views are presented, the psychological security the CWV provides is threatened. This occurs because individuals, when death aware, can minimize their existential anxiety by bolstering their own reality (Solomon et al., 2000). Therefore, individuals respond by derogating the sources that threaten their psychological security (Solomon et al., 2000).

Existential anxiety, CWV bolstering, and fluctuating levels of cultural intolerance are critical for understanding intercultural communication. Of particular interest are areas such as diplomatic and business negotiations where levels of intolerance and threat can greatly impact outcomes. Research could also examine persuasive communication, particularly advertising that uses fear appeals and controlling messages.

Beyond the mechanics of CWV bolstering as a distal defense, understanding cultural variants of death and death rituals is a secondary area important for research. The ways in which we communicate about existential anxiety are one area that TMT and communication can easily intersect and flourish. Arndt, Solomon, Kasser, and Sheldon (2004) further discuss how the rituals of death help the living feel better about their own impending death. Understanding and making meaning of death is very culturally specific. For example, within the Asante tribe in Ghana, their death rituals do not view death as an end; if it is not an end, then there is no reason to fear it. In Mexico, Day of the Dead festivities may appear macabre to outsiders, but they are a celebration of life and a ritual of healing. For communication scholars, future research should investigate death rituals and communication within death rituals that potentially are causing these psychological reactions. This would be an excellent opportunity for ethnographic research to take a different and fresh approach to TMT, and one that has yet to be uncovered.

Culturally different views of mortality, death, and the anxiety levels inspired by TMT research are proving to be a methodological challenge and heuristically provocative. TMT is built upon a very Western notion of what death is and what CWVs should look like. Some studies have encountered methodological issues based on these assumptions of death. Harvell et al (2013) found participants who identify themselves as part of the Mormon religion do not seem to be affected by the death prime the way other religious individuals are. Those individuals who are Mormon seem to have a more positive view of the afterlife than those belonging to other religions. So much so that when asked about what they think happens to them after they die, Mormons have almost nonexistent death-thought accessibility. Thus, the control group holds more death awareness than the group who was reminded of their own death. The investigation into death awareness of different cultures, as well as how it affects social behavior, can provide a deeper and richer understanding of TMT.

Political Communication

While researchers have previously examined the intersection of existential psychology and political attitudes, the application of TMT has only limitedly been utilized in political communication research. Past studies point to two important lines of thought in political TMT: the political worldview defense hypothesis and the conservative shift hypothesis. The political worldview defense hypothesis suggests mortality salience (MS) triggers a bolstering of existing attitudes; thus liberals fall back on liberal views and conservatives rely on conservative views (e.g., Anson, Pyszczynski, Solomon, & Greenberg, 2009; Pyszczynski, Abdollahi, Solomon, Greenberg, Cohen, & Weise, 2006). On the contrary, other research has found MS-induced tendencies toward increasing support of the status quo and/or increased conservatism (e.g., Jost, Glaser, Kruglanski, & Sulloway, 2003). Research in this area has found MS leads to support for maintaining power structures as they currently exist, support for political leaders, greater nationalistic attitudes, and increased negativity toward outgroups. Chapter 3 explores these concepts further.

What is interesting for political communication scholars is an adoption of anxiety-inducing imagery and speech in an attempt to imbue death into political debates. The impact of MS is not always clear cut. Much of the research in this area has focused on political attitudes and political candidates. For instance, Jonas and Greenberg (2004) investigated German attitudes toward the fall of the Berlin wall and German reunification. Results showed, with death awareness, Germans with a more favorable attitude toward the German reunification had more positive attitudes about the fall of the Berlin wall compared to those in the control condition (Jonas & Greenberg, 2004). However, those with a neutral attitude did not show any significant effects (Jonas & Greenberg, 2004).

Cohen and colleagues (2005) investigated how mortality salience affects evaluations of political candidates as a function of leadership style (Cohen et al., 2005). Participants showed an increased preference for a charismatic political candidate and decreased preference for a relationship-oriented political candidate when made aware of their own death (Cohen et al., 2005). They argued these results could lend explanation for why some historically bad electoral decisions were made (e.g., Hitler).

The effects of existential awareness have also been studied in political support for or against a candidate. For example, Landau and colleagues (2004) investigated how existential anxiety affected support for George W. Bush. Interestingly, results showed both conservatives *and* liberals increased their support for President Bush after reminded of 9/11 (Landau et al., 2004). Other studies found similar results (e.g., Cohen, Ogilvie, Solomon, Greenberg, & Pyszczynski, 2005). While this is interesting, other research suggests conservatives have rated liberals harsher than other conservatives when in an MS condition (compared with non-MS condition; Greenberg et al., 1992). Interestingly, in the same study, death-aware liberals rated conservatives less negatively than their non-MS counterparts (Greenberg et al., 1992). However, while other studies have resulted in ideological shifts, Nail and McGregor (2009) found that even though people did become more conservative after 9/11, the shift was not significantly different between conservatives and liberals. While these studies are not a complete list of political TMT research, they serve as good examples of how the political science discipline is using TMT in their research.

Further research in political communication can build on these studies and interweave the important components. In particular, political communication scholars can go beyond ideology and explore how group dynamics and threat influence political attitudes and behaviors. Integrating social media and persuasive message design are critical to understanding MS, CWV, and the impact of death anxiety on political rhetoric.

Mass Communication

TMT in conjunction with mass communication has only been limitedly examined, but offers a context that is heuristically fruitful. Media and mass communication are conduits for shaping culture and our CWV. Moreover, mortality salience via mass or mediated communication has the potential to impact a wide swath of a population. For example, people may be impacted by the news media covering terrorism and world affairs. A study by Das, Bushman, Bezemer, Kerkhof, and Vermeulen (2009) found media-based news coverage instigated anti-Muslim attitudes in the Netherlands. It is unclear how these mediated factors work, especially the amount of MS generated and how people use media to bolster CWV or buffer against anxiety.

There are a number of interesting concepts in mass communication that mirror the main components of TMT. Parasocial interactions or parasocial relationships suggest audiences can have an emotionally deep, yet one-sided attachment to a celebrity or fictitious character. Parasocial mimics close personal relationship aspects of TMT, and it is possible for fandom to work as an anxiety buffer. Chapter 7 in this book explores this concept further.

Social media is also interesting for TMT research in that it can both encapsulate personal connection and impact self-esteem. In many ways, social media helps people stay connected with friends and family, providing a close personal relationship anxiety buffer. On the other hand, there is the potential for social media to be linked with personal isolation and lower self-esteem as people feel detached from other people and unable to fulfill their desired goals in life.

Social Death as a Communication Construct

Much TMT research focuses on the way we evaluate our place within the social structure and how existential anxiety can be predictably manipulated. Based on some unusual findings (Arndt et al., 1997; Harvell, Nisbett, & Miller, 2012), scholars are moving beyond the effects of physical death mortality salience. New research examines the ability to create existential anxiety stemming from a loss of social connection. Given that it is meant to semantically represent a parallel with physical death anxiety, some TMT scholars are referring to the phenomenon as social death.

Social death, specifically priming social death, in communication is interesting for a number of reasons. First, while physical death may seem distant and abstract, social death can feel immediate and concrete. People tend to have an optimistic bias about death, believing the misfortunes of others will not befall them. This is especially true for younger people, who cannot project into the future and keenly imagine their own demise. Thus, priming physical death may not be particularly strong. Social anxiety can take any number of banal and mundane forms that people encounter every day. Getting shunned, bullied, fired, or rejected can all create anxiety about one's inability to live up to his place in the social order. Moreover, social death goes beyond psychological processing of existential anxiety and explores how we act and communicate as a response to primed social isolation.

Second, feelings of social death can integrate within an existing TMT theoretical structure. Specifically, it would be useful to weave together disparate aspects of the psychological impact of anxiety to better understand social interactions. Tackling social death in a similar fashion as physical death can address factors like social cohesion, self-esteem, and social isolation. Levels of self-esteem dictate how a person feels she is living up to her part of the social contract—is she a good person doing the right thing. This directly impacts how well a person's cultural worldview and close relationships act as anxiety buffers. Theoretically and methodologically, examining social death should parallel the process used to examine physical death, allowing for a better understanding of the theory and wider contextual application.

To date, social death is only a concept worth exploring further, though researchers have examined aspects of social death in terms of loss of close personal relationships and low self-esteem. When individuals feel isolated and rejected, they will have a higher level of existential anxiety than individuals who feel connected with others (Koole et al., 2006) and lack all ability to buffer existential anxiety (Mikulincer, Florian, & Hirschberger, 2003). Future studies will need to explore social death manipulation, social death-thought accessibility measures, and social death anxiety levels. Extant literature is lacking in reliable measures for the concept. Future research will also need to explore the application of social death anxiety to areas such as advertising, politics, communication, and consumer behavior.

Conclusion

This chapter examined how TMT can enhance and collaborate with communication theory to gain insight into interpersonal, organizational, intercultural, political, and mass communication. In many ways, the title of the chapter is a misnomer. It is not so much how we communicate about death, but how we socially construct our lives and cultures. Communication functions as a conduit for the mechanics of TMT, be it on the personal or mass scale. Examining TMT in communication can help us understand how the psychological effects of existential anxiety, self-esteem, culture, and relationships work on a wider social (and at times mediated) scale.

References

Anson, J., Pyszczynski, T., Solomon, S., & Greenberg, J. (2009). Political ideology in the 21st century: A terror management perspective on maintenance and change of the status quo. In J. T. Jost, A. C. Kay & H. Thorisdottir (Eds.), *Social and Psychological Bases of Ideology and System Justification* (pp. 210–240). New York: Oxford University Press. http://dx.doi.org/10.1093/acprof:oso/9780195320916.003.009

Arndt, J., Cook, A., & Routledge, C. (2004). The blueprint of terror management: Understanding the cognitive architecture of psychological defense against the awareness of death. In J. Greenberg, S. L. Koole & T. Pyszczynski's (Eds.), *Handbook of Experimental Existential Psychology* (pp. 35–53). New York: Guilford.

Arndt, J., Greenberg, J., Pyszczynski, T., & Solomon, S. (1997). Subliminal exposure to death-related stimuli increases defense of the cultural worldview. *Psychological Science, 8*, 379–385. doi:10.1111/j.1467–9280.1997.tb00429.x

Arndt, J., Solomon, S., Kasser, T., & Sheldon, K. M. (2004). The urge to splurge revisited: Further reflections on applying terror management theory to materialism and consumer behavior. *Journal of Consumer Psychology, 14*(3), 225–229.

Christensen, T., Laegreid, P., & Rykkja, L. H. (2013). After a terrorist attack: Challenges for political and administrative leadership in Norway. *Journal of Contingencies and Crisis Management, 21*(3), 46–68. doi:10.1111/1468–5973.12019

Cohen, F., Ogilvie, D. M., Solomon, S., Greenberg, J., & Pyszczynski, T. (2005). American roulette: The effect of reminders of death on support for George W. Bush in the 2004 presidential election. *Analyses of Social Issues and Public Policy, 5*, 177–187. http://dx.doi.org/10.1111/j.1530–2415.2005.00063.x

Das, E., Bushman, B. J., Bezemer, M. D., Kerkhof, P., & Vermeulen, I. E. (2009). How terrorism news reports increase prejudice against outgroups: A terror management account. *Journal of Experimental Social Psychology, 45*, 453–459. http://dx.doi.org/10.1016/j.jesp. 2008. 12.001

Florian, V., Mikulincer, M., & Hirschberger, G. (2002). The anxiety-buffering function of close relationships: Evidence that relational commitment acts as a terror management mechanism. *Journal of Personality and Social Psychology, 82*(4), 527–542. doi:10.1037// 0022–3514.82.4.527

Goldenberg, J. L., & Arndt, J. (2008). The implications of death for health: A terror management health model for behavioral health promotion. *Psychological Review, 115*, 1032–1053. doi:10.1037/a0013326

Greenberg, J., Simon, L., Pyszczynski, T., Solomon, S., & Chatel, D. (1992). Terror management and tolerance: Does mortality salience always intensify negative reactions to others who threaten one's worldview? *Journal of Personality and Social Psychology, 63*, 212–220. doi:http://dx.doi.org/10.1037%2F%2F0022-3514.63.2.212

Harvell, L. A., Nisbett, G. S., & Miller, C. H. (2012, November). *Plane crashes: The effects of news regarding our fear of death.* Presented at the annual meeting of the National Communication Association in Orlando, FL.

Harvell, L. A., Nisbett, G. S., Wong, N. C. H., & McCloskey, Y. (2013). *Apocalyptic doom: How religion and mortality salience affect fears of the 2013 Mayan prophecy.* Presented at the annual meeting of Central States Communication Association in Kansas City, Missouri.

Jonas, E., & Greenberg, J. (2004). Terror management and political attitudes: The influence of mortality salience on Germans' defense of the German reunification. *European Journal of Social Psychology, 34*, 1–9.

Jost, J. T., Glaser, J., Kruglanski, A. W., & Sulloway, F. J. (2003). Political conservatism as motivated social cognition. *Psychological Bulletin, 129*, 339–375. http://dx.doi.org/10.1037/0033–2909.129.3.339

Koole, S. L., Greenberg, J., & Pyszczynski, T. (2006). Introducing science to the psychology of the soul: experimental existential psychology. *Current Directions in Psychological Science, 15*, 212–216. doi:10.1111/j.1467–8721.2006.00438.x

Landau, M. J., Solomon, S., Greenberg, J., Cohen, F., Pyszczynski, T., Arndt, J., Miller, C. H., Ogilvie, D. M., & Cook, A. (2004). Deliver us from evil: The effects of mortality salience and reminders of 9/11 on support for President George W. Bush. *Personality and Social Psychology Bulletin, 30*, 1136–1150. http://dx.doi.org/10.1177/0146167204267988

Mikulincer, M., Florian, V., & Hirschberger, G. (2003). The existential function of close relationships: Introducing death into the science of love. *Personality and Social Psychological Review, 7*(1), 20–40.

Miller, E. D. (2003). Imagining partner loss and mortality salience: Consequences for romantic-relationship satisfaction. *Social Behavior & Personality, 31*(2), 167–180.

Nail, P., & McGregor, I. (2009). Conservative shift among liberals and conservatives following 9/11/01. *Social Justice Research, 22*, 231–240. http://dx.doi.org/10.1007/s11211–009–0098-z

Pyszczynski, T., Abdollahi, A., Solomon, S., Greenberg, J., Cohen, F., & Weise, D. (2006). Mortality salience, martyrdom, and military might: The Great Satan versus the Axis of Evil. *Personality and Social Psychology Bulletin, 32*, 525–537.

Pyszczynski, T., Greenberg, J., & Solomon, S. (1997). Why do we need what we need? A terror management perspective on the roots of human social motivation. *Psychological Inquiry, 8*, 1–20. doi:10.1207/s15327965pli0801_1

Smieja, M., Kalaska, M., & Adamczyk, M. (2006). Scared to death or scared to love? terror management theory and close relationships seeking. *European Journal of Social Psychology, 36*, 279–296. doi:10.1002/ejsp.301

Solomon, S., Greenberg, J., & Pyszczynski, T. (1998). Tales from the crypt: On the role of death in life. *Zygon, 33*, 9–43. doi:10.1111/0591–2385.1241998124

Solomon, S., Greenberg, J., & Pyszczynski, T. (2000). Pride and prejudice: Fear of death and social behavior. *Current Directions is Psychological Science, 9*, 200–204. doi:10.1111/1467–8721.00094

Solomon, S., Greenberg, J., & Pyszczynski, T. (2004). The cultural animal: Twenty years of terror management theory and research. In J. Greenberg, S. Koole, & T. Pyszczynski (Eds.), *Handbook of experimental existential psychology* (pp. 13–34). New York: Guilford Press.

Solomon, S., Greenberg, J., Schimel, J., Arndt, J., & Pyszczynski, T. (2004). Human awareness of mortality and the evolution of culture. In M. Schaller & C. Crandall's (Eds.), *The Psychological Foundations of Culture* (pp. 15–40). New York: Erlbaum.

Van Tongeren, D. R., Green, J. D., Davis, D. E., Worthington Jr., E. L., & Reid, C. A. (2013). Till death do us part: Terror management and forgiveness in close relationships. *Personal Relationships, 20,* 755–768. doi:10.1111/pere.12013

Wong. N. C. H., Nisbett, G. S., & Harvell, L. A. (2015). *Smoking is so Ew! College smokers' reactions to health vs. social-focused antismoking threat messages.* National Communication Association Conference, Las Vegas, NV.

3

TERROR MANAGEMENT AND POLITICS

Comparing and Integrating the "Conservative Shift" and "Political Worldview Defense" Hypotheses

Spee Kosloff, Mark J. Landau, and Brian Burke

> Civilization, in fact, grows more and more maudlin and hysterical; especially under democracy it tends to degenerate into a mere combat of crazes; the whole aim of practical politics is to keep the populace alarmed (and hence clamorous to be led to safety) by menacing it with an endless series of hobgoblins, most of them imaginary.
> —*H. L. Mencken,* In Defense of Women *(1922, p. 53)*

The role of fear in politics is, in itself, quite frightening. The injection of unchecked emotion into processes by which civilizations rise and fall runs counter to the rationalist principles upon which democracies are founded. But how, in particular, do fear and anxiety govern us? How do real or imagined vulnerabilities influence the content of our political worldviews?

Some insights come from lines of research in social, personality, and political psychology examining the roles of motivational and emotional processes in the formation and maintenance of political beliefs and attitudes (e.g., Rokeach, 1960; Westen, 2007). This work highlights how largely unconscious existential threats—triggered by a political environment of war, murder, and corruption—condition the positions people take on socioeconomic issues, how they vote, and their perceptions of reality as a whole. But important questions remain.

The present chapter endeavors to compare and integrate competing perspectives and research on the impact of these existential threats, particularly those linked to the awareness of death. In one view, death-related threats provoke defensive clinging to distinctively conservative ideologies—clamping down on the status quo for dear life in order to combat the uncertainties of existence, even if doing so runs against the grain of a liberal's preexisting worldview (e.g., Jost, Glaser, Kruglanski, & Sulloway, 2003a). The competing view from terror management theory posits such threats have a polarizing effect, motivating individuals to seize upon whatever political ideology has served their personal death-denying needs in the past, be it liberal or conservative (e.g., Anson, Pyszc-zynski, Solomon, & Greenberg, 2009).

Substantial evidence exists in support of both points of view. Relevant studies examine effects of *mortality salience* (MS)—temporary reminders of one's mortality—on political outcomes. A meta-analysis of these studies ($k = 31$) showed the effect sizes of conservative shifting ($r = .22$) and defense of preexisting political worldviews ($r = .35$) to be significant and statistically equivalent (Burke, Kosloff, & Landau, 2013). Both perspectives thus contribute substantially to the emerging existential psychology of political life, yet they remain unreconciled. The present chapter endeavors to integrate these alternative explanations through consideration of specific research findings, theoretical boundary conditions, and historical context.

Evidence of Conservative Shifting

In the decades since Theodore Adorno's seminal studies of the relationship between personality and political ideology (Adorno, Frenkel-Brunswick, Levinson, & Sanford, 1950), psychologists' attention to ideology has been sporadic. The subject was revived with the publication of a meta-analysis by Jost and colleagues (2003a), which identified associations between political conservatism and an array of individual differences in personality, cognition, and motivation. Ultimately, the review cast political conservatism as a rigid and defensive ideology, characterized by low tolerance for ambiguity, low openness to experience, high personal need for structured knowledge, and chronic fear of death.

Those results appeared consistent with an uncertainty-threat model of political conservatism (Jost & Napier, 2012), according to which resistance to change and opposition to equality are core components of right-wing ideology and function to mitigate uncertainty and threat. Further, Jost and colleagues' (2003a) findings lined up neatly with the claim from system justification theory (e.g., Jost, Banaji, & Nosek, 2004) that people gain certainty and security by perpetuating the social system as it stands—adopting a conservative orientation to the status quo. Progressive left-wing ideologies, by contrast, are considered less reliable bases of security; they embrace change and social equality principles that question the status quo instead of maintaining it, thus implying chaos and unpredictability (Jost & Napier, 2012). These theories form the basis for the *conservative shift hypothesis*: threatening conditions will motivate people to gravitate toward right-wing ideologies and away from left-wing ideologies (cf. Tetlock, 1989).

In support of this perspective, Jost et al. (2007) found perceptions of status quo threat and self-reported death anxiety to predict higher levels of conservatism. Critically, these factors did not predict ideological extremism—that is, endorsement of *either* extremely conservative or extremely liberal ideologies—suggesting conservatism, but not liberalism, is uniquely associated with threat sensitivity. Nail, McGregor, Drinkwater, Steele, and Thompson (2009) provided converging experimental evidence. In their research, participants in a threat condition read an article designed to undermine perception of a just social system (by describing corporate corruption). Self-identified liberals responded to this threat with increased patriotism to levels generally observed among their more conservative counterparts. Similar effects occur even among individuals relatively disadvantaged by existing social systems. For instance, Milojev, Greaves, Osborne, & Sibley (2015) observed New Zealanders of low socioeconomic status to become more conservative following the 2007–2008 global financial crisis.

Failures of social systems thus elicit defense of the status quo, and some terror management research suggests that death reminders may have a similar effect. For example, studies show mortality salience causes people to think about the social world in simple, familiar ways. When reminded of death, people increasingly process social information in a heuristic manner (Landau et al., 2004), rely on stereotypes (Schimel et al., 1999), and proclaim the existing social system to be just (Hirschberger, 2006). MS often seems to promote black-and-white thinking that reinforces established social guidelines. In an early terror management study, for instance, Greenberg and colleagues (1990) observed MS to increase municipal court judges' fines for a prostitute, reflecting a strengthened emphasis on the application of law and opposition to moral violation. Along similar lines, Cuillier (2009) recently found MS to reduce journalism students' favorability to relativistic thinking, motivating them instead to promote clear ethical journalistic duties and harshly punish those who violate them.

Similarly, the well-established effect of MS to amplify preference for ingroups over outgroups may be interpreted as conservative advocacy for the status quo— as championing a comfortable, preset sense of social order and hierarchy. Greenberg et al. (1990), for instance, observed MS to increase Americans' preference for a person expressing positive (vs. negative) opinions of the United States. Similarly, Bassett and Connelly (2011) found MS caused Americans to negatively evaluate an undocumented Mexican immigrant. Mortality-inspired preference for familiar features of one's ingroup and culture may at times be so potent as to overshadow important personality factors, as findings from van der Zee, van Oudenhoven, and Grijs (2004) suggest. They observed Openness (a personality trait associated with more liberal worldviews) to positively predict attraction to foreign cultures; yet under MS, both high and low in Openness individuals showed comparable preference for their own culture over others.

The most commonly cited evidence for conservative shifting in response to existential threat pertains to Westerners' enhanced nationalism following the 9/11 terrorist attacks. As noted by Christie (2006), in the months following 9/11, Americans' nationalistic sentiments reached peak levels,

> with 97 percent agreeing that they would rather be Americans than citizens of any other country (an increase of 7 percentage points) and 85 percent

reporting that America was a better country than others (5-point increase). Nearly half (49 percent) agreed that the 'world would be a better place if people from other countries were more like Americans' (11-point increase), and disagreement with the idea that there are aspects of America to be ashamed of was up 22 points (from 18 percent to 40 percent). The nationalistic climate was fueled by rhetoric that emphasized essentialism, divisiveness, and moral mandates. (p. 22)

This flag-waving proved psychologically protective to many Americans. Kumagai and Ohbuchi (2002) found that, shortly after the attacks, New Yorkers who strongly identified with the United States felt especially secure from terror. Similarly, Dunkel (2002) observed reminders of 9/11 to heighten anxiety among Midwesterners unless they had an established, well-defined identity to keep them buffered.

Tragically, this boost in nationalistic fervor coincided with intensification of a wide range of hate crimes against individuals of Middle Eastern dissent—as well as those who simply did not "look American" by virtue of their appearance (e.g., Sikhs)—including employment discrimination, verbal harassment, racial profiling, and violence (American-Arab Anti-Discrimination Committee, 2002; Singh, 2002). Remnants of Americans' intensified urge to protect their nationalistic identity from perceived terrorist threats can be observed even a decade later. In 2010, Gallup News Service reported that 53% of Americans held a negative view of the Islamic faith and, from 2000 to 2006, the average American's wariness about having a Muslim neighbor increased by 8% (Schafer & Shaw, 2009). In related experimental findings by Kugler and Cooper (2010), mortality-salient Americans advocated for extended detainment and against procedural protections for a fictional terrorist suspect if he was described as Saudi citizen Abdal-Karim Arif, but not if he was described as Jason Lockhart from the United States.

Joint effects of war, terror, and death on motivation to bolster faith in a core nationalistic identity have been observed in studies throughout the world. Chartard et al. (2011) found students living in a staunchly pro-government region of the war-torn Ivory Coast responded to MS with enhanced support of their government and its military action. Dechesne, van den Berg, and Soeters (2007) found Dutch military personnel exhibited greater concern about death while stationed in Afghanistan (compared to when at home in Europe), which predicted decreased willingness to collaborate with citizens from other nations. Similarly, Kökdemir and Yeniçeri (2010) found Muslims in Turkey responded to MS with decreased interest in sustaining international relations with England and Greece.

Similar pro–status quo effects have been shown in response to even subtle mortality reminders, such as those encountered in the media. Das, Bushman, Bezemer, Kerkhof, and Vermeulen (2009) found that, after the highly publicized murder of filmmaker Theo van Gogh by Muslim extremists, exposing

Dutch participants to a terrorism-related news clip increased the accessibility of death-related thoughts, which in turn predicted increased belief that Arabs in the Netherlands remain loyal to their home countries, thus making the Netherlands unsafe. Further, results on an implicit association test showed terrorism-related news amplified White Europeans' implicit anti-Arab attitudes and Muslim participants' implicit anti-European attitudes, suggesting perceived threat led the opposed groups to cling to their respective visions of the status quo. Hong, Wong, and Liu (2001) reported similar findings in China.

Existential threats inspire people to bolster their ties not only to the broad nationalistic system with which they identify, but also to leaders who represent that system's strength and provide inspiration in the face of adversity. Charismatic political figures have often served as bastions of psychological security in trying times, from Winston Churchill and Nelson Mandela to Bashar Al-Assad and Adolph Hitler. Research suggests that, in the wake of 9/11, Americans looked to then-president George W. Bush to affirm the righteousness of the American way of life and ensure its security against terrorist threats. Several studies showed MS to increase Americans' support for Bush and his antiterrorist policies (e.g., Cohen, Ogilvie, Solomon, Greenberg, & Pyszczynski, 2005; Landau et al., 2004). Such findings are typically construed as support for the conservative shift hypothesis, because even liberal participants responded to MS with enhanced favorability to the staunchly Republican Bush.

In sum, a substantial body of work suggests various forms of psychological threat (terrorism, death, deficient government systems) can motivate individuals to adopt a more conservative worldview, one based on a closed style of thinking that shuns outsiders and defends current laws, ethics, national identity, and leaders against anything that undermines their validity.

Evidence of Political Worldview Defense

Conservative shifting may be only part of the total picture, however. Consider the fact that extreme right-wing *and* left-wing ideologies have served as bases for defensive, inflexible thinking and repressive totalitarian regimes (Greenberg & Jonas, 2003). In parallel with corrosive right-wing social movements like Hitler's Nazism and Mussolini's Fascism stand hardline left-wing communist movements from the Stalinist Soviet Union, Mao's China, and Castro's Cuba. Despite pretensions to progressiveness and social equality, communist societies have historically instituted oppressive policies of social control and imprisonment (e.g., the Stasi of the former German Democratic Republic) and developed hierarchical organizations privileging a select few (e.g., Leonhard, 1986). Moreover, extreme communist beliefs and opposition to capitalism—including extreme endorsement of egalitarianism—correlate positively with authoritarianism (e.g., McFarland, Ageyev, & Abalakina-Paap, 1992). These observations are difficult to explain from the conservative shift perspective.

Closer empirical investigations show, in fact, that responses to real-world threats do not inevitably indicate a conservative shift. For instance, in the aftermath of 9/11, many Americans did not exhibit increased prejudice and intolerance, but rather showed the opposite response (Morgan, Wisneski, & Skitka, 2011; Pyszczynski, Solomon, & Greenberg, 2003). Many opened their hearts to close others and sought out new social connections. Blood donations, charitable giving, volunteerism, and political engagement increased (Morgan et al., 2011). In one survey, 57.8% of Americans came to believe 9/11 had some positive consequences, including heightened senses of the preciousness of life, social closeness, and altruism (Poulin, Silver, Gil-Rivas, Holman, & McIntosh, 2009; Yum & Schenck-Hamlin, 2005). Research by Rutjens, van der Pligt, and van Harreveld (2009) supports the idea that such progressive hope is existentially securing. They found having participants think about progressively solving personal, environmental, and social problems in the near or distant future eliminated the effect of MS to elevate death-thought accessibility, and relaxed negative reactions to a worldview-threatening essay.

Just as historical regimes and responses to impactful events do not invariably produce conservative shifting, neither does MS. Rather, a wealth of terror management research supports the *political worldview defense hypothesis*: Reminders of death will cause conservatives to become more conservative while causing liberals to become more liberal.

For instance, MS intensifies conservative leanings among conservatives, but has no such effect among liberals. A dynamic experimental example comes from Pyszczynski et al. (2006), who observed MS and reminders of terrorism to increase conservatives' support for the use of extreme military measures in the War on Terror (e.g., chemical and nuclear weapons), but to have no such effects among liberal participants. Likewise, Lavine, Lodge, and Freitas (2005) observed high-authoritarian Americans (in comparison to low-authoritarians) to respond to MS with increased interest in pro–death penalty arguments and diminished interest in more balanced, two-sided arguments on that issue (cf. Greenberg et al., 1990). Using diverse correlational survey techniques, McCann (2009) found the degree of social, economic, or political unrest perceived as threatening to the American way of life to predict greater state-level support for Republican candidates, but only in conservative states.

Is the reverse true as well—does MS amplify liberal tendencies among liberals, but not among conservatives? Research suggests it can. The earliest such evidence was provided by Greenberg et al. (1992), who found liberals responded to a death reminder with greater tolerance of a person described as conservative, whereas conservatives instead responded with firmer rejection of a liberal. Although liberals' defensiveness in that study appeared weaker than that of conservatives (the effect among liberals was statistically marginal), recent work by Castano et al. (2011) shows threatened liberals do indeed robustly defend diverse aspects of their liberalism. Across several studies of liberals from New

York City (a relatively liberal location), Castano and colleagues (2011) observed MS to amplify left-leaning views on a host of politically charged issues, including endorsement of stem cell research, government-sponsored national health care, and legalization of same-sex marriages. Furthermore, MS prompted the liberal participants to become particularly anticonservative by more avidly rejecting authoritarianism (a well-known correlate of conservatism in Western culture; Altemeyer, 1998) and more strongly opposing strict sentencing for drug offenders, tightened immigration restrictions, abolishing welfare, the idea that abortion is amoral, and reference to God in the pledge of allegiance.

Research thus shows worldview defense can be observed independently among conservatives *or* liberals. Measuring participants' attitudes toward hot-button political issues of a conservative nature (e.g., Pyszczynski et al.'s [2006] measure of extreme military support) detects pronounced defensiveness among conservatives; while measuring attitudes toward hot-button liberal issues detects liberals' defensiveness (Castano et al., 2011). Notably, however, the political landscape frequently features liberals and conservatives acting defensively at the same time. Incessant partisan quibbling and congressional gridlock commonly result from rigidity occurring in tandem on both sides of political debates. When it comes to the broad issue of science, for instance, Nisbet, Cooper, and Garrett (2015) recently found both liberals and conservatives resist information that does not "fit" with their respective party lines: Conservatives exhibit negative emotions and resistance to scientific claims regarding climate change and evolution, while liberals show the same defensive motivational and emotional reactions to scientific claims about nuclear power and fracking.

Many terror management studies similarly show that MS elicits directionally opposite responses among liberals and conservatives—that the same underlying existential concerns provoke diametrically opposed defensive responses. Such effects often occur with respect to the evaluation of those who overtly derogate a person's political orientation or the views associated with it. For example, McGregor et al. (1998) found that, after MS, Democrats and Republicans alike negatively evaluated critics of their respective political beliefs and even aggressed against their political opponents by doling out large amounts of painfully spicy hot sauce for them to ingest in a supposed taste testing study. In a more issue-specific example, Castano et al. (2011) found MS caused conservatives to reject the author of a pro-evolution essay and embrace the author of a pro-creationism essay, yet liberal participants showed precisely the opposite pattern of author evaluations following MS. Further, on the contentious subject of immigration, Weise, Arciszewski, Verlhiac, Pyszczynski, and Greenberg (2012) observed French and American participants with high levels of right-wing authoritarianism to evaluate an immigrant target especially negatively after MS, whereas low authoritarianism participants showed a significant effect in the opposite direction, becoming more positively inclined to the immigrant following MS (cf. Bassett, 2010). Attitudinal polarization even occurs with respect to evaluation of charismatic political figures. In a hypothetical gubernatorial election scenario, Kosloff, Greenberg, Weise, and Solomon (2010) found MS to enhance people's favoritism toward a charismatic candidate of their own (liberal or conservative) political ideology while diminishing their liking for a charismatic candidate of the opposing ideology.

Divergent responses to existential threat also occur with respect to political issues themselves, regardless of their direct linkage to a specific target person. Vail, Arndt, Motyl, and Pyszczynski (2012) found exposure to images of destroyed buildings reminiscent of the 9/11 terrorist attacks heightened liberals' and conservatives' death-thought accessibility and elicited greater dogmatic certainty in their respective preexisting political beliefs about various issues, including women's rights, homosexuality, atheism, authoritarian control, and traditionalism. Nail et al. (2009) obtained similar results, finding MS increased liberals' conviction regarding their preexisting attitudes toward capital punishment and abortion, up to levels comparable to the conviction of conservative participants. Cuillier, Duell, and Joireman (2009) observed attitudes toward national security moderated responses to MS regarding the press's right to access government information. The study found MS decreased support for press access among people who highly valued national security, but increased press access support among those who least valued national security. Further, Routledge, Juhl, and Vess (2010) showed thoughts of terrorism increased traditionalist tendencies and opposition to adoption of the Euro among Brits high in the dispositional tendency to prefer structure, order, and consistency; yet those low in such dispositional tendencies had the opposite response.

Importantly, the politically polarizing effect of death-related concerns has been observed outside the laboratory, in a wide variety of cultural contexts, and consequent of various forms of real-world threats that render mortality salient. For instance, McCann (2008) demonstrated homicide rates influence attitudes toward the death penalty differently in Red states than in Blue states, with more conservative states becoming more pro–death penalty and more liberal states becoming more opposed to it as homicides rates rise. Laufer, Solomon, and Levine (2010) demonstrated that direct exposure to terrorist attacks increased both liberal and conservative Israeli citizens' commitment to engaging in demonstrations supporting their respective parties, as well as their motivations to persuade others of the correctness of their respective views and disdain for those who would fail to do so. Further, a longitudinal study by Chatard, Arndt, and Pyszczynski (2010) found Swiss individuals who had experienced the death of a close other over a 6-year period exhibited increasingly polarized political attitudes, with liberals and conservatives more extremely endorsing their respective party-line views regarding the Swiss army, social programs, joining the European Union, providing opportunities for foreigners, environmental protection, taxing the rich, and nuclear energy policy (notably, though, this effect was weaker among liberals).

In sum, liberal ideologies *and* conservative ideologies can afford existential security. Contrary to Jost et al.'s (2007) findings, a large body of research shows that psychological threats are often polarizing and push people to espouse greater conviction in their preexisting left-leaning or right-leaning beliefs and attitudes. The threat of death can motivate people not simply to become more conservative, but to become more firmly entrenched in whatever bases of value and meaning are of essential importance to them.

Integrating the Worldview Defense and Conservative Shift Hypotheses

Clear differences exist between the terror management theory and uncertainty-threat/system justification models of motivated political cognition. How can we reconcile these findings? One starting point is to reconsider the conceptualization of *status quo*, a phrase that translates roughly as "the existing state of affairs." A central tenet of the conservative shift perspective is that motivation to adhere to or defend the status quo is directly linked to conservatism. Yet this framing may refer to "psychological conservatism"—as in, sustaining the system as it stands—rather than "political conservatism," per se. In this way, this framing may muddy the picture: Are we talking about conserving versus progressing the "system," or bolstering support for conservative versus liberal positions on socioeconomic issues and candidates? Conservative shift advocates often toggle between these distinct dimensions yet arguably are referring to the former. Keeping them distinct, though, points to an illuminating possibility: The motivation to conserve the system may be orthogonal to the specific norms, values, and socioeconomic premises propagated by that system, which can be left or right wing.

Jost, Glaser, Kruglanski, and Sulloway (2003b) proposed the compromise view that "rigidity of the left can and does occur, but it is less common than rigidity of the right" (p. 383). They suggested progressive movements at their early stages (liberal, Democratic, neo-Marxist, radical, socialist) are highly open to change and uncertainty, whereas conservative movements at their early stages (religious right, military rule, fascist, neo-Nazi) are only moderately so. Likewise, so-called "old" progressive regimes (Soviet Union, People's Republic of China, Cuba) are only moderately open to change and uncertainty, whereas old conservative regimes (feudalism, monarchy, religious authority, patriarchy) are not open at all. Moreover, Jost and colleagues' rigorous meta-analytic overview (2003b) showed psychological rigidity to correlate with both extreme right-wing tendencies *and* ideological extremity in either direction, though more studies support the former.

Why then do so many terror management studies show distinct and often comparably strong and opposed defensive responses to MS? And why did Burke and colleagues' (2013) meta-analysis show significant effect sizes for both conservative shifting ($r = .22$) and political worldview defense ($r = .35$), with the latter effect being directionally stronger?

Methods and Mechanisms

One possibility is that Jost et al.'s (2003a, 2003b) hypothesis is only partly correct. Greenberg and Jonas (2003) provided thoughtful counterpoints to the claims that conservatism but not liberalism is historically associated with resistance to change and intolerance of equality. For example, they observed that American social conservatives routinely clamor for systematic change (e.g., reducing consumer safety, environmental, and weapons regulations, taxation, and the size of government) and, as noted earlier, that authoritarian views can emerge on behalf of either type of ideology.

It is feasible that differences between each theoretical camp's research methods may partly explain the lack of fit in their respective findings. An experiment testing how MS impacts political leanings may elicit different psychological processes—and thus produce different psychological outcomes—than a correlational test of the association between political ideology and self-reported death anxiety. Perhaps the former are more unconscious. Terror management research shows conscious death thoughts cause people to seek concrete, literal security, whereas unconscious death thoughts motivate efforts to defend one's worldview (Pyszczynski, Greenberg, & Solomon, 1999). The correlation between subjective death anxiety and conservatism observed by Jost and colleagues (2003a) may therefore reflect motivation to feel literally secure and protected from psychologically overt concerns with uncertainty and vulnerability (e.g., "I want my nation and military to assure my safety!"); conversely, laboratory MS effects instead show reliance on long-standing beliefs and values particular to a person's worldview (e.g., "I will not tolerate the intolerant!"). A simple study to assess this possibility has yet to be done: test whether supraliminal death primes enhance conservative leanings, whereas subliminal death primes have a polarizing effect.

At the theoretical level, Anson and colleagues (2009) importantly noted system justification needs emphasize factors *external* to the individual—such as the perception that the social system is consistent, just, and structured. By contrast, terror management needs emphasize more *internal* factors—that is, motivation to reduce death-related anxiety by finding meaning and value in life. This may be why threats to the perceived certainty/control afforded by external social systems so often elicit generalized system justifying responses in a uniform manner across individuals, whereas death reminders typically elicit defense of worldviews more specific to a given individual's internalized vision of reality.

In line with this view, Rutjens and Loseman (2010) have suggested terror management and system justification operate on the basis of distinct self-regulatory mechanisms. Worldview defense, they claim, is a meaning-seeking response to existential anxiety provoked by MS, while system justification is a control-seeking response to concerns with uncertainty about the world. Indeed, they found MS heightened Dutch participants' death-thought accessibility and elicited highly negative attitudes toward the author of an essay expressing anti-Western sentiments, but had no effect on participants' justification of the Dutch social system. Yet, in another condition, participants completed a taxing task designed to deplete their sense of control instead of inducing MS; neither death-thought accessibility, nor worldview defense were heightened, but system justification was.

Additional research supports the independence of these two processes. Ullrich and Cohrs (2007) found reminding Germans of terrorism heightened their system justification (agreement with items such as "In general the German political system operates as it should"), yet did so without increasing existential concerns (i.e., death-thought accessibility). Conversely, in the terror management literature, numerous studies have shown MS effects are different from uncertainty salience effects (Burke, Martens, & Faucher, 2010) and, further, that MS amplifies risky and thus control-reducing behaviors if they serve a person's strivings for meaning and value (e.g., Landau & Greenberg, 2006; Taubman-Ben-Ari, 2000).

In sum, multiple mechanisms likely come into play where defense of political ideology is concerned, suggesting conservative shifting and political worldview defense may ultimately be best viewed as complementary rather than competing processes.

Historical, Dispositional, and Situational Fluctuations in Perception of the Status Quo

Although different threats may elicit different processes, the research reviewed earlier in this chapter showed the same variable, mortality salience, elicits conservative shifting in some studies but polarizing political worldview defense in others, even when it is manipulated using similar methods and thus likely engaging similar processes. So how can the full body of MS effects be explained?

A crucial factor to consider here is that worldviews fluctuate across history, culture, people, and situations, and thus so do the particular beliefs and values people rely upon for existential security. We have already noted zeitgeists associated with massive historic social movements can precipitate authoritarian tendencies of a left-wing or right-wing nature. However, even within one culture over time, there may be noticeable population-level shifts in preference for liberal or conservative ideology. At those respective historical junctures, the currently dominant ideology may serve as a primary ideological rallying point. For instance, in post-Depression era America, the New Deal created social security and FDR's "fireside chats" presented Americans with a comforting liberal face; whereas, in post-9/11 America, the War on Terror established radical national security measures behind the confident assertions of conservative George W. Bush.

This raises an important question: To what extent do MS-induced conservative shift effects represent clinging to historically and culturally concurrent trends in nationalism rather than conservatism per se? The reader may have noticed most evidence for conservative shifting after MS shows individuals gravitating toward beliefs, attitudes, and figures that are multidimensional in nature, representing not only a conservative worldview but also standing tall on behalf of nationalistic identity and the current president or positions on issues reflecting concerns for the nation as a whole (e.g., terrorism, immigration). For example, as mentioned earlier, portrayals of terrorism in the media amplify people's defense of the status quo against terrorist outsiders (Das et al., 2009). Indeed, Nail and McGregor (2009) found liberals and conservatives alike reported greater conservatism following the 9/11 attacks, but this effect was most pronounced on items assessing support for then-president Bush and increased military spending and much less pronounced on more politically divisive issues like socialized medicine.

Longitudinal research is needed to determine whether responses to death-related thoughts shift people leftward or rightward over time in parallel with the pendulum swings of the political landscape. Yet, it is clear from evidence to date that individual differences in political orientation moderate MS effects at our current moment in history and in many cultures. Perhaps different worldviews render different features of the human experience chronically accessible or salient, including values otherwise generally important to most people—part of a *universal human worldview.* For instance, most people, when pushed, will acknowledge that getting along with others and demonstrating compassion are crucial for human survival; likewise, most will acknowledge that excessive taxation and government overreach are undesirable. Yet long-standing adherence to a particular liberal or conservative ideology is likely to render norms and values associated with each respective point of view chronically accessible, and thus highly likely to condition politically defensive responses to MS. This idea is akin to contemporary positions on attachment, which often attribute secure/insecure attachment to the chronic or situational activation of specific relationship schemas.

Consistent with this view, a wealth of evidence shows salient situational information moderates MS effects (Fritsche, Jonas, Niesta Kayser, & Koranyi, 2010; Gailliot, Sillman, Schmeichel, Maner, & Plant, 2008; Jonas et al., 2008). Findings indicate that when situational primes make liberal principles and positions salient (e.g., prosociality, benevolence, egalitarianism, pacifism, helpfulness, protection of the environment), MS amplifies thought and behavior consistent with those norms. Conversely, when conservative principles and positions are rendered salient (e.g., punitiveness, pro-selfness), MS causes people to act in line with those norms instead.

Greenberg et al. (1992) presented the earliest of such evidence, showing that priming individuals with words related to tolerance eliminated the effect of MS to enhance negative evaluation of the author of an anti–United States essay. More recently, Abdollahi, Henthorn, and Pyszczynski (2009) found that, among Iranian college students, MS increased support for martyrdom attacks against Western targets, but this effect was eliminated if participants were first presented with information indicating the majority of Iranians opposed such violence. Similarly, Rothschild, Abdollahi, and Pyszczynski (2009) found presenting compassion-oriented Biblical verses to American religious fundamentalists reduced the effect of MS to amplify their support for extreme military interventions in the Middle East, and priming compassion-oriented Koran verses to Iranian Shiite Muslims eliminated the ability of MS to heighten anti-Western sentiment. Such moderation effects also occur with respect to support for political figures: During the 2008 U.S. presidential election, Vail, Arndt, Motyl, and Pyszczynski (2009) found MS elevated support for Republican candidate John McCain, but if individuals were first primed with compassionate values advocating love and understanding, MS instead elevated support for Democratic candidate Barak Obama.

In a similar vein, Weise et al. (2008) observed a generalized liberal shift due to situationally salient information, finding that, among American liberals and conservatives primed with thoughts of secure interpersonal attachments, MS decreased support for the use of extreme military measures (e.g., chemical and nuclear weapons) in the War on Terror. Yet Vail et al. (2012) demonstrated salient information can also promote a warmongering mentality, finding that presenting images of destroyed buildings and deadly terrorist attacks heightened the accessibility of death-related thoughts, which in turn mediated intensified support for aggressive military action against Iran among both liberal and conservative Americans.

In sum, predicting whether existential concerns elicit a conservative or a liberal shift requires consideration of factors contributing to changes/differences in perception of the status quo across history, culture, people, and situations. Worldviews are individualized psychological structures internalized over the course of socialization, and, consequently, prevailing views espoused by the culture at large and highlighted by particular historical, social, and situational forces can alter how one perceives and defends the state of affairs.

Conclusion

Regardless of whether they operate in tandem or independently, detrimental effects of terror management and system justification processes on the political landscape are palpable and numerous. Beliefs, attitudes, and voting behavior are skewed by our insecurities and defensive ideological clinging, contradicting the rationalist principles of Jeffersonian democracy and undermining desperately needed efforts for humans to find common understanding before we bring about our own extinction. After reading this chapter, it may not be surprising to learn that emotional and motivational processes interfere with citizens' abilities to rationally examine legitimate evidence of state crimes against democracy and thereby pave the way for governments to manipulate their citizenries (Manwell, 2010). An existentially anxious population is a controllable population. Learning about the various ways in which defensiveness shapes political ideology is an essential step toward reinstating reason in the political world.

References

Abdollahi, A., Henthorn, C., & Pyszczynski, T. (2009). Experimental peace psychology: Priming consensus mitigates aggression against outgroups under mortality salience. *Behavioral Sciences of Terrorism and Political Aggression, 2*(1), 30–37. http://dx.doi.org/10.1080/19434470903319466

Adorno, T. W., Frenkel-Brunswick, E., Levinson, D. J., & Sanford, R. N. (1950). *The authoritarian personality.* New York: Harper. http://dx.doi.org/10.4135/9781446220986.n8

Altemeyer, R. A. (1998). The other "authoritarian personality". In M. P. Zanna (Ed.), *Advances in experimental social psychology* (30, pp. 47–91). New York: Academic Press. http://dx.doi.org/10.1016/S0065–2601(08)60382–2

American-Arab Anti-Discrimination Committee. (2002). *ADC fact sheet: The condition of Arab Americans post-9/11.* Retrieved from http://www.adc.org/2001/11/the-condition-of-arab-americans-post-9–11/

Anson, J., Pyszczynski, T., Solomon, S., & Greenberg, J. (2009). Political ideology in the 21st century: A terror management perspective on maintenance and change of the status quo. In J. T. Jost, A. C. Kay and H. Thorisdottir (Eds.), *Social and psychological bases of ideology and system justification* (pp. 210–240). New York: Oxford University Press. http://dx.doi.org/10.1093/acprof:oso/9780195320916.003.009

Bassett, J. F. (2010). The effects of mortality salience and social dominance orientation on attitudes toward illegal immigrants. *Social Psychology, 41,* 52–55. http://dx.doi.org/10.1027/1864–9335/a000008

Bassett, J. R., & Connelly, J. N. (2011). Terror management and reactions to undocumented immigrants: Mortality salience increases aversion to culturally dissimilar others. *The Journal of Social Psychology, 151,* 117–120. http://dx.doi.org/10.1080/00224540903365562

Burke, B. L., Kosloff, S., & Landau, M. J. (2013). Death goes to the polls: A meta-analysis of mortality salience effects on political attitudes. *Political Psychology, 34,* 183–200. http://dx.doi.org/10.1111/pops.12005

Burke, B. L., Martens, A., & Faucher, E. H. (2010). Two decades of terror management theory: A meta-analysis of mortality salience research. *Personality & Social Psychology Review, 14,* 155–195. http://dx.doi.org/10.1177/1088868309352321

Castano, E., Leidner, B., Bonacossa, A., Nikka, J., Perrulli, R., Spencer, B., et al. (2011). Ideology, fear of death, and death anxiety. *Political Psychology, 32,* 601–621. http://dx.doi.org/10.1111/j.1467–9221.2011.00822.x

Chatard, A., Arndt, J., & Pyszczynski, T. (2010). Loss shapes political views? Terror management, political ideology, and the death of close others. *Basic and Applied Social Psychology, 32,* 2–7. http://dx.doi.org/10.1080/01973530903539713

Chatard, A., Selimbegović, L., N'dri Konan, P., Arndt, J., Pyszczynski, T., Lorenzi-Cioldi, F., & Van Der Linden, M. (2011). Terror management in times of war: Mortality salience effects on self-esteem and governmental support. *Journal of Peace Research, 48,* 225. http://dx.doi.org/10.1177/0022343310397435

Christie, D. J. (2006). 9/11 Aftershocks: An analysis of conditions ripe for hate crimes. In P. R. Kimmel & C. E. Stout (Eds.), *Collateral damage: The psychological consequences of America's war on terrorism* (pp. 19–44). Westport, CT: Praeger Publishers/Greenwood Publishing Group.

Cohen, F., Ogilvie, D. M., Solomon, S., Greenberg, J., & Pyszczynski, T. (2005). American roulette: The effect of reminders of death on support for George W. Bush in the 2004 presidential election. *Analyses of Social Issues and Public Policy, 5*, 177–187. http://dx.doi.org/10.1111/j.1530–2415.2005.00063.x

Cuillier, D. (2009). Mortality morality: Effect of death thoughts on journalism students' attitudes toward relativism, idealism, and ethics. *Journal of Mass Media Ethics, 24*, 40–58. http://dx.doi.org/10.1080/08900520802644394

Cuillier, D., Duell, B., & Joireman, J. (2009). FOI friction: The thought of death, national security values, and polarization of attitudes toward freedom of information. *Open Government, 5*(1). Retrieved from www.opengovjournal.org

Das, E., Bushman, B. J., Bezemer, M. D., Kerkhof, P., & Vermeulen, I. E. (2009). How terrorism news reports increase prejudice against outgroups: A terror management account. *Journal of Experimental Social Psychology, 45*, 453–459. http://dx.doi.org/10.1016/j.jesp.2008.12.001

Dechesne, M., van den Berg, C., & Soeters, J. (2007). International collaboration under threat: A field study in Kabul. *Conflict Management and Peace Science, 24*, 25–36. http://dx.doi.org/10.1080/07388940601102811

Dunkel, C. S. (2002). Terror management theory and identity: The effect of the 9/11 terrorist attacks on anxiety and identity change. *Identity, 2*, 281–301. http://dx.doi.org/10.1207/S1532706XID0204_01

Fritsche, I., Jonas, E., Niesta Kayser, D., & Koranyi, N. (2010). Existential threat and compliance with pro-environmental norms. *Journal of Environmental Psychology, 30*, 67–79. http://dx.doi.org/10.1016/j.jenvp.2009.08.007

Gailliot, M. T., Sillman, T. F., Schmeichel, B. J., Maner, J. K., & Plant, E. A. (2008). Mortality salience increases adherence to salient norms and values. *Personality and Social Psychology Bulletin, 34*, 993–1003. http://dx.doi.org/10.1177/0146167208316791

Gallup News Service. (2010). *In U.S., religious prejudice stronger against Muslims.* Retrieved on February 20, 2015 from http://www.gallup.com/poll/125312/ReligiousPrejudice-Stronger Against-Muslims.aspx

Greenberg, J., & Jonas, E. (2003). Psychological motives and political orientation—The left, the right, and the rigid: Comment on Jost et al. (2003). *Psychological Bulletin, 129*(3), 376–382.

Greenberg, J., Pyszczynski, T., Solomon, S., Rosenblatt, A., Veeder, M., Kirkland, S., & Lyon, D. (1990). Evidence for terror management II: The effects of mortality salience on reactions to those who threaten or bolster the cultural worldview. *Journal of Personality and Social Psychology, 58*, 308–318. http://dx.doi.org/10.1037//0022–3514.58.2.308

Greenberg, J., Simon, L., Pyszczynski, T., Solomon, S., & Chatel, D. (1992). Terror management and tolerance: Does mortality salience always intensify negative reactions to others who threaten one's worldview? *Journal of Personality and Social Psychology, 63*, 212–220. http://dx.doi.org/10.1037//0022–3514.63.2.212

Hirschberger, G. (2006). Terror management and attributions of blame to innocent victims: Reconciling compassionate and defensive responses. *Journal of Personality and Social Psychology, 91*, 832–844. http://dx.doi.org/10.1037/0022–3514.91.5.832

Hong, Y., Wong, R. Y. M., & Liu, J. H. (2001). The history of war strengthens ethnic identification. *Journal of Psychology in Chinese Societies, 2*, 77–105.

Jonas, E., Martens, A., Niesta, D., Fritsche, I., Sullivan, D., & Greenberg, J. (2008). Focus theory of normative conduct and terror management theory: The interactive impact of mortality salience and norm salience on social judgment. *Journal of Personality and Social Psychology, 95*, 1239–1251. http://dx.doi.org/10.1037/a0013593

Jost, J. T., Banaji, M. R., & Nosek, B. A. (2004). A decade of system justification theory: Accumulated evidence of conscious and unconscious bolstering of the status quo. *Political Psychology, 25*, 881–919. http://dx.doi.org/10.1111/j.1467–9221.2004.00402.x

Jost, J. T., Glaser, J., Kruglanski, A. W., & Sulloway, F. J. (2003a). Political conservatism as motivated social cognition. *Psychological Bulletin, 129*, 339–375. http://dx.doi.org/10.1037/0033–2909.129.3.339

Jost, J. T., Glaser, J., Kruglanski, A. W., & Sulloway, F. J. (2003b). Exceptions that prove the rule—Using a theory of motivated social cognition to account for ideological incongruities and political anomalies: Reply to Greenberg and Jonas (2003). *Psychological Bulletin, 129*, 383–393.

Jost, J. T., & Napier, J. L. (2012). The uncertainty-threat model of political conservatism. In M. A. Hogg & D. L. Blaylock (Eds.), *Extremism and the psychology of uncertainty* (pp. 90–111). New York: Wiley-Blackwell. http://dx.doi.org/10.1002/9781444344073.ch6

Jost, J. T., Napier, J. L., Thorisdottir, H., Gosling, S. D., Tibor, P. P., & Ostafin, B. (2007). Are needs to manage uncertainty and threat associated with political conservatism or ideological extremity? *Personality and Social Psychology Bulletin, 33*, 989–1007. http://dx.doi.org/10.1177/0146167207301028

Kökdemir, D., & Yeniçeri, Z. (2010). Terror Management in a Predominantly Muslim Country: The effects of mortality salience on university identity and on preference for the development of international relations. *European Psychologist, 15*, 165–174. http://dx.doi.org/10.1027/1016–9040/a000012

Kosloff, S., Greenberg, J., Weise, D., & Solomon, S. (2010). Mortality salience and political preferences: The roles of charisma and political orientation. *Journal of Experimental Social Psychology, 46*, 139–145. http://dx.doi.org/10.1016/j.jesp.2009.09.002

Kugler, M. B., & Cooper, J. (2010). Still an American? Mortality salience and treatment of suspected terrorists. *Journal of Applied Social Psychology, 40*, 3130–3147. http://dx.doi.org/10.1111/j.1559–1816.2010.00694.x

Kumagai, T., & Ohbuchi, K. (2002). Changes in social cognition and social behavior after the September 11th affair: An interpretation from terror management theory. *Tohoku Psychologica Folia, 61*, 22–28.

Landau, M. J., & Greenberg, J. (2006). Play it safe or go for the gold? A terror management perspective on self-enhancement and protection motives in risky decision making. *Personality and Social Psychology Bulletin, 32*, 1633–1645. http://dx.doi.org/10.1177/0146167206292017

Landau, M. J., Solomon, S., Greenberg, J., Cohen, F., Pyszczynski, T., Arndt, J., Miller, C. H., Ogilvie, D. M., & Cook, A. (2004). Deliver us from evil: The effects of mortality salience and reminders of 9/11 on support for President George W. Bush. *Personality and Social Psychology Bulletin, 30*, 1136–1150. http://dx.doi.org/10.1177/0146167204267988

Laufer, A., Solomon, Z., & Levine, S. Z. (2010). Elaboration on posttraumatic growth in youth exposed to terror: The role of religiosity and political ideology. *Social Psychiatry and Psychiatric Epidemiology, 45*, 647–653. http://dx.doi.org/10.1007/s00127–009–0106–5

Lavine, H., Lodge, M., & Freitas, K. (2005). Threat, authoritarianism, and selective exposure to information. *Political Psychology, 26*, 219–244. http://dx.doi.org/10.1111/j.1467–9221.2005.00416.x

Leonhard, W. (1986). *The Kremlin and the West*. New York: Norton.

Manwell, L. A. (2010). In denial of democracy: Social psychological implications for public discourse on state crimes against democracy post-9/11. *American Behavioral Scientist, 53*, 848–884. http://dx.doi.org/10.1177/0002764209353279

McCann, S. J. H. (2008). Social threat, authoritarianism, conservativism, and U.S. state death penalty sentencing (1977–2004). *Journal of Personality and Social Psychology, 94*, 913–923.

McCann, S. J. H. (2009). Political conservatism, authoritarianism, and societal threat: Voting for Republican representatives in U.S. congressional elections from 1946 to 1992. *Journal of Psychology: Interdisciplinary and Applied, 143*, 341–358. http://dx.doi.org/10.3200/JRLP.143.4.341–358

McFarland, S., Ageyev, V. S., & Abalakina-Paap, M. A. (1992). Authoritarianism in the former Soviet Union. *Journal of Personality and Social Psychology, 63*, 1004–1010. http://dx.doi.org/10.1037//0022–3514.63.6.1004

McGregor, H., Lieberman, J. D., Solomon, S., Greenberg, J., Arndt, J., Simon, L., & Pyszczynski, T. (1998). Terror management and aggression: Evidence that mortality salience motivates aggression against worldview threatening others. *Journal of Personality and Social Psychology, 74*, 590–605. http://dx.doi.org/10.1037//0022–3514.74.3.590

Mencken, H. L. (1922). *In defense of women*. New York: A. A. Knopf. Retrieved from http://pds.lib.harvard.edu/pds/view/2573491?n=71&s=4&imagesize=1200&rotation=0

Milojev, P., Greaves, L., Osborne, D., & Sibley, C. G. (2015). Stability and Change in Political Conservatism Following the Global Financial Crisis. *Personality and Social Psychology Bulletin, 41*(1), 127–139. http://dx.doi.org/10.1177/0146167214559710

Morgan, G. S., Wisneski, D. C., & Skitka, L. J. (2011). The expulsion from Disneyland: The social psychological impacts of 9/11. *American Psychologist, 66*, 447–454. http://dx.doi.org/10.1037/a0024772

Nail, P., & McGregor, I. (2009). Conservative shift among liberals and conservatives following 9/11/01. *Social Justice Research, 22*, 231–240. http://dx.doi.org/10.1007/s11211–009–0098-z

Nail, P., McGregor, I., Drinkwater, A. E., Steele, G., & Thompson, A. W. (2009). Threat causes liberals to think like conservatives. *Journal of Experimental Social Psychology, 45*, 901–907. http://dx.doi.org/10.1016/j.jesp.2009.04.013

Nisbet, E. C., Cooper, K. E., Garrett, R. K. (2015). The Partisan Brain: How dissonant science messages lead conservatives and liberals to (dis)trust science. *The ANNALS of the American Academy of Political and Social Science, 658*, 36–66. http://dx.doi.org/10.1177/0002716214555474

Poulin, M. J., Silver, R. C., Gil-Rivas, V., Holman, E. A., & McIntosh, D. N. (2009). Finding social benefits after a collective trauma: Perceiving societal changes and well-being following 9/11. *Journal of Traumatic Stress, 22*, 81–90. http://dx.doi.org/10.1002/jts.20391

Pyszczynski, T., Abdollahi, A., Solomon, S., Greenberg, J., Cohen, F., & Weise, D. (2006). Mortality salience, martyrdom, and military might: The Great Satan versus the Axis of Evil. *Personality and Social Psychology Bulletin, 32*, 525–537. http://dx.doi.org/10.1177/0146167205282157

Pyszczynski, T., Greenberg, J., & Solomon, S. (1999). A dual-process model of defense against conscious and unconscious death-related thoughts: An extension of terror management theory. *Psychological Review, 106*, 835–845. http://dx.doi.org/10.1037/0033–295X.106.4.835

Pyszczynski, T., Solomon, S., & Greenberg, J. (2003). *In the wake of 9/11: The psychology of terror.* Washington, DC: American Psychological Association. http://dx.doi.org/10.1037/10478-000

Rokeach, M. (1960). *The open and closed mind.* New York: Basic Books

Rothschild, Z. K., Abdollahi, A., & Pyszczynski, T. (2009). Does peace have a prayer? The effect of mortality salience, compassionate values, and religious fundamentalism on hostility toward out-groups. *Journal of Experimental Social Psychology, 45,* 816–827. http://dx.doi.org/10.1016/j.jesp.2009.05.016

Routledge, C., Juhl, J., & Vess, M. (2010). Divergent reactions to the terror of terrorism: Personal need for structure moderates the effects of terrorism salience on worldview-related attitudinal rigidity. *Basic and Applied Social Psychology, 32,* 243–249. http://dx.doi.org/10.1080/01973533.2010.495667

Rutjens, B. T., & Loseman, A. (2010). The society-supporting self: System justification and cultural worldview defense as different forms of self-regulation. *Group Processes and Intergroup Relations, 13,* 241–250. http://dx.doi.org/10.1177/1368430209351703

Rutjens, B. T., van der Pligt, J., & van Harreveld, F. (2009). Things will get better: The anxiety-buffering qualities of progressive hope. *Personality and Social Psychology Bulletin, 35,* 535–543. http://dx.doi.org/10.1177/0146167208331252

Schafer, C. E., & Shaw, G. M. (2009). Trends: Tolerance in the United States. *Public Opinion Quarterly, 73,* 404–431. http://dx.doi.org/10.1093/poq/nfp022

Schimel, J., Simon, L., Greenberg, J., Pyszczynski, T., Solomon, S., Waxmonski, J., & Arndt, J. (1999). Stereotypes and Terror Management: Evidence that mortality salience enhances stereotypic thinking and preferences. *Journal of Personality and Social Psychology, 77,* 905–926. http://dx.doi.org/10.1037//0022-3514.77.5.905

Singh, A. (2002). "We are not the enemy": Hate crimes against Arabs, Muslims, and those perceived to be Arab or Muslim after September 11. *Human Rights Watch Report, 14,* 6(G).

Taubman-Ben-Ari, O. (2000). The effect of death reminders on reckless driving: A terror management perspective. *Current Directions in Psychological Science, 9,* 196–199.

Tetlock, P. E. (1989). Structure and function in political belief systems. In A. R. Pratkanis, S. J. Breckler & A. G. Greenwald (Eds.), *Attitude structure and function* (pp. 129–151). Hillsdale, NJ: Erlbaum.

Ullrich, J., & Cohrs, J. C. (2007). Terrorism salience increases system justification: Experimental evidence. *Social Justice Research, 20,* 117–139. http://dx.doi.org/10.1007/s11211-007-0035-y

Vail, K. E., Arndt, J., Motyl, M., & Pyszczynski, T. (2009). Compassionate values and presidential politics: Mortality salience, compassionate values and support for Barack Obama and John McCain in the 2008 Presidential election. *Analyses of Social Issues and Public Policy, 9,* 255–268. http://dx.doi.org/10.1111/j.1530-2415.2009.01190.x

Vail, K. E., Arndt, J., Motyl, M., & Pyszczynski, T. (2012). The aftermath of destruction: Images of destroyed buildings increase support for war, dogmatism, and death thought accessibility. *Journal of Experimental Social Psychology, 48,* 1069–1081. http://dx.doi.org/10.1016/j.jesp.2012.05.004

van der Zee, K., van Oudenhoven, J. P., & Grijs, E. (2004). Personality, threat, and cognitive and emotional reactions to stressful intercultural situations. *Journal of Personality, 72,* 1069–1096. http://dx.doi.org/10.1111/j.0022-3506.2004.00290.x

Weise, D. R., Arciszewski, T., Verlhiac, J., Pyszczynski, T., & Greenberg, J. (2012). Terror management and attitudes toward immigrants: Differential effects of mortality salience for low and high right-wing authoritarians. *European Psychologist, 17,* 63–72. http://dx.doi.org/10.1027/1016-9040/a000056

Weise, D. R., Pyszczynski, T., Cox, C. R., Arndt, J., Greenberg, J., Solomon, S., & Kosloff, S. (2008). Interpersonal politics: The role of terror management and attachment processes in shaping political preferences. *Psychological Science, 19*, 448–455. http://dx.doi.org/10.1111/j.1467–9280.2008.02108.x

Westen, D. (2007). *The political brain: The role of emotion in deciding the fate of the nation.* New York: Public Affairs Books.

Yum, Y., & Schenck-Hamlin, W. (2005). Reactions to 9/11 as a function of terror management and perspective taking. *Journal of Social Psychology, 145*, 265–286. http://dx.doi.org/10.3200/SOCP.145.3.265–286

4

BRIDGING HEALTH AND DEATH

Insights and Questions From a Terror Management Health Model

Melissa Spina, Jamie Arndt, Patrick Boyd, and Jamie Goldenberg

Terror management theory (TMT; Greenberg et al., 1986) is predicated on the assumption that much of human social behavior is fueled by efforts to manage the troubling psychological implications associated with an awareness of the inevitability of death (see Chapter 1 of this volume). Yet every day people make physical health decisions that work against this presumed motivation to avoid mortality. Consider how in the United States people spend upwards of $4.9 billion on indoor tanning each year (Huber, 2012) and that an estimated 42.1 million people smoke cigarettes (CDC, 2012) despite the health risks posed by ultraviolet radiation and, especially, tobacco use (ACS, 2015). While such decisions seem ironic in light of TMT, these ironies can be illuminating. Indeed, Kurt Lewin's (1951, p.169) classic quote, "There is nothing so practical as a good theory," is often taken to suggest a theory can inform the complex interplay of everyday social circumstances. But there is also nothing so *theoretical* as a practical *problem*. A practical problem—as evidenced by ironic, self-defeating health decisions—provides an opportunity from which basic theory can be expanded and enriched by evaluating, not just what *can* happen, but also what *does* happen in the world (Rothman & Salovey, 2007).

In this vein, an interdisciplinary application of TMT to health behavior presents a unique opportunity to explore both the underlying factors influencing harmful and beneficial health decisions, as well as the fundamental processes of how people manage existential insecurity. Yet until the terror management health model (TMHM) was proposed (Goldenberg & Arndt, 2008), TMT had little to say about how the awareness of one's mortality can impact health decisions. And the silence was reciprocal. Health psychology had little to say about how health decisions might be influenced by existential concerns about mortality. The TMHM thus represents a bridge that brings TMT into the health world, and at the same time, brings health into the world of TMT.

This chapter begins with a general overview of the model and the research it has inspired, and then takes stock of what the study of how people manage their awareness of mortality has taught us about health decisions and what the study of health decisions has taught us about how people manage their awareness of mortality; finally, we consider emerging issues and directions that can further inform the intersection between death and health.

Terror Management Health Model: Core Propositions and Basic Research

As you are disrobing to step into the shower you notice a lump where a lump should not be. Many of us may have experienced this kind of scenario (or will in the future), and the knot that arises in one's stomach at least partly reflects the deep connection between perceptions of physical health and concerns about mortality. This example highlights one core proposition of the TMHM: Confrontations with health relevant events can cause people to think about death—either consciously or nonconsciously.

A growing literature demonstrates how health and death are cognitively intertwined. For instance, having people explicitly think about cancer (Arndt et al., 2007), communicating the risks of smoking (Hansen et al., 2010) or unprotected sun exposure (Cooper et al., 2014), all have been shown to activate death-related cognitions. Performing screening behaviors, such as breast exams for women, similarly increase death-related thoughts (Goldenberg et al., 2008). Even subliminal presentations of the word *cancer*—that participants report not having seen—increase death-thought accessibility (Arndt et al., 2007).

These examples all implicate cancer, one of the leading causes of death. In this context, it is perhaps not surprising that over 60% of people in a population-level survey reported that when they think of cancer they automatically think of death (Moser et al., 2014). Yet, while cancer may have an especially potent association with death, it is just one of many health domains that share this connection. Appeals about the consequences of binge drinking (Jessop & Wade, 2008), risky sex (Grover et al., 2010), and even insurance advertisements (Fransen et al., 2008) also increase death-thought accessibility. Such findings highlight a critical question: How do cognitions about mortality influence health decision-making and behavior?

The dual defense model of TMT (e.g., Pyszczynski et al., 1999), which distinguishes how people manage conscious and nonconscious reminders of mortality, provides the foundation for the TMHM. Research indicates, for example, when explicitly confronted with the thought of death, people try to remove such thoughts from conscious awareness (e.g., by suppressing them; Greenberg et al., 1994). These types of responses are referred to as *proximal* defenses. In contrast, *distal* defensive strategies occur when thoughts of death are highly accessible but outside of conscious awareness. Distal responses to death reminders include bolstering one's self-esteem and/or faith in a meaningful, shared cultural worldview (see e.g., Greenberg et al., 2008).

Building from both the dual-defense model of TMT and literature on behavioral health motivations, the TMHM posits when mortality concerns are conscious, health decisions are largely guided by the proximal motivational goals of reducing perceived vulnerability to health threats to remove death-related cognitions from focal attention. These efforts can either engage adaptive health behaviors (e.g., exercising) or less adaptive responses including avoidance of, minimization of risks associated with, and denial of one's vulnerability to health threats. In contrast, when mortality concerns are active but outside of focal attention, health-relevant decisions are guided by the distal motivational goals of bolstering self-esteem and maintaining one's symbolic conception of self. These responses can also be conducive or harmful to health (e.g., sun protection or tanning) depending on the constellation of one's worldview and how one derives self-worth. To date over 50 studies have utilized the TMHM, examining the merits of these basic propositions.

The Effects of Conscious Death Thoughts

When a person's mortality is rendered conscious, whether through the media (e.g., antismoking commercial) or a trip to the emergency room, people may take (or at least intend to take) steps that might reasonably forestall this inevitability. A number of studies highlight this kind of response. For example, individuals explicitly reminded of their mortality report increased intentions to exercise and engage in sun-protective behavior (Arndt et al., 2003; Routledge et al., 2004). From the perspective of the TMHM, by engaging in behaviors that make one healthier (e.g., wearing sunblock), death cognitions can temporarily be cast aside because individuals perceive they have reduced the risk associated with the threatening health situation.

However, to the extent the *perception* of threat is critical, rather than a reality, individuals have flexibility to reduce the threat with biased and avoidant processing of health risks. For instance, people deny their vulnerability to factors that purportedly decrease life expectancy (e.g., heightened emotionality) when death thoughts are conscious (Greenberg et al., 2000). Of course, people are replete with biases when it comes to assessing their risk for negative health consequences. One such bias is the underaccumulation bias, wherein people fail to appreciate how risk accumulates over time (Linville et al., 1993). Klein and colleagues (2015) examined whether reminders of mortality influence the way young adult smokers perceive their risk of dying from lung cancer risk at age 35, 45, and 55 (when relative lung cancer risk accumulates dramatically). Although smokers acknowledged they were at greater risk than nonsmokers at all three time points, reminders of mortality led to lower estimates compared with smokers not reminded of mortality. This kind of biased processing may also extend to actual behavior. Arndt and colleagues (2013) measured smoking craving among light smokers, as individuals craving smoking are prone to discount future health risks and focus more on positive aspects of smoking (e.g., Sayette et al., 2005). The light smokers were then reminded of their mortality or not. Smokers who were high in smoking craving smoked with greater intensity, as measured by the topography of their inhalations (e.g., puff duration), when they were primed with the notion of their own death.

These studies illustrate the counterintuitive, health defeating responses that sometimes occur following conscious reminders of mortality. They also raise the importance of discerning factors that instead promote productive behaviors that reduce health risks. Two factors that have been identified are health optimism and response efficacy. Arndt et al. (2006) and Cooper et al. (2010) showed that participants high in health optimism, or with expectations that a health behavior (i.e., sun protection) is effective, increase health-related intentions (e.g., to get mammograms or wear sunscreen) in response to conscious death thoughts. Productive health behaviors may be endorsed by these individuals because their efficacy and optimism help to mitigate a sense of vulnerability and attenuate conscious death-related concerns. Consistent with these findings, when paired with health communications that make death conscious, intervention approaches (e.g., beachgoers in South Florida receiving information that enhanced instead of undermined sun protection efficacy; Cooper et al., 2014) have been found to be especially effective.

Taken together, research indicates conscious contemplation of death can influence both adaptive health-oriented behaviors as well as threat avoidant, maladaptive behaviors. However, because these types of defensive responses remove death thoughts from consciousness (see e.g., Greenberg et al., 2008), it is critical to consider the role nonconscious death thoughts play in health decision-making.

The Effects of Nonconscious Death Thoughts

TMT's most generative hypothesis is that people cope with the unconscious reverberations of death-related thoughts with psychological defenses that address the threat at more distal levels of abstraction, symbolically affirming the value and validity of their cultural worldview and sense of personal significance within that worldview. The TMHM builds on this tenet to offer a novel hypothesis concerning health behavior: When death cognitions are activated but nonconsciously accessible, people are especially motivated to protect and enhance the self, even at the expense of their health.

Tanning behavior among college students provides a prime example. Recall the study by Routledge et al. (2004) wherein participants boosted their sun protection intentions immediately following mortality reminders. In contrast, when participants were distracted from the mortality reminder (through an intervening exercise that allowed thoughts of death to fade from focal attention), participants actually decreased their interest in sun protection, presumably because a tan complexion is socially valued and offers a pathway to self-esteem. Similar ironic effects are found in other health domains, such as binge drinking and smoking (Jessop & Wade, 2008; Hansen et al., 2010).

On the flip side, when individuals derive self-worth from health-benefiting behaviors, distal responses to death reminders stand to benefit health. In Arndt and colleagues' (2003) study on fitness intentions, for example, participants deriving self-esteem from exercise exhibited increased exercise intentions when they were distracted from thoughts of mortality. Boyd and colleagues (2015) recently expanded this perspective by measuring the extent to which some people, more so than others, derive self-esteem from being healthy, one of numerous domains from which people should be able to draw self-esteem (e.g., contingencies of self-worth; Crocker & Wolfe, 2001). As predicted, participants who had stronger health-relevant esteem contingencies were especially likely to endorse health behaviors across a variety of health domains (e.g., nutrition) after being reminded of and then distracted from mortality.

While the aforementioned examples illustrate the influence of dispositional differences in bases of self-esteem, a growing body of research also suggests, especially in the face of nonconscious thoughts of death, health-relevant decisions can be swayed by the esteem-relevant framing of the health behaviors. This was first revealed in Routledge et al.'s (2004) work on tanning. When participants were shown an advertisement that associated tanning with an attractive appearance (a tanned attractive woman vs. a beach ball), mortality reminders led participants to express greater interest in tanning products. Moreover, whereas increased tanning intentions were exhibited by participants who were reminded of their mortality and told "bronze is beautiful," beachgoers reminded of their mortality and given information conveying "pale can be pretty" requested higher levels of protective sunscreen as compensation for participating in the study (Cox et al., 2009).

The malleability of health responses following mortality reminders has also been explored with experiments utilizing celebrities, who have the capacity to steer perceptions of health-relevant behavior as being culturally valued or not (e.g., Dalton et al., 2003). McCabe et al. (2014) extended this work to examine the interactive effect of mortality reminders and celebrity endorsement on attitudes related to alcohol consumption and smoking, as well as intentions to drink water and get influenza vaccinations. Whereas product or appeal endorsements by medical doctors were more potent after conscious death reminders, when dealing with nonconscious thoughts of death, celebrity endorsement more effectively shifted water consumption behavior, willingness to engage in risky drinking, antismoking attitudes, and influenza vaccination intentions.

Of course, cultural representations not only stem from iconic celebrities but also typical people who encapsulate what is seen as culturally normative and affirming. Thus, another mechanism for shifting the relevance of a health behavior involves reminding individuals of prototypically healthy people (see Gibbons & Gerrard, 1995). Priming prototypes can especially alter the contingencies of value associated with a health behavior when participants have been reminded of mortality (Arndt, Vess, Cox, Goldenberg, and Lagle 2009), thereby promoting behavior in line with these contingencies. Accordingly, McCabe et al. (2015) reminded grocery shoppers of their mortality (or not) and asked them to visualize a prototypical healthy eater (or a neutral person) before they shopped. Coding of actual grocery receipts revealed shoppers reminded of mortality and primed with the healthy eater prototype purchased foods with greater nutritional value.

The tendency to engage in certain (health) behaviors as a distal defense can also vary as a function of people's more global esteem orientations and their connection to how vested an individual is in cultural standards. Arndt et al. (2009) found that, in response to nonconscious reminders of death, individuals with higher extrinsic self-esteem (i.e., basing self-worth on extrinsic evaluations; Williams et al., 2010) exhibited greater engagement in health decisions related to valued societal standards. Specifically, they were especially interested in purchasing tanning products, and smokers were more interested in quitting after viewing a commercial that touted negative social consequences of smoking (e.g., people who smoke smell bad).

There are, of course, other ways in which people's cultural belief systems can affect health decisions when death thoughts are active and outside of consciousness. For example, Vess and colleagues (2009) found that when distracted from thoughts of death, highly religious fundamentalists were more inclined to support religiously motivated decisions to refuse medical treatment and endorse prayer as a medical substitute. This suggests an ironic tendency for death thoughts on the brink of consciousness to push individuals to uphold their worldviews at the potential expense of their health.

The TMHM also elucidates other ways in which worldviews can work against what the medical field would prescribe as effective health procedures. The model builds from the recognition that worldviews often imbue physical aspects of the body (e.g., sex and other natural bodily functions) with symbolic meaning (e.g., love, beauty) because reminders of one's physicality threaten the uniquely human meaning that people rely on to defend against mortality concerns (see e.g., Goldenberg et al., 2000). The TMHM integrates these insights to suggest individuals should be more uncomfortable with, and avoidant of, health procedures that bring them in closer contact with the body's physicality when mortality concerns are activated (perhaps by the procedure itself). In support of this, women report lower breast exam intentions, conduct shorter breast exams, and report more discomfort during mammograms under such conditions (Goldenberg et al., 2008, 2009). This in turn suggests a certain amount of detachment from the body may actually decrease reluctance to conduct risk-preventative physical examinations that are themselves creaturely (e.g., prodding, pulling, poking at parts of one's body). Consistent with this possibility, women high in trait self-objectification responded to an objectified depiction of a woman's body with increased breast exam intentions after being reminded of mortality (Morris et al., 2013). This work was not intended to condone objectification, but to highlight the motive and defense inherent in construing the body symbolically.

Taking Stock

As noted at the outset, theoretically applied work can enrich understanding of both the target domain as well as the basic theory (Rothman & Salovey, 2007). In this section, insights from the TMHM for understanding health decisions and how the study of health decisions has informed the fundamental processes associated with the management of existential insecurity are considered. Finally, the generativity of a theoretically applied perspective is highlighted by reviewing a few issues that merit further research and theoretical articulation.

How Studying Terror Management Enhances Understanding of Health Decisions

Traditional research in behavioral health has long shown that while people can take a rational approach to their health, they often do not (e.g., maladaptive coping; Rippetoe & Rogers, 1987). By programmatically exploring the role of existential motivation in health judgments, the TMHM provides insights into the underlying forces that can engage and direct the biases that manifest. People are motivated by factors of more direct relevance to health, considering or at times denying, for example, risk relevant information. But their health decisions also occur within the context of motivations for esteem, social appeal, and a symbolic social identity that helps to define who they are. What are the catalysts that render these different classes of motivation more or less operative? The TMHM illuminates one such factor in the consciousness of death-related thought. Thus, TMHM affords greater understanding of when health cognitions and esteem/identity factors are likely to be more or less influential in health decisions.

This basic understanding, in turn, has implications for efforts to change health behavior. Consider the classic formula for an effective fear appeal: an appropriate amount of fear juxtaposed with a recommendation of how to avoid the feared outcome (Leventhal, 1971; Witte & Allen, 2000). The present analysis offers the insight that not all fear appeals are created equal, nor is the fear likely to be equally attenuated by different health appeals. When a fear appeal engages conscious concerns with mortality, it is likely best addressed with behavior change strategies that bolster the health cognitions (e.g., response efficacy, health optimism) of more proximal relevance to the behavior in question. Yet when a fear appeal engages nonconscious concerns with mortality, it may be better addressed with strategies that reinforce the esteem-enhancing consequences of relevant behavior change.

The TMHM therefore advises caution in how health communication that features reminders of death should be used. To the extent an appeal more subtly primes death-related thought and targets a behavior that is esteem relevant, such as smoking or alcohol consumption (especially for some young adults), reminders of mortality have the potential to ironically increase the very behavior one seeks to reduce (e.g., Hansen et al., 2010; Jessop & Wade, 2008). The same type of process is observed, for example, with sun protection (e.g., Cox et al., 2009). When mortality concerns are active but outside of awareness, the more effective route focuses on the appearance or social appeal dynamics of the health behavior in question (e.g., Arndt et al., 2009). Morris et al. (2014) make this point clearly. When participants were reminded and then distracted from thoughts of mortality and subsequently exposed to a photograph of themselves that depicted areas of skin damage from ultraviolet exposure, framing the photo as revealing health consequences of tanning had little effect on participants' tanning intentions. Yet when the same photo was framed as reflecting appearance consequences, it markedly reduced tanning intentions.

The existential orientation of the TMHM thus allows one to appreciate the broader motivational network in which health decisions occur and the relevance of a wider range of factors than perhaps would otherwise be recognized. Whether it is the influence of cultural and religious beliefs systems (e.g., Vess et al., 2009) or aversion to confronting the creatureliness of the human body (e.g., Goldenberg et al., 2008), the TMHM offers an integrative framework for understanding diverse influences on health decisions.

Further, one strength of the TMHM is it highlights a core psychological process applicable to a variety of health decisions, from choices to imbibe excessively, exercise, or get a recommended screening exam. Although there are certainly unique factors that influence particular health domain decisions, and the TMHM thus likely needs to be supplemented with other more focused perspectives, a broad theoretical framework offers both integrative and generative possibilities for understanding health (Klein et al., 2014).

How Studying Health Decisions Enhances Understanding of Terror Management

What has the study of health decisions unveiled about how people manage awareness of their own mortality? Just as the study of terror management processes can increase understanding of health behavior, studying health can increase understanding of the fundamental ways in which people manage existential insecurity. A few examples may help to illustrate.

Initial efforts to understand the cognitive architecture of terror management showed that when explicitly reminded of mortality, people tended to suppress death-related thoughts (e.g., Greenberg et al., 1994). But health research has revealed a wider repertoire of responses. People at times deny vulnerability and at other times increase desires to do that which might reasonably reduce their vulnerability, such as sun protection, exercise, or reducing smoking. Moreover, studying these processes has revealed individual differences that predict the types of defenses employed in response to conscious death-related cognition. Thus, we see that what Pyszczynski and colleagues (1999) defined as *proximal* defenses are broader and more variable than originally conceived.

Health-related research has also revealed with perhaps the starkest clarity the divergent responses to conscious and nonconscious death-related thoughts. Whereas initial research on this distinction muddied domain (e.g., vulnerability denial; worldview bolstering) with type of defense (i.e., proximal; distal), certain health behaviors lend themselves to being influenced by reminders of mortality in different directions as a function of the consciousness of the death cognition. For example, intentions to tan decrease when people are consciously thinking about death, but increase when participants have been distracted from such thoughts (Routledge et al., 2004). This kind of research in turn contributes a basic level of understanding to the fundamental ways in which people respond to their underlying awareness of mortality when it does or does not bubble to the surface.

A third example of how health-focused research has enriched understanding of terror management processes concerns the socially infused flexibility of esteem-based defenses to deal with awareness of mortality. TMHM research has showcased a variety of ways in which esteem contingencies shift with the influences that emanate from the surrounding world. Whether societal standards of the "thin ideal" (Goldenberg et al., 2005), the endorsement of a popular celebrity (McCabe et al. 2014), or the prototypical representations of a behavior (McCabe et al, 2015), there is malleability to terror management processes that has been uniquely revealed by TMHM research. Indeed, health research has further revealed that susceptibility to these external influences is most likely among those who derive self-esteem from extrinsic, as opposed to, intrinsic sources (Arndt et al., 2009).

These are just a few of the ways a health context provides a bridge for TMT to connect with basic perspectives in social and health psychology. These connections have in turn enhanced the depth and scope of the original theory.

Challenges of Bridging TMT to Health

As stated in the introduction, an interdisciplinary approach to TMT and health invites one to consider what actually *does* happen in the environment and to detach oneself, to an extent, from examining what *can* happen. A laboratory setting affords tight control over key variables, including whether a person is consciously or nonconsciously thinking about death. However, when one adopts an interdisciplinary health focus, the situation becomes more muddled. As people navigate through their daily affairs, and perhaps especially when they entertain an important health decision, they are likely to oscillate back and forth between conscious and nonconscious death-related cognition. Thus, to the extent these cognitions have divergent effects on health decisions, more naturalistic studies of these processes are warranted. Whereas the lack of such research to date can be seen as a weakness to the overall research program, it can also be viewed as a generative opportunity for theoretical and, perhaps especially, methodological advance. Real-time data capture and ecological momentary assessments have considerable potential as research strategies, particularly when juxtaposed with the causal insights merited by experimental design. But to take advantage of these techniques, advances are needed in the conceptualization and the measurement of routine manifestations of death-related thought.

Another challenge to the interdisciplinary health application of TMT is how to facilitate sustainable health behavior change. This requires the conceptualization of more extended durations of terror management effects and processes. However, the vast majority of TMT studies have only examined short-term effects, manifesting a few minutes after a mortality-salience manipulation or other everyday inductions of death-related thought (e.g., proximity to a funeral home; Pyszczynski et al., 1996). Certainly there are exceptions (e.g., terror management work related to trauma; see Abdollahi et al., 2011), but in general, interdisciplinary applications to health invite the development of new extended duration models of terror management processes, lest one be left with the possibility that reminders of mortality just produce a brief blip on the behavior change radar.

Although there is much to be done in this area, research by Morris and colleagues (2015) provides an encouraging start. These studies were guided by the idea that there may be a reinforcing dialectic whereby behavior that is engaged in response to mortality concerns can then become further integrated into one's lexicon of self-value and in so doing further guide behavior. A first study found that pairing a mortality-salience induction with an opportunity to exercise increased (reports of) exercise over the ensuing 2 weeks, and this increase in behavior promoted stronger fitness-related esteem contingencies. A second study observed that reminding smokers of their mortality and having them visualize negative social prototypes of smokers predicted increased quit intentions 3 weeks later, and these increased quit intentions in turn predicted greater cessation success 3 weeks after that. These findings offer an important foundation for understanding how terror management processes can be utilized to facilitate sustained health behavior change.

Other Areas of TMT and Health

Whereas many areas of health decisions have been examined from a terror management perspective, there are some areas of interface that are ripe for further development. One concerns the impact of terror management processes on health care provision. To date, the majority of TMHM research has focused on how people make health-relevant decisions for themselves. But what about those who make decisions for others? One study found that, after being reminded of mortality, Christian medical students gave a (hypothetical) Christian patient complaining of chest pains more serious cardiac risk assessments than a Muslim patient (Arndt et al., 2009), suggesting biased risk assessments by future medical providers through the reliance on cultural worldviews to mitigate their own existential concerns. This study is a possible starting point for future research to examine the influence of terror management processes on health care biases.

Another area ripe for interdisciplinary integration concerns terror management processes among the elderly. Certainly knowing one is going to die is troubling, but to know one's expiration date is just around the corner is another matter entirely. Thus, there may be implications associated with the aging body and more frequent reminders of its frailty and creatureliness. Emerging research suggests those approaching the end of life engage in different forms of terror management, and instead of conventional worldview defense, affirm a greater interest in generativity (e.g., Maxfield et al., 2014), and with overall intentions to be healthy (Bevan et al., 2014). The interdisciplinary integration with gerontological health perspectives is an exciting direction for TMT.

In a similar vein, the operation of terror management processes among people with terminal illness merits more programmatic study. For example, some research suggests that death-related cognition undermines psychological and functional well-being among those with a serious illness (Cox et al., 2012), especially when confronted with such thoughts soon after diagnosis (Luszczynska et al., 2012). Therefore, the accessibility of death-related thought and how people manage those cognitions may play a key role in the emotional well-being of individuals facing serious illness. Indeed, among individuals with end-stage congestive heart failure, having religious comfort predicted lower concerns about death. But for those experiencing religious struggle, death concerns were elevated and contributed to greater depressive symptoms (Edmonson et al., 2008). In short, there seems to be considerable potential for a terror management health interface to offer novel insights into physical and psychological health outcomes for individuals with life-threatening illness.

Conclusion

TMT is by its very roots (e.g., building from the work of cultural anthropologist Ernest Becker) an interdisciplinary endeavor, and thus it is apropos to see this volume recognizing the interdisciplinary trajectories along which TMT has begun to flow. But in the domain of health, while much has been learned, there is much more to do. Whereas the intersection of death and health seems rather obvious, existential concerns were not examined in the context of health until recently, and the scope of this relationship has yet to be fully examined. In doing so, it is anticipated that an informative feedback loop will continue to ensue, allowing practical health issues to expand on the foundations of TMT and for terror management processes to enhance understanding of health decisions and behavior.

References

Abdollahi, A., Pyszczynski, T., Maxfield, M., & Luszczynska, A. (2011). Posttraumatic stress reactions as a disruption in anxiety-buffer functioning: Dissociation and responses to mortality salience as predictors of severity of posttraumatic symptoms. *Psychological Trauma: Theory, Research, Practice, and Policy, 3*, 329–341. http://dx.doi.org/10.1037/a0021084

American Cancer Society (2015). Retrieved from http://www.cancer.org/

Arndt, J., Cook, A., Goldenberg, J. L., & Cox, C. R. (2007). Cancer and the threat of death: The cognitive dynamics of death-thought suppression and its impact on behavioral health intentions. *Journal of Personality and Social Psychology, 92*, 12–29. http://dx.doi.org/10.1037/0022–3514.92.1.12

Arndt, J., Cox, C. R., Goldenberg, J. L., Vess, M., Routledge, C., Cooper, D. P., & Cohen, F. (2009). Blowing in the (social) wind: Implications of extrinsic esteem contingencies for terror management and health. *Journal of Personality and Social Psychology, 96*, 1191–1205. http://dx.doi.org/10.1037/a0015182

Arndt, J., Routledge, C., & Goldenberg, J. L. (2006). Predicting proximal health responses to reminders of death: The influence of coping style and health optimism. *Psychology and Health, 21*, 593–614. http://dx.doi.org/10.1080/14768320500537662

Arndt, J., Schimel, J., & Goldenberg, J. L. (2003). Death can be good for your health: Fitness intentions as a proximal and distal defense against mortality salience. *Journal of Applied Social Psychology, 33*(8), 1726–1746. http://dx.doi.org/10.1111/j.1559–1816.2003.tb01972.x

Arndt, J., Vail III, K. E., Cox, C. R., Goldenberg, J. L., Piasecki, T. M., & Gibbons, F. X. (2013). The interactive effect of mortality reminders and tobacco craving on smoking topography. *Health Psychology, 32*, 525–532. http://dx.doi.org/10.1037/a0029201

Arndt, J., Vess, M., Cox, C. R., Goldenberg, J. L., & Lagle, S. (2009). The psychosocial effect of thoughts of personal mortality on cardiac risk assessment by medical students. *Medical Decision Making, 29*, 175–181. http://dx.doi.org/10.1177/0272989X08323300

Bevan, A. L., Maxfield, M., & Bultmann, M. N. (2014). The effects of age and death awareness on intentions for healthy behaviours. *Psychology & Health, 29*, 405–421. http://dx.doi.org/10.1080/08870446.2013.859258

Boyd, P. E. K., Goldenberg, J. L., & Arndt, J. (2015). *Health as a basis of self-esteem: Validation of a new measure of health contingent self-worth.* Manuscript in preparation.

Centers for Disease Control and Prevention (CDC). (2012). Current cigarette smoking among adults-United States, 2011. *MMWR: Morbidity and Mortality Weekly Report, 61*, 889–894.

Cooper, D. P., Goldenberg, J. L., & Arndt, J. (2010). Examining the terror management health model: The interactive effect of conscious death thought and health-coping variables on decisions in potentially fatal health domains. *Personality and Social Psychology Bulletin, 36*, 937–946. http://dx.doi.org/10.1177/0146167210370694

Cooper, D. P., Goldenberg, J. L., & Arndt, J. (2014). Perceived efficacy, conscious fear of death and intentions to tan: Not all fear appeals are created equal. *British Journal of Health Psychology, 19*, 1–15. http://dx.doi.org/10.1111/bjhp.12019

Cox, C. R., Cooper, D. P., Vess, M., Arndt, J., Goldenberg, J. L., & Routledge, C. (2009). Bronze is beautiful but pale can be pretty: The effects of appearance standards and mortality salience on sun-tanning outcomes. *Health Psychology, 28*, 746–752. http://dx.doi.org/10.1037/a0016388

Cox, C. R., Reid-Arndt, S. A., & Arndt, J. (2012). Considering the unspoken: The role of death cognition in quality of life among women with and without breast cancer. *Journal of Psychosocial Oncology, 30*, 128–139. http://dx.doi.org/10.1080/07347332.2011.633980

Crocker, J., & Wolfe, C. T. (2001). Contingencies of self-worth. *Psychological Review, 108*, 593–623. http://dx.doi.org/10.1037/0033–295X.108.3.593

Dalton, M. A., Sargent, J. D., Beach, M. L., Titus-Ernstoff, L., Gibson, J. J., Ahrens, M. B., Tickle, J. J., & Heatherton, T. F. (2003). Effect of viewing smoking in movies on adolescent smoking initiation: a cohort study. *The Lancet, 362*, 281–285. http://dx.doi.org/10.1016/S0140–6736(03)13970–0

Edmondson, D., Park, C. L., Chaudoir, S. R., & Wortmann, J. H. (2008). Death without God: Religious struggle, death concerns, and depression in the terminally ill. *Psychological Science, 19*, 754–758. http://dx.doi.org/10.1111/j.1467–9280.2008.02152.x

Fransen, M. L., Fennis, B. M., Pruyn, A. T. H., & Das, E. (2008). Rest in peace? Brand-induced mortality salience and consumer behavior. *Journal of Business Research, 61*, 1053–1061. http://dx.doi.org/10.1016/j.jbusres.2007.09.020

Gibbons, F. X., & Gerrard, M. (1995). Predicting young adults' health risk behavior. *Journal of Personality and Social Psychology, 69*, 505–517. http://dx.doi.org/10.1037/0022–3514.69.3.505

Goldenberg, J. L., & Arndt, J. (2008). The implications of death for health: A terror management health model for behavioral health promotion. *Psychological Review, 115*, 1032–1053. http://dx.doi.org/10.1037/a0013326

Goldenberg, J. L., Arndt, J., Hart, J., & Brown, M. (2005). Dying to be thin: The effects of mortality salience and body mass index on restricted eating among women. *Personality and Social Psychology Bulletin, 31*, 1400–1412. http://dx.doi.org/10.1177/0146167205277207

Goldenberg, J. L., Arndt, J., Hart, J., & Routledge, C. (2008). Uncovering an existential barrier to breast self-exam behavior. *Journal of Experimental Social Psychology, 44*, 260–274. http://dx.doi.org/10.1016/j.jesp.2007.05.002

Goldenberg, J. L., McCoy, S. K., Pyszczynski, T., Greenberg, J., & Solomon, S. (2000). The body as a source of self-esteem: The effect of mortality salience on identification with one's body, interest in sex, and appearance monitoring. *Journal of Personality and Social Psychology, 79*, 118–130. http://dx.doi.org/10.1037/0022–3514.79.1.118

Goldenberg, J. L., Routledge, C., & Arndt, J. (2009). Mammograms and the management of existential discomfort: Threats associated with the physicality of the body and neuroticism. *Psychology and Health, 24*, 563–581. http://dx.doi.org/10.1080/08870440701864546

Greenberg, J., Arndt, J., Simon, L., Pyszczynski, T., & Solomon, S. (2000). Proximal and distal defenses in response to reminders of one's mortality: Evidence of a temporal sequence. *Personality and Social Psychology Bulletin, 26*, 91–99. http://dx.doi.org/10.1177/0146167200261009

Greenberg, J., Pyszczynski, T., & Solomon, S. (1986). The causes and consequences of a need for self-esteem: A terror management theory. In R. F. Baumeister (Ed.), *Public self and private self* (pp. 189–212). New York: Springer. http://dx.doi.org/10.1007/978–1–4613–9564–5_10

Greenberg, J., Pyszczynski, T., Solomon, S., Simon, L., & Breus, M. (1994). Role of consciousness and accessibility of death-related thoughts in mortality salience effects. *Journal of Personality and Social Psychology, 67,* 627–637. http://dx.doi.org/10.1037/0022-3514.67.4.627

Greenberg, J., Solomon, S., & Arndt, J. (2008). A uniquely human motivation: Terror management. In J. Shah & W. Gardner (Eds.), *Handbook of motivation science* (pp.113–134). New York: Guilford.

Grover, K. W., Miller, C. T., Solomon, S., Webster, R. J., & Saucier, D. A. (2010). Mortality salience and perceptions of people with AIDS: Understanding the role of prejudice. *Basic and Applied Social Psychology, 32,* 315–327. http://dx.doi.org/10.1080/0197 3533.2010.519252

Hansen, J., Winzeler, S., & Topolinski, S. (2010). When the death makes you smoke: A terror management perspective on the effectiveness of cigarette on-pack warnings. *Journal of Experimental Social Psychology, 46,* 226–228. http://dx.doi.org/10.1016/j.jesp.2009.09.007

Huber, B. (2012). Burned by health warnings, defiant tanning industry assails doctors, 'sun scare' conspiracy. *Fair warning.* Retrieved from http://www.fairwarning.org/2012/08/burned-by-health-warnings-defiant-tanning-industry-assails-doctors-sun-scare-conspiracy/

Jessop, D. C., & Wade, J. (2008). Fear appeals and binge drinking: A terror management theory perspective. *British Journal of Health Psychology, 13,* 773–788. http://dx.doi.org/10.1348/135910707X272790

Klein, W. M., Bloch, M., Hesse, B. W., McDonald, P. G., Nebeling, L., O'Connell, M. E., Riley, W. T., Taplin, S. H., & Tesauro, G. (2014). Behavioral research in cancer prevention and control: A look to the future. *American Journal of Preventative Medicine, 46,* 301–311. http://dx.doi.org/10.1016/j.amepre.2013.10.004

Klein, W. M. P., Koblitz, A. R., Kaufman, A. E., Vail, K. E., & Arndt, J. (2015). *Ironic effects of mortliaty salience on relative risk perceptions in smokers.* Manuscript under review. National Cancer Institute.

Leventhal, H. (1971). Fear appeals and persuasion: The differentiation of a motivational construct. *American Journal of Public Health, 61,* 1208–1224. http://dx.doi.org/10.2105/AJPH.61.6.1208

Lewin, K. (1951). Theory-directed nursing practice (2nd ed.). In D. Cartwright (Ed.), *Field theory in social science: Selected theoretical papers* (pp. vii–xv). New York: Harper & Brothers.

Linville, P. W., Fischer, G. W., & Fischhoff, B. (1993). AIDS risk perceptions and decision biases. In J. B. Pryor & G. D. Reeder (Eds.), *The social psychology of HIV infection* (pp. 5–38). Hillsdale, NJ: Erlbaum.

Luszczynska, A., Durawa, A. B., Dudzinska, M., Kwiatkowska, M., Knysz, B., & Knoll, N. (2012). The effects of mortality reminders on posttraumatic growth and finding benefits among patients with life-threatening illness and their caregivers. *Psychology & Health, 27,* 1227–1243. http://dx.doi.org/10.1080/08870446.2012.665055

Maxfield, M., Greenberg, J., Pyszczynski, T., Weise, D. R., Kosloff, S., Soenke, M., Abeyta, A., & Blatter, J. (2014). Increases in generative concern among older adults following reminders of mortality. *The International Journal of Aging and Human Development, 79,* 1–21. http://dx.doi.org/10.2190/AG.79.1.a

McCabe, S., Arndt, J., Goldenberg, J. L., Vess, M., Vail III, K. E., Gibbons, F. X., & Rogers, R. (2015). The effect of visualizing healthy eaters and mortality reminders on nutritious grocery purchases: An integrative TMHM and PWN analysis. *Health Psychology, 34,* 279–282. http://dx.doi.org/10.1037/hea0000154

McCabe, S., Vail, K. E. III, Arndt, J., & Goldenberg, J. L. (2014). Hails from the crypt: A terror management health model investigation of health and celebrity endorsements. *Personality and Social Psychology Bulletin, 40,* 289–300. http://dx.doi.org/10.1177/0146167213510745

Morris, K. L., Cooper, D. P., Goldenberg, J. L., Arndt, J., & Gibbons, F. X. (2014). Improving the efficacy of appearance-based sun exposure intervention with the terror management health model. *Psychology and Health, 29,* 1245–1264. http://dx.doi.org/10.1080/08870446.2014.922184

Morris, K. L., Cooper, D. P., Goldenberg, J. L., Arndt, J., & Routledge, C. (2013). Objectification as self-affirmation in the context of a death-relevant health threat. *Self and Identity, 12,* 610–620. http://dx.doi.org/10.1080/15298868.2012.718862

Morris, K. L., Goldenberg, J. L., Arndt, J., Spina, M., McCabe, S., & Vail III, K. E. (2015). *Longitudinal effects of mortality salience on exercise and smoking related behavior and esteem-contingencies.* Manuscript in preparation.

Moser, R. P., Arndt, J., Han, P., Waters, E., Amsellem, M., & Hesse, B. (2014). Perceptions of cancer as a death sentence: Prevalence and consequences. *Journal of Health Psychology, 19,* 1518–1524. http://dx.doi.org/10.1177/1359105313494924

Pyszczynski, T., Greenberg, J., & Solomon, S. (1999). A dual-process model of defense against conscious and unconscious death-related thoughts: An extension of terror management theory. *Psychological Review, 106,* 835. http://dx.doi.org/10.1037/0033-295X.106.4.835

Pyszczynski, T., Wicklund, R. A., Floresku, S., Koch, H., Gauch, G., Solomon, S., & Greenberg, J. (1996). Whistling in the dark: Exaggerated consensus estimates in response to incidental reminders of mortality. *Psychological Science, 7,* 332–336. http://dx.doi.org/10.1111/j.1467-9280.1996.tb00384.x

Rippetoe, P. A., & Rogers, R. W. (1987). Effects of components of protection-motivation theory on adaptive and maladaptive coping with a health threat. *Journal of Personality and Social Psychology, 52*(3), 596–604.

Rothman, A. J., & Salovey, P. (2007). The reciprocal relation between principles and practice: Social psychology and health behavior. In A.W. Kruglanski & E. T. Higgins (Eds.), *Social Psychology: Handbook of Basic Principles* (pp. 826–848). New York: Guilford.

Routledge, C., Arndt, J., & Goldenberg, J. L. (2004). A time to tan: Proximal and distal effects of mortality salience on sun exposure intentions. *Personality and Social Psychology Bulletin, 30,* 1347–1358. http://dx.doi.org/10.1177/0146167204264056

Sayette, M. A., Loewenstein, G., Kirchner, T. R., & Travis, T. (2005). Effects of smoking urge on temporal cognition. *Psychology of Addictive Behaviors, 19,* 88–93. http://dx.doi.org/10.1037/0893-164X.19.1.88

Vess, M., Arndt, J., Cox, C. R., Routledge, C., & Goldenberg, J. L. (2009). Exploring the existential function of religion: The effect of religious fundamentalism and mortality salience on faith-based medical refusals. *Journal of Personality and Social Psychology, 97,* 334. http://dx.doi.org/10.1037/a0015545

Williams, T., Schimel, J., Hayes, J., & Martens, A. (2010). The moderating role of extrinsic contingency focus on reactions to threat. *European Journal of Social Psychology, 40,* 300–320. http://dx.doi.org/10.1002/ejsp.624

Witte, K., & Allen, M. (2000). A meta-analysis of fear appeals: Implications for effective public health campaigns. *Health Education & Behavior, 27,* 591–615. http://dx.doi.org/10.1177/109019810002700506

5

TERROR MANAGEMENT, CRIME, AND LAW

Miliaikeala Heen, Joel D. Lieberman, and Jamie Arndt

As the nature of this volume attests, underlying concerns about mortality potently impact people's efforts to maintain, and live up to, cultural standards of value in ways that affect diverse areas of social life. Terror management theory (TMT; Greenberg, Pyszczynksi, & Solomon, 1986) provides an integrative conceptual vehicle that predicts and explains these relationships, and offers key insights into the dynamics of the human existential condition. In this chapter, the application of TMT to the legal arena is examined. Given the influence of people's awareness of mortality on culturally valued behavior, TMT is inherently relevant to understanding legal transgressions and judgments because the law provides a codified articulation of society's morals and values (Arndt, Lieberman, Cook, & Solomon, 2005). Thus, TMT has the potential to contribute a unique perspective when trying to understand how and why people engage in lawful or unlawful behavior, as well as how individuals react to, adjudicate, and punish criminal offenses.

Terror Management Theory

Given the introduction to TMT in this volume (see Chapter 1), only a few aspects of the theory especially relevant to the research on legally oriented judgment and behavior are highlighted here. TMT argues that people manage the potential anxiety that an awareness of mortality might otherwise engender by embedding themselves in a world of meaning and value, whereby they have the potential to be significant contributors to a symbolic, if not literal, enduring cultural experience. Accordingly, over two decades of research have shown, in a variety of ways and with a number of different paradigms, how people's culturally derived beliefs about the world (i.e., a cultural worldview), and their strivings for personal value within the context of that worldview, help them manage underlying psychological concerns about the inevitably of death (see e.g., Greenberg, Solomon, & Arndt, 2008; Hayes, Schimel, Arndt, & Faucher, 2010; Pyszczynski, Greenberg, Solomon, Arndt, & Schimel, 2004 for qualitative reviews; Burke, Martens, & Faucher, 2010, for a meta-analytic review).

The paradigm most relevant to the research discussed in this chapter is referred to as the *mortality-salience* paradigm, and involves examining the effects of reminding participants of their mortality (or some other, generally aversive, control topic) on attitudes and behavior (Rosenblatt, Greenberg, Solomon, Pyszczynski, & Lyon, 1989; see Burke et al., 2010). This work demonstrates how mortality reminders (mortality salience; MS) increase efforts to identify with, live up to, and defend culturally derived beliefs. Briefly, because cultural worldviews are fragile social constructions, we need to surround ourselves with individuals who share similar values, and who reinforce our beliefs about the importance of our behaviors and accomplishments (Greenberg et al., 1986). Accordingly, when reminded of mortality, people are more positive in their reaction to those who support their beliefs, and more negative toward those who threaten them (i.e., worldview defense; see e.g., Greenberg et al., 2008).

The nature of such defenses allows us to understand the importance of existential motivation in a range of legal affairs. Indeed, an exploration of the motivations elicited by people's awareness of death, and the psychological defenses that result, provides insight into factors related to the commission, prosecution, and punishment of offences (Arndt et al., 2005). However, the TMT-legal relationship has been shown to be both broad and complex.

Commission of Offences

The specific connection between awareness of death and the commission of offences has rarely been directly studied, perhaps partly because of the ethical challenges of examining people's engagement in illegal behavior with the experimental paradigms that typify TMT research. However, it is possible to generate some insights and predictions based on TMT's principles, combined with suggestive evidence from other legally relevant judgments. For example, later in the chapter research is reviewed that elucidates how reminders of mortality influence people's reactions to others who face criminal allegations or commit offences. To the extent that reminders of mortality increase (or decrease) the harshness with which the perpetration of such action is viewed, one may infer some likelihood of an individual committing such acts. Yet this is speculative ground and merits serious caution. Clearly, this is an area ripe for direct empirical scrutiny.

Lawful Behavior

To the extent the awareness of death motivates behavior that affirms cultural values, one would generally expect reminders of mortality to promote lawful behavior, given that laws codify societal values and morals. A number of research lines are consistent with this idea. For example, death reminders have been found to encourage judgment and behavior that is consistent with salient societal norms (Jonas et al., 2008). Further, as is later discussed more fully, death reminders increase justice and fairness concerns (van den Bos, 2001), albeit often for purposes of self- or worldview-serving justifications (e.g., Landau et al., 2004). However, broadly construed, prevailing cultural worldviews advocate the value of justice, and thus, cognitions about mortality should increase interest in justice and, perhaps by extension, lawful behavior.

Media choices offer an interesting forum in which to examine these ideas. From *Perry Mason* to the contemporary onslaught of *Law & Order* and *CSI* variants, people seem fascinated by portrayals of justice. Consistent with a terror management function of such interest, Taylor (2012) found that death reminders increased interest in TV shows that feature justice (e.g., *Law & Order*). Further, following reminders of death, individuals who watched TV portrayals of justice being carried out (vs. being thwarted) were less likely to exhibit other (i.e., self-enhancing) defensive reactions. This research suggests that the awareness of death not only motivates an interest in justice, but that the affirmation of justice helps manage mortality-based concerns.

Illegal Behavior

Although there are theoretical and empirical grounds for expecting mortality-based concerns to promote lawful behavior, research demonstrates that the relationship between MS and legal attitudes and behavior is complex. Consequently, several caveats must be considered to fully understand the conditions in which individuals adhere to or violate legal regulations for behavior. The first caveat relates to the effect of the specific content of an individual's (subcultural or individualized) worldview on behavior. The second pertains to how death awareness creates a need to respond to those who threaten core worldview beliefs. Finally, the third caveat pertains to how individuals compensate for inadequate or failing cultural anxiety buffers. Each caveat is briefly discussed in turn.

Esteem Contingencies and Illegal Behavior

A considerable amount of research shows that reminders of mortality increase self-esteem striving (Pyszczynski et al., 2004). Thus, if the individual's worldview and "esteem contingencies" (i.e., the manner in which self-esteem is derived) prescribe behavior that entails illegal activity, the theory would suggest that reminders of death might encourage unlawful behavior. Consider, for example, research showing that reminders of mortality increase risk-taking (e.g., risky and reckless driving) to the extent the person derives self-esteem from their driving ability (e.g., Ben-Ari, Florian, & Mikulincer, 1999). Similar types of effects are seen with respect to alcohol, drug, and tobacco use (see McCabe & Arndt, in press, for a review). When people derive self-esteem from these respective domains, MS (often ironically induced via health appeals intended to reduce the relevant behavior) increases smoking intentions (Hansen, Winzeler, & Topolinski, 2010), willingness to binge drink and drive drunk (Jessop & Wade, 2008; Shehryar & Hunt, 2005), and willingness to engage in other forms of recreational drug use (Hirschberger, Florian, Mikulincer, Goldenberg, & Pyszczynski, 2002; see also Nagar & Rabinovitz, 2015). Although each of these activities may directly result in illegal behavior for certain populations (e.g., young adults under the legal drinking or tobacco use age), they also converge to suggest that when individuals hold esteem contingencies associated with the illegal behavior, efforts to manage concerns about mortality via terror management processes may contribute to unlawfulness.[1]

Responses to Worldview Threats

The second facet of the caveat pertains to individuals' reactions to worldview threatening others. People often respond quite negatively—and at times even violently—to those who threaten their worldview, and this tendency can be clearly seen in experimental studies that heighten concerns about mortality. Not only does MS increase negative and discriminatory reactions to those who espouse or represent different beliefs (e.g., Greenberg et al., 1990), but it also fuels overall aggression toward worldview-threatening targets (McGregor et al., 1998) as the individual seeks to demonstrate the superiority of his or her belief system. Consequently, efforts to manage concerns about mortality may contribute to even more extreme forms of aggression such as the commission of hate crimes and terrorist acts.

Hate crimes are unusual offences, because attacks are typically committed in a spontaneous manner by a group of people who have no prior direct contact with the victim, and who generally do not take any items of monetary value from the victim. Thus, from a rational standpoint, hate crimes make little sense. However, regardless of whether hate crime attacks involve the commission of either violent or property crimes, they serve as an opportunity to devalue the victim, because of the victim's group identity (e.g., homosexual, Jewish, African American, etc.). By devaluing the victim, the offender is able to reinforce the perception of the superiority of his or her own cultural worldview group. Consequently, TMT can be used to explain motivations for hate crimes (Lieberman, 2010; Lieberman, Arndt, Personius, & Cook, 2001). Hate crimes can provide a mechanism for several avenues of worldview defense, including derogation (e.g., racial slurs combined with threats used to intimidate particular group members) and annihilation (e.g., physically attacking and even killing worldview threatening outgroup members).

Similarly, TMT can explain the motivation behind terrorist acts, and why individuals have the propensity to inflict destruction and death upon innocent victims, simply because they do not share common religious, political, or cultural views (see Pyszczynski, Motyl, & Abdollahi, 2009, for a review). Research has shown that reminders of death lead individuals to express greater support of violent resistance against those who undermine one's ideology (Hirschberger & Ein-Dor, 2006), increased support for military interventions and martyrdom (Pyszczynski et al., 2006), support for counterterrorism policies (Landau et al., 2004), and increased support for extreme and violent approaches to terrorism (Weise et al., 2008). The importance of upholding one's worldviews is so significant that there is an increased willingness for self-sacrifice in the name of one's beliefs or nation (Routledge & Arndt, 2008). Although self-sacrifice is contradictory to death avoidance, this behavior is seen as securing symbolic immortality and is overall an honorable death, thus bolstering one's self-esteem and personal significance. This is evident with the extreme actions of militant Islamic groups as well as being a cross-cultural phenomenon with occurrences in Saudi Arabia, Pakistan, Afghanistan, Britain, Egypt, and Jordan (Crenshaw, 2007).

The role of religion is particularly important when discussing terrorism as it provides a justification for many to engage in this behavior. When faced with reminders of mortality, religious fundamentalists have been found to have higher levels of prejudice, militarism, and ethnocentrism (Rothschild, Abdollahi, & Pyszczynski, 2009). Adhering to strict religious beliefs often provides a sense of serving one's God, adding pressures of a greater cause to protect one's people and culture. Scriptural depictions of violence and violence sanctioned by God have been found to produce aggressive responses to threats by religious individuals (Bushman, Ridge, Das, Key, & Busath, 2007). As religion has been assumed to be the root of Islamic terrorism, it is no surprise that this behavior is often justified by one's religious beliefs (Silke, 2008).

Acts of terrorism also have the potential to foster feelings of hostility and aggression toward outgroups. Evidence of this is shown through research examining the psychological impacts and reactions to the events of the September 11th attacks, which served as an extreme reminder of death for many Americans. After the attacks, there was a surge of intolerance, prejudice, discrimination, and violence, against Arab Americans and Muslims, as well as a call for greater surveillance and restrictions of civil rights of these individuals (Huddy, Feldman, Taber, & Lahav, 2005; Singh, 2002).

Violent Behavior as Compensation for Inadequate Anxiety Buffers

A third caveat for the propensity for people to manage death-related concerns in ways that uphold cultural norms for lawful behavior pertains to how individuals may compensate for poorly functioning anxiety buffers. Similar to the proposition that engaging in risky behavior increases one's self-esteem, reacting to feelings of shame and inadequacy with aggression and violence provides a sense of power and independence. Violent and overly aggressive behavior can mask feelings of low self-esteem to create a cover of inflated "false" self-esteem (Walker & Bright, 2009). Individuals with this trait may respond to threatening situations, particularly if it is a threat to an important cultural belief, with anger and aggression to portray strength. Thus, those who feel large amounts of shame or humiliation, combined with low self-esteem, appear to be more likely to engage in violent and/or bullying behavior (Gilligan, 2003; Walker & Bright, 2009).

From a TMT standpoint, self-esteem serves as an anxiety buffer against the terror of mortality-related cognitions. TMT studies have generally shown that individuals with low self-esteem often engage in greater levels of worldview defensive behavior, than those with high self-esteem, following MS manipulations (e.g., Harmon-Jones et al., 1997; Pyszczynski et al., 2004). In addition, mortality-salient individuals may respond to worldview threats with aggressive and violent behavior (McGregor et al., 1998). TMT may be useful in not only understanding generalized aggression toward worldview threatening others, but also for understanding how threats to self-esteem and sense of shame can shed light on motivations for specific types of crimes, such as domestic violence and sexual abuse.

In the case of domestic violence, for example, abusive husbands tend to have lower self-esteem than nonabusive husbands and also perceive more martial situations as damaging to their self-esteem (Goldstein & Rosenbaum, 1985; Shackelford, 2001). Further, many such men may believe they must be powerful, dominant, successful, and superior. Often feelings of inadequacy within any of these characteristics result in a blow to self-esteem (Coleman, 1980). These characteristics appear to form important values within cultural worldviews for males and when threatened, acts of aggression and violence are one way for men to regain power and control (Brown, 2004; Coleman, 1980). Thus, aggression within an intimate partner context may serve to achieve worldview components of male strength and domination for domestic violence offenders. Similar TMT principles and concepts can also be used to explain motivations behind the commission of sexual violence. Much like domestic abuse and violence, sexual violence often serves to provide an individual with power and control after an offender has experienced feelings of vulnerability, inadequacy, and low self-esteem (Cowan & Mills, 2004; Marshall & Marshall, 2000). From a TMT perspective, sexual violence is viewed as a coping and defense mechanism for individuals who developed feelings of vulnerability and poor self-esteem. Further, sexual attraction can also be viewed as threatening to the extent that it implicates existential concerns with the physicality and corporeality of the body. As such, when threatened with reminders of mortality and primed with lustful thoughts, men actually show greater tolerance for aggression against women (Landau et al., 2006).

MS and Legal Decision-Making

Awareness of Death and Judgments Toward Criminal Offenders

Whereas the role of terror management concerns in the commission of illegal behavior is admittedly speculative, a growing body of research has examined how, and to what extent, reminders of death influence reactions and judgments toward defendants inside the courtroom. As will be discussed, there is considerable nuance to these effects, and MS has the potential to increase both punitive and lenient attitudes toward criminal offenders.

The first experimental study on TMT, conducted by Rosenblatt and colleagues (1989), utilized judges because they have a duty, and likely a belief, to uphold legal statues. In the study, the (municipal court) judges were first reminded of their own death or not. They were then presented with arrest information for an alleged prostitute and asked to set bail. The judges gave significantly higher bail amounts to an alleged prostitute after being exposed to an MS manipulation, compared to those who were in a control condition. These findings were replicated with college students who held negative beliefs about prostitution (Rosenblatt et al., 1989, Study 2).

The work by Rosenblatt et al. (1989) became a catalyst for researchers to manipulate MS and judgments toward offenders in a variety of contexts and settings. Indeed, this and related paradigms have been used to examine a variety of moderators and processes associated with MS effects, often with little or no interest in legal judgments per se. For example, studies examined MS effects on legal judgments within the context of beliefs about symbolic immortality (Florian & Mikulincer, 1998) and interpersonal attachments and needs (e.g., Mikulincer & Florian, 2000). These studies manipulated a variety of crimes (e.g., assault, fraud, and robbery), and generally found that MS leads individuals to have increased punitive judgments toward offenders. However, the results also demonstrate that the tendency for MS to increase punitive judgments depends on a variety of individual difference and situational variables (see Arndt et al., 2005). In short, people who possess stronger mechanisms for managing death-related thoughts (e.g., those with secure relational attachments) do not tend to manifest such reactions.

Further, although there is a general tendency for death-related cognition to cause more punitive reactions and harsher judgments toward lawbreakers across a wide range of criminal offenses, research also demonstrates the potential for leniency toward defendants (Arndt et al., 2005). The critical determining factor seems to be whether it is the defendant or the victim who poses more of a worldview threat to the individual making a judgment. For example, whereas people are generally more punitive toward hate-crime offenders, when reminded of mortality, they show greater tolerance for a hate crime offender if the victim poses a worldview threat (Lieberman et al., 2001). Similar results were obtained by Greenberg, Schimel, Martens, Solomon, & Pyszczynski (2001) in a study exploring perceptions of individuals expressing racist beliefs, that found MS White participants to be more tolerant of racist statements made by a White supremacist, than control participants were. Thus, it appears that reminders of death activate stereotypic perceptions of victims who may pose a worldview threat and intensify positive ingroup identification. However, it is important to note that these types of reactions are only present in MS conditions when a specific victim is presented. When there is no information about a specific victim who potentially poses a worldview threat, individuals exhibit negative reactions toward bias-motivated attacks (Lieberman et al., 2001).

Such findings reveal a disturbing degree of subjectivity within the justice system. If legal decision-making can be significantly influenced by extralegal factors, do defendants ever receive a fair and unbiased trial? Fortunately, as mentioned earlier, TMT research has found MS can also enhance procedural fairness concerns.

Procedural Fairness Concerns

The previous discussion demonstrates MS has the power to create subjective perceptions of criminal offenders that are shaped by extralegal factors. Research has also shown that fairness is an important cultural value, and consequently, MS tends to increase fair process concerns. For example, van den Bos and Miedema (2000) first manipulated MS and then manipulated fair process concerns by asking individuals for their recommendation on how the amount and distribution of rewards for a task should be allocated. Participants were either allowed or not allowed to give a recommendation for a task that they and another individual completed independently, but equally well. The participants, who were allowed to voice their opinion for the reward, recommended that it should be distributed evenly in both the MS and control conditions, which demonstrates a belief in outcomes based on fair and equal performance. However, when MS participants were given the option to voice their opinion, they exhibited more positive feelings and less negative reactions overall compared to participants in the control conditions. This suggests that when reminded of mortality, participants were more pleased with a fair distribution of rewards.

An interesting extension of this reasoning occurs in the context of juror compliance to judicial admonitions. During a trial, a judge may instruct jurors to ignore certain testimony and refrain from using it in their decision-making. Jurors typically ignore this admonition, and may actually pay more attention to the testimony after it is ruled inadmissible (a phenomenon known as the "backfire effect"; Wolf & Montgomery, 1977). Jurors' attention to, and consideration of, inadmissible evidence and testimony, of course, ultimately threatens a defendant's right to a fair trial.

However, Cook, Arndt, and Lieberman (2004) hypothesized that reminders of death might increase a juror's willingness to follow the law and obey judicial instruction in contexts where inadmissible evidence is present. Further, Cook et al. reasoned that that jurors' personal beliefs regarding their inclination to rely on their own sense of justice (known as *nullification* jurors) or to strictly adhere to the law, would predict the likelihood of the backfire effect occurring, with nullification jurors being more likely to utilize incriminating inadmissible evidence. However, because MS has been shown to increase fair process concerns, individuals exposed to inadmissible evidence and asked to contemplate their own mortality would be more likely than non-MS jurors to adhere to judicial instructions to ignore the evidence, because doing so would allow for a more fair trial for the defendant. In a series of studies, Cook et al. found that MS did indeed increase the effectiveness of inadmissible evidence instructions, and that this effect occurred for nullification-prone jurors regardless of whether this perspective was obtained through personality measures or by manipulation of judicial instructions. Consequently, Cook et al. provide further evidence that the relationship between MS and legal judgments is complex and may depend on jurors' sense of fairness and justice. As discussed later in this chapter, additional research (Lieberman, Shoemaker, & Krauss, 2014) has demonstrated that this tendency extends to the consideration of both mitigating and aggravating factors, within the highly mortality-salient context of capital punishment trials.

Trial Strategy and Jury Selection

TMT may have utility for attorneys when developing overall trial strategy and for making jury selection decisions. As noted earlier, MS effects are moderated by a wide array of individual differences. These demographic and personality factors can be considered during the voir dire (i.e., jury selection) process, if attorneys are permitted sufficient latitude by the judge to ask jurors relevant questions. During the trial attorneys may want to emphasize factors in the case that would make mortality salient to jurors, or may want to try to use the voir dire process to identify and select (or more accurately, not exclude) jurors who possess certain personality factors that may ameliorate or intensify MS effects. It is well beyond the present scope to discuss all relevant personality factors, but a few examples are provided to illustrate the interaction between personality and MS during trial.

Characteristics such as authoritarianism have been found to influence jury decision-making, including within the context of TMT (Greenberg et al., 1990). Traditionally, research has found that authoritarians are more conviction prone, as they have a strong belief in abiding by rules and laws and maintaining order, and have negative perceptions of individuals who deviate from society's conventional norms, unless the defendant is viewed as an authority figure (Lamberth, Krieger, & Shay, 1982; Lieberman & Sales, 2007). In the same respect, individuals who believe in a just world (i.e., that people get what they deserve in life) are found to be more punitive (Lieberman & Sales, 2007; Rubin & Peplau, 1975). Consequently, those who have faith in a just world believe outcomes are a function of one's behavior, and violating a law should result in a negative, but just, outcome. Thus, defendants who violate or threaten a juror's worldview or beliefs may be perceived especially negatively, and potentially receive harsher punishments, by these types of individuals compared to defendants who share similar qualities and beliefs. This possibility is supported by research indicating that MS increases participants' preference for just world interpretations of information (Landau et al., 2004).

These are just two examples of the powerful influence personality characteristics might have in a trial, especially when concerns about mortality are active (but, see Lieberman & Sales, 2007, for a discussion of the overall influence of personality factors). Further, the manipulation of emotional or rational factors in the courtroom may enhance or reduce any TMT based effects. Research has demonstrated that MS effects are more likely to emerge when individuals are in an "experiential mode" of processing information where gut level emotions and intuitive thinking influence decisions (Simon et al., 1997). Experiential processing may occur when very emotionally oriented testimony and exhibits are presented. Consequently, it may be beneficial for attorneys to encourage jurors to think, and ultimately deliberate, in a logical and rational way, potentially by reminding them to base their verdict decision on an objective evaluation of the evidence and presented case facts, if the attorneys want to reduce MS effects.

Death Reminders in the Courtroom

Reminders of death have the potential to become salient during the course of a trial without explicitly being stated to jurors. Indeed, a large body of research points to the diverse types of psychological threats that can increase the accessibility of death-related cognition (see Hayes et al., 2010, for a review). Consequently, charges such as murder, involuntary manslaughter, negligent homicide, or attempted murder all have the potential to be death reminders. In addition, mortality can become salient through statements by attorneys or witnesses, as well as during the punishment phase of a capital murder trial. These blatant reminders of death have the potential to increase conscious awareness of mortality and activate defensive mechanisms within a courtroom context.

Further, there is also potential for death-related cognition to become active outside of conscious awareness and motivate TMT processes. In fact, the vast majority of terror management effects that involve efforts to maintain and defend one's worldview occur in response to thoughts of death that occur outside focal awareness (see e.g., Martens, Burke, Schimel, & Faucher, 2011, for a meta-analytic review). In the content of research relevant to legal matters, Nelson, Moore, Olivetti, and Scott (1997) presented participants with a liability case where either an American or Japanese auto manufacturer was being sued over defective car brakes. As evidence in the case, participants were shown a video of a fatal car accident and were then asked to provide judgments of blame toward the company. They found more favorable judgments toward the American manufacturers and less favorable judgments of the foreign manufacturer. The results demonstrate that often more subtle thoughts of death, such as viewing a fatal car accident, have the power to engage efforts to protect cultural worldviews. This may be of particular concern when considering the multitude of ways death-related cognition may occur within the courtroom through charges, exhibits, and testimony.

In addition, legal decision-making may be influenced by events outside the courtroom that claim the lives of large numbers of people. For example, the terrorist attacks of September 11, 2001, are particularly noteworthy. To the extent that such events foster widespread concerns with mortality, TMT predicts that they would also trigger hyper-punitive worldview defenses in many contexts (Pyszczynksi, Solomon, & Greenberg, 2003), and result in more severe sentences for particular types of crimes for a sustained period after the event (Rowland, 2002).

Death Penalty Decision-Making

There is no greater setting where mortality plays more of a role in legal proceedings than capital punishment trials. Jurors must contemplate actions that led to the victim's death, and if a defendant is convicted, must consider whether to impose a sentence that would lead to his or her death (Judges, 1999; Kirchmeier, 2008; Lieberman et al., 2014). However, jurors' contemplation of mortality may be directed externally (toward the defendant and victim) rather than internally (toward themselves). Several TMT studies have found that MS effects are more pronounced when people consider their personal mortality rather than the mortality of others (e.g., Greenberg, Pyszczynski, Solomon, & Breus, 1994; Nelson et al., 1997). Lieberman et al. (2014) explored the impact of self- versus other-focused mortality on mock juror perceptions of aggravating factors (which make a sentence of death appropriate) and mitigating factors (which make a sentence of life imprisonment appropriate). Across two studies, Lieberman et al. found that MS effects were heightened when participants were instructed to focus on their own mortality.

More specifically, participants were either exposed to the evidence in the case that had an inherent mortality component (e.g., evidence regarding the victim's death, consideration of the defendant's fate) or exposed to the same trial information, but also asked to contemplate their own death. In Study 1, the strength of aggravating factors (i.e., aspects of the case that make death an appropriate sentence) was manipulated, and Lieberman et al. (2014) found that self-focused mortality participants were more likely to sentence the defendant to death when aggravating factors were strong (i.e., had not been undermined by cross-examination), than other participants. In a second study, self-focused mortality participants were more likely to render a life imprisonment sentence when strong mitigating factors (i.e., aspects of the case that make life in prison, rather than death, an appropriate sentence) were present. However, this effect was limited to jurors who had a high level of comprehension of the jury instructions, which included an explanation of mitigating factors. Lieberman et al. interpreted these findings as further evidence that the effects of MS on legal decisions may be complex, and often derive from aforementioned fair process concerns, which are reflected in a more appropriate weighing of the evidence.

Conclusions

The last three decades have seen TMT applied to a wide range of social behavior, including legal judgments. This work has generally shown that MS can create a hyper-punitive desire to punish lawbreakers, but importantly, also heightens concerns for the fair treatment for parties involved in litigation. Although this may sometimes produce negative reactions to moral transgressors, it may also lead to greater adherence to judicial instructions that serve to protect defendants (e.g., mitigating factors or admonitions to ignore inadmissible evidence).

Although initial TMT legal research primarily focused on perceptions of offenders (often from the perspective of jurors or judges), the theory is useful in understanding offender motivations as well. To date, research has typically utilized the worldview defensive mechanism of annihilation for understanding the motivation of terrorists and hate-crime offenders, as well as general aggression to worldview threats. However, the breadth of the theory also encourages consideration of how other factors, such as inadequate anxiety buffers reflected in low self-esteem, can impact specific crimes such as domestic and sexual violence.

Further, the findings of studies exploring procedural fairness may have important implications for understanding underlying motivations behind social protests in cities like Ferguson, Missouri, and Baltimore. Mortality may be made salient through community members' identification with the victim in these instances. Further, citizens may feel that dynamics regarding the administration of local police forces, or the legal system in general, may impede their ability to obtain what they perceive as a procedurally fair outcome. Police officers may, in turn, then be viewed as worldview violators, and may be dealt with in a worldview defensive reaction including derogation or aggression, in an attempt to manage the worldview threat, or to create conditions where greater procedural fairness may occur in the future. Of course, such an interpretation is purely speculative; however, this example illustrates that there is much that can be done to foster a broader application of TMT in the legal arena. Hopefully, work in this area will continue to evolve and extend beyond identifying terror management–based causes of antisocial behavior and legal judgments, and extend to crime prevention and rehabilitation of offenders. Ultimately, TMT may not only be useful in understanding the general relationship between morality and legality, but may provide a means of motivating greater adherence to moral and legal standards.

Note

1. Whereas many if not most of the effects discussed here stem from nonconscious concerns with mortality (see Chapter 1 of this volume), conscious thoughts of death have also been found to impact substance use, potentially for some people, as a form coping (see McCabe & Arndt, in press). Consideration of these effects is beyond the scope of this chapter, but it is noted here simply as another way in which mortality concerns may potentially contribute to illegal behaviors.

References

Arndt, J., Lieberman, J. D., Cook, A., & Solomon, S. (2005). Terror management in the courtroom: Exploring the effects of mortality salience on legal decision making. *Psychology, Public Policy, and Law, 11*, 407–438. doi:10.1037/1076–8971.11.3.407

Ben-Ari, O. T., Florian, V., & Mikulincer, M. (1999). The impact of mortality salience on reckless driving: A test of terror management mechanisms. *Journal of Personality and Social Psychology, 76*, 35–45. doi:10.1037/0022–3514.76.1.35

Brown, J. A. C. (2004). Shame and domestic violence: Treatment perspectives for perpetrators from self psychology and affect theory. *Sexual and Relationship Therapy, 19*, 39–56. doi:10.1080/14681990410001640826

Burke, B. L., Martens, A., & Faucher, E. H. (2010). Two decades of terror management theory: A meta-analysis of mortality salience research. *Personality and Social Psychology Review, 14*, 155–195. doi:10.1177/1088868309352321

Bushman, B. J., Ridge, R. D., Das, E., Key, C. W., & Busath, G. L. (2007). When god sanctions killing effect of scriptural violence on aggression. *Psychological Science, 18*, 204–207. doi:10.1111/j.1467–9280.2007.01873.x

Coleman, K. H. (1980). Conjugal violence: What 33 men report. *Journal of Marital and Family Therapy, 6*, 207–213. doi:10.1111/j.1752–0606.1980.tb01307.x

Cook, A., Arndt, J., & Lieberman, J. D. (2004). Firing back at the backfire effect: The influence of mortality salience and nullification beliefs on reactions to inadmissible evidence. *Law and Human Behavior, 28*, 389–410. doi:10.1023/B:LAHU.0000039332.21386.f4

Cowan, G., & Mills, R. D. (2004). Personal inadequacy and intimacy predictors of men's hostility toward women. *Sex Roles, 51*, 67–78. doi:10.1023/B:SERS.0000032310.16273.da

Crenshaw, M. (2007). Explaining suicide terrorism: A review essay. *Security Studies, 16*, 133–162. doi:10.1080/09636410701304580

Florian, V., & Mikulincer, M. (1998). Symbolic immortality and the management of the terror of death. *Journal of Personality and Social Psychology, 74*, 725–734. doi:10.1037/0022–3514.74.3.725

Gilligan, J. (2003). Shame, guilt, and violence. *Social Research: An International Quarterly, 70*, 1149–1180.

Goldstein, D., & Rosenbaum, A. (1985). An evaluation of the self-esteem of maritally violent men. *Family Relations, 34*, 425–428.

Greenberg, J., Pyszczynski, T., & Solomon, S. (1986). The causes and consequences of a need for self-esteem: A terror management theory. In R. F. Baumeister (Ed.), *Public self and private self* (pp.189–212). New York: Springer-Verlag. doi:10.1007/978–1–4613–9564–5_10

Greenberg, J., Pyszczynski, T., Solomon, S., & Breus, M. (1994). Role of consciousness and accessibility of death-related thoughts in mortality salience effects. *Journal of Personality and Social Psychology, 67*, 627–637. doi:10.1037/0022–3514.67.4.627

Greenberg, J., Pyszczynski, T., Solomon, S., Rosenblatt, A., Veeder, M., Kirkland, S., & Lyon, D. (1990). Evidence for terror management theory II: The effects of mortality salience on reactions to those who threaten or bolster the cultural worldview. *Journal of Personality and Social Psychology, 58*, 308–318. doi:10.1037/0022–3514.58.2.308

Greenberg, J., Schimel, J., Martens, A., Solomon, S., & Pyszczynski, T. (2001). Sympathy for the devil: Evidence that reminding Whites of their mortality promotes more favorable reactions to White racists. *Motivation and Emotion, 25*, 113–133. doi:10.1023/A:1010613909207

Greenberg, J., Solomon, S., & Arndt, J. (2008). A basic but uniquely human motivation: Terror management. In J. Shah & W. Gardner (Eds.), *Handbook of motivation science* (pp. 113–134). New York: Guilford.

Hansen, J., Winzeler, S., & Topolinski, S. (2010). When the death makes you smoke: A terror management perspective on the effectiveness of cigarette on-pack warnings. *Journal of Experimental Social Psychology, 46*, 226–228. doi:10.1016/j.jesp.2009.09.007

Harmon-Jones, E., Simon, L., Greenberg, J., Pyszczynski, T., Solomon, S., & McGregor, H. (1997). Terror management theory and self-esteem: Evidence that increased self-esteem reduces mortality salience effects. *Journal of Personality and Social Psychology, 72*, 24–36. doi:10.1037/0022–3514.72.1.24

Hayes, J., Schimel, J., Arndt, J., & Faucher, E. (2010). A theoretical and empirical review of the death-thought accessibility concept in terror management research. *Psychological Bulletin, 136*, 699–739. doi:10.1037/a0020524

Hirschberger, G., & Ein-Dor, T. (2006). Defenders of a lost cause: Terror management and violent resistance to the disengagement plan. *Personality and Social Psychology Bulletin, 32*, 761–769. doi:10.1177/0146167206286628

Hirschberger, G., Florian, V., Mikulincer, M., Goldenberg, J. L., & Pyszczynski, T. (2002). Gender differences in the willingness to engage in risky behavior: A terror management perspective. *Death Studies, 26*, 117–141. doi:10.1080/074811802753455244

Huddy, L., Feldman, S., Taber, C., & Lahav, G. (2005). Threat, anxiety, and support of antiterrorism policies. *American Journal of Political Science, 49*, 593–608. doi:10.1111/j.1540–5907.2005.00144.x

Jessop, D. C., & Wade, J. (2008). Fear appeals and binge drinking: A terror management theory perspective. *British Journal of Health Psychology, 13*, 773–788. doi:10.1348/135910707X272790

Jonas, E., Martens, A., Niesta, D., Fritsche, I., Sullivan, D., & Greenberg, J. (2008). Focus theory of normative conduct and terror management theory: The interactive impact of mortality salience and norm salience on social judgment. *Journal of Personality and Social Psychology, 95*, 1239–1251. doi:10.1037/a0013593

Judges, D. P. (1999). Scared to death: Capital punishment as authoritarian terror management. *UC Davis Law Review, 33*, 155–248.

Kirchmeier, J. L. (2008). Our existential death penalty: Judges, jurors, and terror management. *Law & Psychology Review, 32*, 55–108.

Lamberth, J., Krieger, E., & Shay, S. (1982). Juror decision making: A case of attitude change mediated by authoritarianism. *Journal of Research in Personality, 16*, 419–434. doi:10.1016/0092–6566(82)90003–4

Landau, M. J., Goldenberg, J., Greenberg, J., Gillath, O., Solomon, S., Cox, C., Martens, A., & Pyszczynski, T. (2006). The siren's call: Terror management and the threat of men's sexual attraction to women. *Journal of Personality and Social Psychology, 90,* 129–146. doi:10.1037/0022–3514.90.1.129

Landau, M. J., Johns, M., Greenberg, J., Pyszczynski, T., Martens, A., Goldenberg, J. L., & Solomon, S. (2004). A function of form: Terror management and structuring the social world. *Journal of Personality and Social Psychology, 87,* 190–210. doi:10.1037/0022–3514.87.2.190

Landau, M. J., Solomon, S., Greenberg, J., Cohen, F., Pyszczynski, T., Arndt, J., & Cook, A. (2004). Deliver us from evil: The effects of mortality salience and reminders of 9/11 on support for President George W. Bush. *Personality and Social Psychology Bulletin, 30,* 1136–1150. doi:10.1177/0146167204267988

Lieberman, J. D. (2010). Inner terror and outward hate: The effects of mortality salience on bias motivated attacks. In B. H. Bornstein & R. L. Wiener (Eds.), *Emotion and the law* (pp. 133–155). New York: Springer. doi:10.1007/978–1–4419–0696–0_5

Lieberman, J. D., Arndt, J., Personius, J., & Cook, A. (2001). Vicarious annihilation: The effect of mortality salience on perceptions of hate crimes. *Law and Human Behavior, 25,* 547–566. doi:10.1023/A:1012738706166

Lieberman, J. D., & Sales, B. D. (2007). *Scientific jury selection.* Washington, DC: American Psychological Association.

Lieberman, J. D., Shoemaker, J., & Krauss, D. A. (2014). The effects of mortality salience and evidence strength in death penalty sentencing decisions. *Psychology, Crime, & Law, 20,* 199–221. doi:10.1080/1068316X.2013.770853

Marshall, L. E., & Marshall, W. (2000). The origins of sexual offending. *Trauma, Violence, & Abuse, 1,* 250–263. doi:10.1177/1524838000001003003

Martens, A., Burke, B. L., Schimel, J., & Faucher, E. H. (2011). Same but different: meta-analytically examining the uniqueness of mortality salience effects. *European Journal of Social Psychology, 41,* 6–10. doi:10.1002/ejsp.767

McCabe, S., & Arndt, J. (in press). The psychological threat of mortality and the implications it has for tobacco and alcohol misuse. In Victor Preedy (Ed.), *The neuropathology of drug addictions and substance misuse.* London: Academic Press.

McGregor, H. A., Lieberman, J. D., Greenberg, J., Solomon, S., Arndt, J., Simon, L., & Pyszczynski, T. (1998). Terror management and aggression: Evidence that mortality salience motivates aggression against worldview-threatening others. *Journal of Personality and Social Psychology, 74,* 590–605. doi:10.1037/0022–3514.74.3.590

Mikulincer, M., & Florian, V. (2000). Exploring individual differences in reactions to mortality salience: Does attachment style regulate terror management mechanisms? *Journal of Personality and Social Psychology, 79,* 260–273. doi:10.1037/0022–3514.79.2.260

Nagar, M., & Rabinovitz, S. (2015). Smoke your troubles away: Exploring the effects of death cognitions on cannabis craving and consumption. *Journal of Psychoactive Drugs, 47,* (published online May 7, 2015). doi: 10.1080/02791072.2015.1029654

Nelson, L. J., Moore, D. L., Olivetti, J., & Scott, T. (1997). General and personal mortality salience and nationalistic bias. *Personality and Social Psychology Bulletin, 23,* 884–892. doi:10.1177/0146167297238008

Pyszczynski, T., Abdollahi, A., Solomon, S., Greenberg, J., Cohen, F., & Weise, D. (2006). Mortality salience, martyrdom, and military might: The great Satan versus the axis of evil. *Personality and Social Psychology Bulletin, 32,* 525–537. doi:10.1177/0146167205282157

Pyszczynski, T., Greenberg, J., Solomon, S., Arndt, J., & Schimel, J. (2004). Why do people need self-esteem? A theoretical and empirical review. *Psychological Bulletin, 130*, 435–468. doi:10.1037/0033–2909.130.3.435

Pyszczynski, T., Motyl, M., & Abdollahi, A. (2009). Righteous violence: Killing for god, country, freedom, and justice. *Behavioral Sciences of Terrorism and Political Aggression, 1*, 12–39. doi:10.1080/19434470802482118

Pyszczynski, T., Solomon, S., & Greenberg, J. (2003). *In the wake of 9/11: Rising above the terror.* Washington, DC: American Psychological Association. doi:10.1037/10478–009

Rosenblatt, A., Greenberg, J., Solomon, S., Pyszczynski, T., & Lyon, D. (1989). Evidence for terror management theory I: The effects of mortality salience on reactions to those who violate or uphold cultural values. *Journal of Personality and Social Psychology, 57*, 681–690. doi:10.1037/0022–3514.57.4.681

Rothschild, Z. K., Abdollahi, A., & Pyszczynski, T. (2009). Does peace have a prayer? The effect of mortality salience, compassionate values, and religious fundamentalism on hostility toward out-groups. *Journal of Experimental Social Psychology, 45*, 816–827. doi:10.1016/j.jesp.2009.05.016

Routledge, C., & Arndt, J. (2008). Self-sacrifice as self-defense: Mortality salience increases efforts to affirm a symbolic immortal self at the expense of the physical self. *European Journal of Social Psychology, 38*, 531–541. doi:10.1002/ejsp.442

Rowland, C. K. (2002). Psychological perspectives on juror reactions to the September 11 events. *Defense Counsel Journal, 69*, 180–184.

Rubin, Z., & Peplau, A. (1975). Who believes in a just world? *Journal of Social Issues, 29*, 73–93. doi:10.1111/j.1540–4560.1975.tb00997.x

Shackelford, T. K. (2001). Self-esteem in marriage. *Personality and Individual Differences, 30*, 371–390. doi:10.1016/S0191–8869(00)00023–4

Shehryar, O., & Hunt, D. M. (2005). A terror management perspective on the persuasiveness of fear appeals. *Journal of Consumer Psychology, 15*, 275–287. doi:10.1207/s15327663jcp1504_2

Silke, A. (2008). Holy warriors exploring the psychological processes of Jihadi radicalization. *European Journal of Criminology, 5*, 99–123. doi:10.1177/1477370807084226

Simon, L., Greenberg, J., Harmon-Jones, E., Solomon, S., Pyszczynski, T., Arndt, J., & Abend, T. (1997). Terror management and cognitive-experiential self-theory: Evidence that terror management occurs in the experiential system. *Journal of Personality and Social Psychology, 72*, 1132–1146. doi:10.1037/0022–3514.72.5.1132

Singh, A. (2002). *"We are not the enemy": Hate crimes against Arabs, Muslims, and those perceived to be Arab or Muslim after September 11.* Vol. 14(6). New York: Human Rights Watch.

Taylor, L. D. (2012). Death and television: Terror management theory and themes of law and justice on television. *Death Studies, 36*, 340–359. doi:10.1080/07481187.2011.553343

Van den Bos, K. (2001). Reactions to perceived fairness: The impact of mortality salience and self-esteem on ratings of negative affect. *Social Justice Research, 14*, 1–23. doi:10.1023/A:1012501506803

Van den Bos, K., & Miedema, J. (2000). Toward understanding why fairness matters: The influence of mortality salience on reactions to procedural fairness. *Journal of Personality and Social Psychology, 79*, 355–366. doi:10.1037/0022–3514.79.3.355

Walker, J. S., & Bright, J. A. (2009). False inflated self-esteem and violence: A systematic review and cognitive model. *The Journal of Forensic Psychiatry & Psychology, 20*, 1–32. doi:10.1080/14789940701656808

Weise, D. R., Pyszczynski, T., Cox, C. R., Arndt, J., Greenberg, J., Solomon, S., & Kosloff, S. (2008). Interpersonal politics the role of terror management and attachment processes in shaping political preferences. *Psychological Science, 19*, 448–455. doi:10.1111/j.1467–9280.2008.02108.x

Wolf, S., & Montgomery, D. A. (1977). Effects of inadmissible evidence and level of judicial admonishment to disregard on the judgments of mock jurors. *Journal of Applied Social Psychology, 7*, 205–219. doi:10.1111/j.1559–1816.1977.tb00746.x

6

MARKETING, MONEY, AND MORTALITY

Tyler F. Stillman and Lindsey A. Harvell

Coffins. They come in all shapes and sizes, some plain and some extravagant. A typical coffin costs over $2,000, with many people choosing to spend $5,000, and still others spending up to $10,000 (Federal Trade Commission, 2015). To put these numbers in perspective, $2,000 is enough money to feed an average American family of four for about three and a half months; $5,000 can feed the same family for almost nine months; $10,000 approaches one and a half years (United States Department of Agriculture, 2014). To be sure, most Americans spend money on a variety of things, such as cars, that can be considered expensive or even wasteful when one considers the family-of-four equivalent. However, cars are rarely deliberately buried under dirt within hours of purchase—with the hope they will never be seen again. This is not to suggest that spending lavishly for things is always purely irrational. There are some benefits to spending money in a seemingly frivolous manner, such as attracting or keeping a mate (Sundie, Kenrick, Griskevicius, Tybur, Vohs, & Beal, 2011; Wang & Griskevicius, 2014). It seems unlikely that purchasing coffins—even the most lavish ones—has much mate-attracting value. So why do people spend lavishly on coffins?

The answer may be that confronting the reality of human mortality is a powerful and disruptive event, and doing so causes a change in people's behavior across a broad spectrum of domains. Therefore, this chapter investigates consumer spending and marketing and how death salience, in the theoretical grounding of terror management theory (TMT), can help explain these spending phenomena.

Terror Management Theory

One might plausibly suggest that Americans are the only ones to spend lavishly when someone dies. However, citizens of Borneo and Ghana also participate in expensive death rituals (Bonsu & Belk, 2003; Metcalf, 1981). Observing these patterns of spending in the aftermath of death across cultures suggests that something fundamentally human is occurring, rather than something fundamentally American. TMT holds that people's understanding that they will eventually die produces unpleasant death-related feelings, and people try to alleviate these unpleasant feelings through a variety of means, including their economic and consumer behavior (Becker, 1973; Greenberg et al., 1990; Greenberg, Pyszczynski, & Solomon, 1986).

Crucial to managing the anxiety associated with an awareness of one's mortality is one's cultural worldview. Cultural worldviews are "beliefs about the nature of reality shared by groups of people that developed (quite unconsciously) as a means by which individuals manage the potential for terror provoked by the human consciousness of mortality" (Arndt, Solomon, Kasser, & Sheldon, 2004, p. 199). One's cultural worldview may include his or her religious beliefs, political views, cultural heritage, nationalistic pride, or anything else that addresses existential questions about the purposes and reasons for existence. Cultural worldviews are at the heart of how people cope with unpleasant death-related cognitions (Arndt, Greenberg, Solomon, Pyszczynski, & Simon, 1997; Greenberg et al., 1990; Greenberg, Solomon, & Pyszczynski, 1997). However, simply having a cultural worldview is not enough to buffer one from the anxiety and fear associated with knowing one will die—everyone has a worldview, regardless of whether they are confronting thoughts of death or not. TMT holds that people buffer themselves from the discomfort of knowing they are going to die through worldview defense—that is, asserting the correctness and superiority of one's worldview. Worldview defense often entails distancing oneself from people who have a different cultural worldview and approaching those with a similar worldview (Greenberg, Solomon, & Pyszczynski, 1997) or adhering to cultural norms (Gailliot, Stillman, Schmeichel, Maner, & Plant, 2008). For instance, participants from a Christian background who have been asked to write about their own death subsequently formed more positive impressions of a Christian and less positive impressions of a Jew (Greenberg et al., 1990). That is, being made aware of their mortality caused participants to embrace Christianity and distance themselves from a different worldview, namely, Judaism. Likewise, a different study found that Christian participants demonstrated an increased reluctance to use a crucifix as a hammer when they were asked to think about their own deaths (Greenberg, Simon, Porteus, et al., 1995), consistent with embracing their worldview. A meta-analysis of 277 experiments revealed consistent evidence that death-related thoughts increased worldview defense, using a variety of worldview-defense measures such as denigrating people from other cultures (Burke, Martens, & Faucher, 2010).

Mortality, Materialism, and Worldview Defense

Arndt and colleagues (2004) describe childhood psychosocial development as a process of internalizing values espoused by parents, such that what the parents consider valuable becomes what children consider valuable. Children consider themselves as being worthy and behaving properly to the extent that they do as their parents want them to. As children develop into adults, however, the basis for what is considered valuable shifts from parents to the broader culture, at which point people consider themselves worthy to the extent they behave according to the demands of the broader culture.

Most observers agree that modern Western culture, and perhaps especially American culture, values the acquisition of wealth and the display of material possessions (Kasser, 2003; Kasser & Ryan, 1993; Shi, 1985). Consequently, worldview defense as a response to mortality salience should entail materialistic pursuits for Westerners. That is, to the extent that materialistic pursuits are part of Western culture, Westerners may find solace from death anxiety in getting rich and buying luxury goods.

Empirical evidence is supportive of these ideas. In one study, participants were randomly assigned to write about their thoughts and feelings associated with their own death (mortality-salience condition) or to write about their thoughts and feelings associated with listening to music (control condition; Kasser & Sheldon, 2000). Those who wrote about death anticipated having greater financial worth 15 years later. In a second study, participants completed a forest-management simulation in which personal financial benefits had to be balanced against public good. Those in the mortality-salience condition proposed harvesting 62% of the forest in one year, as compared to 49% of those in the control condition. Hence mortality salience caused American participants to prioritize personal wealth.

In addition to accumulating money, the purchase and display of luxury goods is an important part of Western culture. Accordingly, brand preferences also change when people think about death. Awareness of mortality caused American participants to view luxury brands, such as Lexus, more favorably. It caused them to view lower-status brands, such as Chevy, somewhat less favorably (Mandel & Heine, 1999). That is, thinking about death caused participants to become more eager for luxury goods as well as the accumulation of wealth, both of which are part of modern Western culture.

Two notes of caution are worth mentioning with respect to worldview defense. First, Western culture is not alone in spending in response to death awareness (Bonsu & Belk, 2003; Metcalf, 1981). Likewise, Western culture is not alone in spending on luxury goods (Zhan & He, 2012). However, given the strong emphasis placed on material and financial acquisition in Western culture, one would expect that acquisition would figure prominently in worldview defense among individuals from Western cultures. In other words, it seems likely that mortality salience would prompt materialistic strivings among Westerners above what is observed elsewhere. Second, worldview defense is not necessarily the only way of explaining increased acquisitiveness and emphasis on branded goods following mortality salience. There are complementary explanations, which are considered next.

Mortality, Materialism, and Insecurity

Highly materialistic people experience different dreams than less materialistic people (Kasser & Kasser, 2001). In particular, highly materialistic people are more likely to dream of threats (such as dying and falling) than others. While it is plausible that materialism causes threatening dreams, the authors' explanation that an underlying insecurity led to materialistic pursuits—as a way of providing a sense of security. That is, they viewed insecurity as bringing about materialism. Developmental research provides additional evidence that materialism can function to overcome insecurity, as people whose childhoods were insecure (e.g., those who experienced a family disruption, such as divorce) are more likely to grow to be materialistic (John 1999; Kasser, Ryan, Zax, & Sameroff, 1995). In short, insecurity seems to cause increased materialism.

Existential Insecurity and Brands

Rindfleisch and colleages (2009) proposed that the reason people who experience mortality salience demonstrate an interest in accumulating wealth and a fondness for luxury brands (as described earlier; Kasser & Sheldon, 2000; Mandel & Heine, 1999) is to restore a sense of psychological security. They described awareness of one's mortality as existential insecurity, and they suggested that material objects perform a compensatory function, in that they could restore a feeling of security. In particular, they proposed that being bonded to a brand could reestablish the security that death awareness disrupts. Two studies supported this existential insecurity perspective (Rindfleisch et al., 2009). In one study, survey research showed that materialistic people who also demonstrated existential insecurity were more likely than others (those low in materialism and/or low in existential insecurity) to feel a deep and abiding connection to a brand they owned (such as jeans or automobiles; Rindfleisch et al., 2009). In other words, materialistic people with a pronounced fear of death were especially likely to love their pants.

In a second study, these researchers employed an experimental design, such that some participants were assigned to think about their own death and others were assigned to think about listening to music. Among materialistic participants, those who were in the death-awareness condition were more likely than those in the control condition to report a strong bond to their MP3 player or sunglasses. Death awareness did not bring about changes in brand-bondedness among participants low in materialism. In sum, there is merit to the idea that people become more bonded to brands as a means of buffering existential distress, although this seems not to generalize to people low in materialism.

Spending and Self-Esteem

Terror management theory holds that the primary function of self-esteem is to be a buffer to existential fear and anxiety (Pyszczynski, Greenberg, Solomon, Arndt, & Schimel, 2004). This contention is supported empirically. In three studies, researchers replicated the finding that mortality salience increases worldview defense, but the effect was not observed among those high in self-esteem (Schmeichel, Gailliot, Filardo, McGregor, Gitter, & Baumeister, 2009). These researchers also found that experimentally increased self-esteem resulted in reduced worldview defense. These findings are supportive of the notion that the purpose of self-esteem is to buffer existential fears.

The notion that people choose products and brands as a means of communicating information about themselves is well established (Belk, 1988; Escalas & Bettman, 2003, 2005; Levy, 1959; Mead, Baumeister, Stillman, Rawn, & Vohs, 2011). What do people communicate about themselves when they buy luxury brands? According to Arndt and colleagues (2004), luxury brands "represents a culturally sanctioned symbolic testimony to one's value" (p. 203). Based on this view, luxury brands provide the buyer with self-esteem and a sense of value, the purpose of which is to buffer existential dread. Indeed, survey evidence has found that higher self-esteem does correspond to a preference for luxury goods (Truong & McColl, 2011).

One important consideration is that self-esteem does not develop in a vacuum—it develops within the context of a culture (Pyszczynski et al., 2004). People develop self-esteem related to things that are valued within that culture, which in some cases may be owning luxury goods or in others it may be one's proficiency as a hunter. In other words, different cultures produce different sources of self-esteem.

Virtuous Spending

Even within the same country people develop different sources of self-esteem. Research has assessed how mortality salience differentially impacted people with different sources of self-esteem, namely, those for whom virtue was critical to their self-esteem and those for whom virtue was less important to their self-esteem (Ferraro, Shiv, & Bettman, 2005). Among people for whom virtue was an important source of self-esteem, those who experienced mortality salience offered a higher portion of their compensation for participating in the study to charity, relative to those for whom virtue was not an important source of self-esteem. The researchers also assessed participants' intentions to engage in socially conscious consumer behaviors, such as refusing to buy products that were made using child or sweatshop labor. Again, among participants for whom virtue was an important source of self-esteem, those exposed to death awareness demonstrated increased determination to consume in a socially conscious manner, compared to participants for whom virtue was a less important source of self-esteem.

Cigarettes

For some people who smoke, smoking cigarettes is a source of self-esteem. For other smokers, it is not. Based on the findings described earlier, one could expect that death awareness would affect these groups differently, and research has supported this expectation (Hansen, Winzeler, & Topolinski, 2009). When exposed to cigarette warnings in which death is mentioned, those for whom cigarette smoking is a source of self-esteem consider smoking more positively. In contrast, when exposed to a cigarette warning not mentioning death, such participants came to view the practice more negatively. In sum, mortality salience prompts donations and product affinity, but only when consistent with an individual's basis for self-esteem, which is consistent with the notion that self-esteem serves to buffer existential dread.

Money as Symbolic Immortality

Becker (1975) described the accumulation of money as a means of buffering fears of death in a manner consistent with the concept of symbolic immortality: "It can be accumulated and passed on, and so radiates its powers even after one's death" (p. 81). Money can be a means of achieving symbolic immortality, as people can continue to affect the lives of others, through their accumulated money, after death.

One means of quelling death-related anxiety is through symbolic immortality. Whereas literal immortality is the belief one will continue to exist after the death of the body (as a spirit or other form of consciousness), symbolic immortality is the belief that some aspect of the self will continue to exist after the death of the body (Lifton & Olson, 1974; Martin, 1999). According to Lifton (1979), symbolic immortality allows people to maintain a sense of continuity, or an ongoing connection to others, after death. Among the most common ways of achieving symbolic immortality is through continuous biological attachment, such as by having children who presumably will continue one's genes. Research has found that people who have a sense of symbolic immortality, as compared to those who do not, are less fearful of death and less reactive to explicit reminders of mortality (Florian & Mikulincer, 1998). This supports the notion that symbolic immortality reduces existential fears.

The symbolic nature of money, as well as the symbolic nature of one's product choices, has been established in the literature, as money and products often fill symbolic needs rather than filling strictly instrumental needs (Belk, 1988; Furnham & Argyle, 1998; Kasser, Ryan, Couchman, & Sheldon, 2004; Stillman, Fincham, Vohs, Lambert, & Phillips, 2012). In a series of experiments, researchers tested whether mortality salience affected people's perceptions of money (Zaleskiewicz, Gasiorowska, Kesebir, Luszczynska, & Pyszczynski, 2013b). Results revealed that participants assigned to the mortality-salience condition perceived money differently from those in the control condition in several ways. Death awareness increased people's perception of the physical size of money, such that money came to be perceived as occupying a larger physical space. The perception of large physical space is suggestive of greater value being attached to money. Death awareness also altered people's answers to a question about how much money one needs to earn in order to be considered rich, such that death-aware participants had a higher threshold for wealth. This, too, is consistent with the notion that existential fears provoke acquisitiveness, presumably to assuage those fears. These researchers also tested the notion that money reduces fear of death explicitly. Participants were assigned either to count real money or to count money-sized papers with numbers on them. Those who counted real money (and therefore were thinking about money at some level) reported being less fearful of death, as compared to participants who counted nonmoney papers. In sum, death awareness also seems to increase the value attached to money, and thinking about money seems to reduce existential fears (Zaleskiewicz et al., 2013b).

However, does death awareness increase the desire to accumulate money, so that it can "radiate its powers even after one's death" (Becker, 1975, p. 81)? Recent research suggests that it does (Zaleskiewicz, Gasiorowska, & Kesebir, 2013a). Participants who were faced with a spend-or-save dilemma were more likely to choose saving money after having experienced an experimental mortality-salience induction. This indicates that mortality salience promotes the accumulation of money. In a separate study, these researchers also found that inducing participants to think about saving decreased their fear of death. These findings are consistent with the accumulation of money as a means of reducing existential fears. In sum, money seems to buffer existential fears in a manner consistent with the concept of symbolic immortality.

There is a consideration that is worth repeating with respect to money as a means of symbolic immortality, namely, that culture is crucial in managing existential fears. The means of achieving symbolic immortality are not innate but are acquired through culture. As Becker (1973) stated, culture is "more than merely an outlook on life: it is an immortality formula" (p. 255). For some cultures, the accumulation of money is part of that formula, and it is likely that for some cultures the accumulation of money is not part of that formula.

Gender Norms and Consumer Behavior

Evidence indicates that women have more death anxiety than men do (Dattel & Neimeyer, 1990; Ens & Bond, 2007; Rose & O'Sullivan, 2002; Russac, Gatliff, Reece, & Spottswood, 2007). Do men and women respond differently to mortality salience? There have been some studies in which gender moderated mortality-salience effects (e.g., Arndt, Greenberg, & Cook, 2002). However, a meta-analysis concluded that gender does not moderate mortality-salience effects in a generalized way (Burke et al., 2010). This does not mean that one cannot anticipate some cases where gender might moderate mortality-salience effects. While many cultural expectations are identical for men and women, some expectations differ for men and women (Money, Hampson, & Hampson, 1955). These expectations, or gender roles, are acquired through culture and can lead men and women to behave differently when death awareness is activated.

Gambling

One cultural expectation of men is that they behave in a riskier manner than women (e.g., Kelling, Zerkes, & Myerowitz, 1976; see also Zuckerman, 1979). Research has found that men, but not women, who were exposed to a mortality-salience induction subsequently showed an increased willingness to engage in some risky behaviors, such as skydiving and taking psychoactive drugs (Hirschberger, Florian, Mikulincer, Goldenberg, & Pyszczynski, 2002). A second cultural expectation of men is that they act as "bread-winners" (Gerson, 1993). Gambling is an endeavor that captures both getting money and behaving in a risky manner. Hence mortality salience should cause men, but not women, to want to gamble. Recently, researchers conducted a field experiment to understand the gender differences in how death awareness affects consumer behavior outside a laboratory setting, and in particular how gender moderated the effects of mortality salience on gambling (Harvell, Stillman, Nisbett, Cranney, & Marabella, 2015). The research was conducted using travelers at McCarran International Airport in Las Vegas. Rather than asking participants explicitly to write about death, participants in the death-awareness condition were asked to describe their "main fears or anxieties about air travel." Participants in the control condition were asked about their experience at the airport. As expected, participants who wrote about their main fears related to air travel frequently wrote about death in the form of air disasters (whereas those who wrote about the airport did not). Participants were subsequently asked about the likelihood that they would gamble in the next hour. Results indicated that male travelers, but not female travelers, who were made death-aware showed a substantially increased intention to gamble. Mortality salience caused a change in participants' intended consumer behavior, and it did so according to gender norms.

Conclusions—Do *You* Want the Elaborate Coffin?

This chapter began by describing a pattern of behavior that seems irrational: spending substantial amounts of money on an item that is literally going to be buried and never seen again. Irrational though it may be, spending money on coffins is not senseless. When a loved one dies, those who grieve must confront death in an unambiguous way. This may entail seeing and touching a lifeless body, watching an interment, and witnessing the resulting emotional upheaval. The death of a loved one makes the reality of mortality unavoidable. Such thoughts are literally dreadful. Research on terror management theory described herein suggests that people spend as a means of quelling the dreadful thoughts. Spending lavishly on a coffin may allow people a measure of comfort and reassurance of their continued existence. Therefore, as long as there is death anxiety, there will be lavish spending. The question is, is this something that marketing agencies will start taking advantage of? Only time will tell.

References

Arndt, J., Greenberg, J., & Cook, A. (2002). Mortality salience and the spreading activation of worldview-relevant constructs: Exploring the cognitive architecture of terror management. *Journal of Experimental Psychology: General, 131*, 307–324.

Arndt, J., Greenberg, J., Solomon, S., Pyszczynski, T., & Simon, L. (1997). Suppression, accessibility of death-related thoughts, and cultural worldview. *Journal of Personality and Social Psychology, 73*(1), 5–18.

Arndt, J., Solomon, S., Kasser, T., & Sheldon, K. M. (2004). The urge to splurge: A terror management account of materialism and consumer behavior. *Journal of Consumer Psychology, 14*(3), 198–212.

Becker, E. (1973). *The denial of death.* New York: Free Press.

Becker, E. (1975). *Escape from evil.* New York: Free Press.

Belk, R. W. (1988). Possessions and the Extended Self. *Journal of Consumer Research, 15*, 139–167. doi:10.1086/209154

Bonsu, S. K., & Belk, R. W. (2003) Do not go cheaply into that good night: Death-ritual consumption in Asante, Ghana. *Journal of Consumer Research, 30*(1), 41–55. doi:10.1086/74699

Burke, B. L., Martens, A., & Faucher, E. H. (2010). Two decades of terror management theory: A meta-analysis of mortality salience research. *Personality and Social Psychology Review, 14*(2), 155–195. doi:10.1177/1088868309352321

Dattel, A. R., & Neimeyer, R. A. (1990). Sex differences in death awareness: Testing the emotional expressiveness hypothesis. *Death Studies, 14*, 1–11.

Ens, C., & Bond, J. B. (2007). Death anxiety in adolescents: The contributions of bereavement and religiosity. *Omega, 55*, 169–184. doi:10.2190/OM.55.3.a

Escalas, J. E., & Bettman, J. R. (2003). You are what they eat: The influence of reference groups on consumer connections to brands. *Journal of Consumer Psychology, 13*(3), 339–348. doi:10.1207/S15327663JCP1303_14

Escalas, J. E., & Bettman, J. R. (2005). Self-construal, reference groups, and brand meaning. *Journal of Consumer Research, 32*, 378–389. doi:10.1086/497549

Federal Trade Commission. (2015). *Funeral costs and pricing checklist.* Retrieved from http://www.consumer.ftc.gov/articles/0301-funeral-costs-and-pricing-checklist

Ferraro, R., Shiv, B., & Bettman, J. R. (2005). Let us eat and drink, for tomorrow we shall die: Effects of mortality salience and self-esteem on self-regulation in consumer choice. *Journal of Consumer Research, 32*(1), 65–75. doi:10.1086/429601

Florian, V., & Mikulincer, M. (1998). Symbolic immortality and the management of the terror of death. *Journal of Personality and Social Psychology, 74*, 725–734.

Furnham, A., & Argyle, M. (1998). *The psychology of money.* London: Routledge.

Gailliot, M. T., Stillman, T. F., Schmeichel, B. J., Maner, J. K., & Plant, E. A. (2008). Mortality salience increases adherence to salient norms and values. *Personality and Social Psychology Bulletin, 34*(7), 993–1003.

Gerson, K. (1993). *No man's land.* New York: Basic Books.

Greenberg, J., Pyszczynski, T., & Solomon, S. (1986). The causes and consequences of a need for self-esteem: A terror management theory. In R. E. Baumeister (Ed.), *Public self and private self* (pp. 189–212). New York: Springer-Verlag.

Greenberg, J., Pyszczynski, T., Solomon, S., Rosenblatt, A., Veeder, M., Kirkland, S., & Lyon, D. (1990). Evidence for terror management II: The effects of mortality salience on reactions to those who threaten or bolster the cultural worldview. *Journal of Personality and Social Psychology, 58*, 308–318. doi:10.1037/0022–3514.58.2.308

Greenberg, J., Simon, L., Porteus, J., Pyszczynski, T., & Solomon, S. (1995). Evidence of a terror management function of cultural icons: The effects of mortality salience on the inappropriate use of cherished cultural symbols. *Personality and Social Psychology Bulletin, 21*, 1221–1228. doi:10.1177/01461672952111010

Greenberg, J., Solomon, S., & Pyszczynski, T. (1997). Terror management theory of self-esteem and cultural worldviews: Empirical assessments and conceptual refinements. *Advances in Experimental Social Psychology, 29*, 61–139. doi:10.1016/S0065–2601 (08)60016–7

Hansen, J., Winzeler, S., & Topolinski, S. (2009). When the death makes you smoke: A terror management perspective on the effectiveness of cigarette on-pack warnings. *Journal of Experimental Social Psychology, 46*(1), 226–228. doi:10.1016/j.jesp.2009.09.007

Harvell, L. A., Stillman, T. F., Nisbett, G. S., Cranney, K., & Marabella, A. (2015). *A field investigation of flight anxiety: Evidence of gender differences in consumer behaviors among Las Vegas passengers.* Manuscript under review.

Hirschberger, G., Florian, V., Mikulincer, M., Goldenberg, J. L., & Pyszczynski, T. (2002). Gender differences in the willingness to engage in risky behavior: A terror management perspective. *Death Studies, 26*, 117–141. doi:10.1080/074811802753455244

John, D. J. (1999). Consumer socialization of children: A retrospective look at twenty-five years of research. *Journal of Consumer Research, 26*(December), 183–213. doi:10.1086/209559

Kasser, T. (2003). *The high price of materialism.* Cambridge, MA: MIT Press.

Kasser, T., & Kasser, V. G. (2001). The dreams of people high and low in materialism. *Journal of Economic Psychology, 22*, 693–719.

Kasser, T., & Ryan, R. M. (1993). The dark side of the American Dream: Correlates of intrinsic and extrinsic goals. *Journal of Personality and Social Psychology, 65*(2), 410–422.

Kasser, T., Ryan, R. M., Couchman, C. E., & Sheldon, K. M. (2004). Materialistic values: Their causes and consequences. In T. Kasser & A. D. Kanner (Eds.), *Psychology and consumer culture* (pp. 11–28). Washington, DC: American Psychological Association.

Kasser. T., Ryan, R. M., Zax, M., & Sameroff., A. J. (1995). The relations of maternal and social environments to late adolescents' materialistic and prosocial values. *Developmental Psychology, 31*(6), 907–914. doi:10.1037/0012–1649.31.6.907

Kasser, T., & Sheldon, K. M. (2000). Of wealth and death: Materialism, mortality salience, and consumption behaviors. *Psychological Science, 11*, 348–351.

Kelling, G. W., Zerkes, R., & Myerowitz, D. (1976). Risk as value: A switch of set hypothesis. *Psychological Reports, 38*, 655–658. doi:10.2466/pr0.1976.38.2.655

Levy, S. J. (1959). Symbols for sale. *Harvard Business Review, 33*, 117–124. doi:10.4135/9781452231372.n18

Lifton, R. J. (1979). *The broken connection: On death and the continuity of life.* Washington, DC: American Psychiatric Press, Inc.

Lifton, R. J., & Olson, E. (1974). *Living and dying.* New York: Praeger.

Mandel, N., & Heine, S. J. (1999). Terror management and marketing: He who dies with the most toys wins. In E. J. Arnold & L. M. Scott (Eds.), *Advances in consumer research Vol.26*, (pp. 527–532). Provo, UT: Association for Consumer Research.

Martin, L. L. (1999). I-D compensation theory: Some implications of trying to satisfy immediate-return needs in a delayed-return culture. *Psychological Inquiry, 10*, 195–208. doi:10.1207/S15327965PLI1003_1

Mead, N., Baumeister, R. F., Stillman, T. F., Rawn, K., & Vohs, K. D. (2011). Social exclusion causes people to spend and consume strategically in the service of affiliation. *Journal of Consumer Research, 37*, 902–919. doi:10.1086/656667

Metcalf, P. (1981). Meaning and materialism: The ritual economy of death. *Man, 16*(4), 586–578. doi:10.2307/2801488

Money, J., Hampson, J. G., & Hampson, J. (1955). An examination of some basic sexual concepts: The evidence of human hermaphroditism. *Bulletin of the Johns Hopkins Hospital, 97*(4), 301–319.

Pyszczynski, T., Greenberg, J., Solomon, S., Arndt, J., & Schimel, J. (2004). Why do people need self-esteem? A theoretical and empirical review. *Psychological Bulletin, 130*(3), 435–468. doi:10.1037/0033-2909.130.3.435

Rindfleisch, A., Burroughs, J. E., & Wong, N. (2009). The safety of objects: Materialism, existential insecurity, and brand connection. *Journal of Consumer Research, 36*, 1–16. doi:10.1086/595718

Rose, B. M., & O'Sullivan, M. J. (2002). Afterlife beliefs and death awareness: An exploration of the relationship between afterlife expectations and fear of death in an undergraduate population. *Omega, 45*, 229–243.

Russac, R., Gatliff, C., Reece, M., & Spottswood, D. (2007). Death awareness across the adult years: An examination of age and gender effects. *Death Studies, 2*, 549–561.

Schmeichel, B. J., Gailliot, M. T., Filardo, E. A., McGregor, I., Gitter, S., & Baumeister, R. F. (2009). Terror management theory and self-esteem revisited: The roles of implicit and explicit self-esteem in mortality salience effects. *Journal of Personality and Social Psychology, 96*(5), 1077–1087. doi:10.1037/a0015091

Shi, D. (1985). *The simple life.* New York: Oxford University Press.

Stillman, T. F., Fincham, F. D., Vohs, K. D., Lambert, N. M., & Phillips, C. A. (2012). The material and immaterial in conflict: Spirituality reduces conspicuous consumption motives. *Journal of Economic Psychology, 102*, 291–305.

Sundie, J. M., Kenrick, D. T., Griskevicius, V., Tybur, J. M., Vohs, K. D., & Beal, D. J., (2011). Peacocks, Porsches, and Thorstein Veblen: Conspicuous consumption as a sexual signaling system. *Journal of Personality and Social Psychology, 100*(4), 664–680.

Truong, Y., & McColl, R. (2011). Intrinsic motivations, self-esteem, and luxury goods consumption. *Journal of Retailing and Consumer Services, 18*(6), 555–561. doi:10.1016/j.jretconser.2011.08.004

United States Department of Agriculture. (2014). *USDA food plans: Cost of food report for December 2014.* Retrieved from: http://www.cnpp.usda.gov/sites/default/files/CostofFoodDec2014_0.pdf

Wang, Y., & Griskevicius, V. (2014). Consumption, relationships, and rivals: Women's luxury products as signals to other women. *Journal of Consumer Research, 40*(5), 834–854. doi:10.1086/673256

Zaleskiewicz, T., Gasiorowska, A., & Kesebir, P. (2013a). Saving can save from death anxiety: Mortality salience and financial decision-making. *PLoS ONE, 8*(11), e79407. doi:10.1371/journal.pone.0079407

Zaleskiewicz, T., Gasiorowska, A., Kesebir, P., Luszczynska, A., & Pyszczynski, T. (2013b). Money and the fear of death: The symbolic power of money as an existential anxiety buffer. *Journal of Economic Psychology, 36*, 55–67. doi:10.1016/j.joep.2013.02.008

Zhan, L., & He, Y. (2012). Understanding luxury consumption in China: Consumer perceptions of best-known brands. *Journal of Business Research, 65*(10), 1452–1460. doi:10.1016/j.jbusres.2011.10.011

Zuckerman, M. (1979). *Sensation seeking: Beyond the optimal level of arousal.* Hillsdale, NJ: Erlbaum.

7

THE EXISTENTIAL FUNCTION OF PARASOCIAL RELATIONSHIP INTERACTION

Shane M. Semmler

Millions celebrate the life and death of well-known media figures as though they were close intimates (Meyrowitz, 1994). Approximately 161 million people, from around the globe, watched and celebrated the wedding of the United Kingdom's Prince William and Kate Middleton (Harris, 2011). On the day pop singer Michael Jackson died, fans created 500 commemorative Facebook pages and crashed Internet sites like Twitter and *The Los Angeles Times* (Skok, 2009). Even the demise of fictional mediated others inspires authentic mourning. After the death of *Breaking Bad*'s (2008–2013) Walter White, fans honored his memory with an obituary and authentic funeral services held at Albuquerque's Memorial Park, complete with a tombstone commemorating him as a "Beloved Husband, Father, Teacher, & Entrepreneur" (Grow, 2013). Psychologists (Horton & Wohl, 1956) and communication scholars (Rubin et al., 1985) use the terms *parasocial relationship* and *parasocial interaction* to describe the process of thinking and feeling about mediated performers as though they were interpersonal friends.

Parasocial relationship interaction (PSRI) is the imaginary application of interpersonal relationship considerations to liked mediated others (Giles, 2002; Horton & Wohl, 1956; Rubin et al., 1985). Despite early theorizing that PSRI is a compensatory response to chronic loneliness and inadequate social skills (Nordlund, 1978), empirical researchers have found that PSRI complements normal social interaction (Kanazawa, 2002; Tsao, 1996), motivates media use (Conway & Rubin, 1991), and even inspires intergroup cooperation (Schiappa, Gregg, & Hewes, 2005). Current theorizing proposes that PSRI analogizes to the functions and outcomes of actual interpersonal relationship interaction (Giles, 2002; Knowles, 2007; Perse & Rubin, 1989; Rubin & McHugh, 1987). The current study extends that proposition to terror management theory (Pyszczynski,

Greenberg, & Solomon, 1999). Using Mikulincer, Florian, and Hirschberger'
(2003) demonstration that thinking about one's own death elicits relationship
striving, this study tests the capacity of death-thought accessibility (DTA) to
elicit PSRI.

Literature Review and Hypotheses

Parasocial relationship interaction is a productive and useful construct. It has
been demonstrated with talk radio hosts (Rubin & Step, 2000), soap opera characters (Rubin & Perse, 1987), television newscasters (Rubin et al., 1985), and even
athletes (Hartmann, Stuke, & Daschmann, 2008). As a motivation for media
use, PSRI might be more important than programming content (Conway &
Rubin, 1991). Thus, media producers seeking to enhance audience loyalty should
improve the PSRI potential of their programming with variations in program-
ming form (Auter, 1992; Semmler, Loof, & Berke, 2015) and content (Auter &
Moore, 1993; Horton & Wohl, 1956). More broadly PSRI has been used to help
explain and predict media effects in a variety of domains, including entertainment education (Moyer-Gusé, Jain, & Chung, 2012), intergroup relations (Schiappa et al., 2005), and political communication (Rubin & Step, 2000). Despite
PSRI's practical and theoretical usefulness, however, it has been criticized for
being under theorized (Giles, 2002). One response to that criticism has been to
analogize PSRI to theories of face-to-face interpersonal relationship interaction
(Giles, 2002; Schiappa et al., 2005).

This study examines PSRI as an extended form of face-to-face interpersonal
communication with respect to PSRI's capacity to manage the terror of death
awareness. The following sections review terror management theory (Pyszczynski et al., 1999), DTA's elicitation of relationship striving (Mikulincer et al.,
2003), and the interpersonal functions of PSRI (Derrick, Gabriel, & Hugenberg,
2009; Knowles, 2007).

Terror Management Theory

Based on the work of Ernest Becker (1973), terror management theory (TMT)
acknowledges the anxiety associated with humanity's recognition of its own
mortality. The theory axiomatically posits that humanity's awareness of death
motivates a search for symbolic immortality, defined as alliance with a cultural
worldview (Burke, Martens, & Faucher, 2010; Rosenblatt, Greenberg, Solomon,
Pyszczynski, & Lyon, 1989), pursuit of self-esteem (Harmon-Jones et al., 1997),
expressing loyalty to a political leader (Landau et al., 2004), or striving for interpersonal relationships (Mikulincer et al., 2003). These symbolic buffers have
a common basis in some significant perspective, like a set of socially defined
moral values (Rosenblatt et al., 1989) or even more directly from other people
(Harmon-Jones et al., 1997; Mikulincer et al., 2003).

TMT is considered a dual process theory (Pyszczynski et al., 1999). In other words, death awareness elicits two stages of drive reduction. Immediately after one's death is made salient (i.e., proximal mortality salience), one is driven to distraction with reminders of longevity or non-death-related cognitions. After death thoughts are pushed out of conscious awareness, mortality nevertheless remains highly accessible in the subconscious (i.e., distal mortality salience). The concomitant DTA can be suppressed by reinforcing one's symbolic immortality, like by recommending harsh punishments for transgressors against a moral worldview (Rosenblatt et al., 1989), expressing support for a nationalistic political leader (Landau et al., 2004), or connecting to a community of others (Taubman-Ben-Ari, Findler, & Mikulincer, 2002). These three particular mechanisms do not exhaust the options for death-thought suppression, but all forms of such suppression are linked to assertions of one's value in a social context, either within a socially constructed worldview (Rosenblatt et al., 1989) or from a significant social perspective (Harmon-Jones et al., 1997; Mikulincer et al., 2003).

Typical validations of TMT use an experimental design to prime mortality salience. As Burke and colleagues (2010) reported, researchers have devised several methods for eliciting death awareness, including close-ended questions about death, requests to describe one's own death, subliminally presented death words, being near a funeral home, or viewing advertisements featuring car crashes or films about the Holocaust. Following mortality-salience induction, subjects are given a series of distracting tasks and penultimately presented with a manipulation check designed to measure DTA. Finally, subjects are given the opportunity to buffer death anxiety through some form of symbolic immortality. Across more than 250 experiments, the strength of DTA's impact on embracing symbolic immortality is in the top 25% of effects for psychology (Burke et al., 2010).

The Existential Function of Relationship Striving

Mikulincer et al.'s (2003) explanation for relationship striving's amelioration of DTA is initially founded on the assumption of humanity's inherent need to belong. Maslow (1943) ranked belongingness as more important than self-esteem or self-actualization. Aristotle (trans. 1943) famously claimed that humans are social animals, arguing that people living outside society are either beasts or gods. Consistent with Aristotle's assertions of human sociality, Baumeister and Leary (1995) articulated a fundamental need to belong, which has subsequently received considerable empirical validation (see Leary, Kelly, Cottrell, & Schreindorfer, 2013). On a purely material/biological level, the human species could not physically survive without society. Berger and Luckmann (1966) observed that humanity's extended period of neoteny requires a complex and stable system of social relationships. As they reasoned, the absence of such relationships would most certainly result in the failure of the species. Families must both nurture their children's physical survival and prepare them for adulthood, during which time protection and continued socialization expand to include a broader society of significant and generalized others. Those in good standing with society's others thrive in the glow of self-esteem (Maslow, 1943), which is another mechanism of buffering death awareness grounded in the maintenance of social relationships (see Harmon-Jones et al., 1997). In part, self-esteem is "reputation or prestige (defining it as respect from other people) recognition, attention, importance or appreciation" (Maslow, 1943, p. 382). Not incidentally, striving for self-esteem is merely another form of relationship striving. Beyond general social esteem, particular cultures connect much of their symbolic worldview to the meaning of specific relationships. For Catholics, marriage is a sacrament and analogous to the love of Christ for humanity. Thus, the psychological need to belong, physical need for society, pleasure of self-esteem, and cultural functions of close relationships explain why DTA elicits relationship strivings (Mikulincer et al., 2003).

A substantial body of empirical evidence supports the association between DTA and relationship strivings (Mikulincer et al., 2003). DTA predicts relationship striving in terms of an expressed desire for romantic intimacy (Mikulincer & Florian, 2000). DTA even enhances existing relationship bonds. As Florian, Mikulincer, and Hirschberger (2002) found, people in committed relationships respond to mortality salience with more attraction-based commitment to their existing romantic partners. DTA is also associated with relationship striving in platonic relationships. As Taubman-Ben-Ari and colleagues (2002) found, subjects asked to think about their personal death expressed a greater willingness to invite same-sex acquaintances out for coffee. They also rated themselves as more interpersonally competent and were more optimistic about their interpersonal communication competence. Given mortality salience's association with relationship strivings for both romantic (Florian et al., 2002; Mikulincer & Florian, 2000) and platonic relationships (Taubman-Ben-Ari et al., 2002), DTA should reliably predict greater levels of Baumeister and Leary's (1995) general concept of the need to belong (H1).

The Social Functions of Parasocial Relationship Interaction

The society of human friendships and acquaintances extends to hundreds of mediated others (Meyrowitz, 1994). Some are actual people, like John F. Kennedy, and others are merely imaginary, like the deities and demigods of ancient Greece. Caughy (1984) empirically documented imaginary social relationships with characters in novels and television performers. Kanazawa (2002) concluded that humans "fail to distinguish between real friends and the imaginary ones they see on TV" (p. 167). Using General Social Survey data, he found that women who watched more family-based television programs and men who watched more work-based television programs were subjectively more satisfied with their actual friendships. Kanazawa (2002) inferred that people confounded their actual friendships with parasocial friendships. Indeed, the feelings associated with parasocial relationships are qualitatively similar to the emotional prerequisites of interpersonal friendships: When subliminally primed with images of a parasocial friend, subjects experience increased feelings of empathy and a desire to self-disclose (Knowles, 2007).

Parasocial attachments function like actual friendships. Awareness of a parasocial friend is associated with comfort after a social rejection or after performing a frustrating task (Knowles, 2007). As Derrick, Gabriel, and Tippen (2008) revealed, focusing on one's favored celebrity even reduces ideal/actual discrepancies (see Higgins, 1987), meaning people bask in the reflected glow of their parasocial friends. Like being in the presence of attractive others (see Rowatt, Cunningham, & Druen, 1999), the mere presence of admired mediated others elicits self-consciousness: Priming subjects with their favorite television performers predicts better performance on well-learned tasks and worse performance on novel tasks (Gardner & Knowles, 2008; Knowles, 2007).

The difference between parasocial and actual friends is one of degree, not kind. The most preferred television performers are experienced as more real, more likable, and more similar to the self (Gardner & Knowles, 2008). The high fidelity of those performers is reflected in the distress of losing a parasocial friend to a casting change or a cancelled program. Cohen (2003) adapted an interpersonal relationship dissolution scale to measure how people respond when their favorite television characters are no longer on the air. Eyal and Cohen (2006) used the parasocial breakup scale (Cohen, 2003) to measure how fans of NBC's *Friends* (1994–2004) reacted when the program was canceled. Although scores on the scale were lower than for actual interpersonal break ups, PSRI with the *Friends* characters was significantly and positively related to the distress associated with losing a valued interpersonal relationship. Even if parasocial friends are not rated as closer than interpersonal friends, they are experienced as significantly closer than acquaintances (Koenig & Lessan, 1985).

The intermediate nature of parasocial friends combines with findings about the existential function of relationships to suggest a positive relationship between DTA and PSRI. In other words, the potential of relationship striving to buffer death anxiety might not be limited to actual friends and intimate lovers. Findings reviewed earlier show that death anxiety is assuaged by asking same-sex acquaintances to study over coffee (Taubman-Ben-Ari et al., 2002). Because parasocial friends are perceived as real (Eyal & Cohen, 2006; Gardner & Knowles, 2008; Kanazawa, 2002), function to recover from rejection (Knowles, 2007), and are closer than acquaintances (Eyal & Cohen, 2006; Koenig & Lessan, 1985), it is expected that DTA elicits relationship striving in terms of PSRI with a favorite television performer (H2).

Confirming hypothesis 2 could provide substantial construct validation for the social surrogacy hypothesis positing that parasocial relationships offer a functional complement to interpersonal relationships (Derrick et al., 2009; Gardner &

Knowles, 2008; Knowles, 2007). Early articulations of that hypothesis (Knowles, 2007) were based on cross-sectional studies relating the need to belong with greater levels PSRI. Therefore and in the interests of providing additional construct validation for the social surrogacy hypothesis, it was posited that the need to belong is associated with more PSRI with a favorite television performer (H3).

Method and Results

Students in an introduction to communication studies course at a public Midwestern university received course credit for participating in a study entitled *Communication and Personality Pre-Test*. It was administered in three 35- to 40-minute sessions (March 5, 2014, and March 6, 2014) with each including 70 to 90 recruits ($N = 241$). Respondents were instructed to not change their answers, work forward, and sit quietly when completed. Some respondents were removed for failing to complete the packet, providing response sets, or including nonsense responses ($n = 8$). The final sample included 233 respondents. Multiple hierarchical regression techniques were used to analyze the three hypotheses. Cases with missing data were excluded listwise.

Experimental Procedure and Measures

Respondents were randomly assigned to a control ($n = 119$) or experimental ($n = 114$) version of a questionnaire packet containing a variety of measures, including Rosenblatt et al.'s (1989) Mortality Attitudes Personality Survey (MAPS). The MAPS (Burke et al., 2010) asks subjects to describe their own death (experimental condition) or personal dental pain (control). The MAPS was unobtrusively included in the packet of ordered measures. Except for categorical measures and the death-thought accessibility (0 to 6) scale, all measures were operationalized with 1 to 7 scales where 1 was less of the concept and 7 was more of the concept. In the following order, the packet's items included biological sex (female = 130, 55.8%); Mikulincer, Florian, and Tolmacz's (1990) attachment styles inventory (secure: $M = 4.63$, $SD = 1.01$, $\alpha = .55$; avoidant: $M = 3.92$, $SD = 1.25$, $\alpha = .70$; anxious: $M = 3.14$, $SD = 1.33$, $\alpha = .70$); Watson and Clark's (1991) positive ($M = 3.67$, $SD = 1.28$, $\alpha = .88$) and negative ($M = 2.41$, $SD = 1.10$, $\alpha = .83$) affect schedule; a DTA (see Burke et al., 2010) word-stem completion task ($M = 1.97$, $SD = 1.12$); Rubin and Perse's (1987) parasocial relationship interaction scale ($M = 4.55$, $SD = 1.27$, $\alpha = .86$); and Leary and colleagues' (2013) need to belong scale ($M = 4.40$, $SD = 1.13$, $\alpha = .77$).

Preliminary Analysis

Three hierarchical regression models were constructed to examine the influence of the control block and the MAPS (0 = dental-pain essay, 1 = death-thought essay) on positive mood, negative mood, and DTA. Because biological sex (Cohen, 2003; Eyal & Cohen, 2006) and attachment style (Cohen, 1997; Taubman-Ben-Ari et al., 2002) have been shown to influence this study's proposed outcomes, they were included in the control block. In the first analysis, positive mood was regressed on control block in the first step (Adj. $R^2 = .019$, $R^2\Delta = .036$, $F\Delta[4, 224] = 2.08$, $p = .084$) and the mortality-salience prime in the second step (Adj. $R^2 = .021$, $R^2\Delta = .007$, $F\Delta[1, 223] = 1.61$, $p = .205$, $B = .22$, $SE = .17$). The second analysis regressed negative mood on the block of control variables in the first step (Adj. $R^2 = .103$, $R^2\Delta = .119$, $F\Delta[4, 224] = 7.58$, $p < .001$) and the mortality-salience prime in the second step (Adj. $R^2 = .101$, $R^2\Delta = .002$, $F\Delta[1, 223] = .504$, $p = .478$, $B = .10$, $SE = .14$). Based on results of the first two analyses, the mortality-salience prime did not significantly influence positive or negative mood. The final preliminary multiple hierarchical regression analysis examined the influence of the mortality-salience prime on DTA. In the first step, DTA was regressed on the control block including positive and negative mood (Adj. $R^2 = .032$, $R^2\Delta = .057$, $F\Delta[6, 222] = 2.25$, $p = .040$) and the mortality-salience prime in a second step (Adj. $R^2 = .041$, $R^2\Delta = .013$, $F\Delta[1, 221] = 3.12$, $p = .079$, $B = .26$, $SE = .15$). The predicted influence of the mortality-salience prime on DTA was only marginally significant. Therefore, the following hypothesis tests should be considered to be very conservative.

Primary Analysis

Multiple hierarchical regression analyses were used to analyze H1 and H2. The model statistics and regression coefficients are on display in Table 7.1. H1 was analyzed with a two-step multiple hierarchical regression analysis in which the need for belonging was regressed on the block of control variables in step 1 and DTA in step 2. H1 was not confirmed: DTA did not significantly predict higher levels of the need to belong. H2 was analyzed by regressing PSRI on the control block in step 1 and DTA in step 2. It was confirmed. DTA predicted greater levels of relationship striving in terms of more PSRI.

H3 was analyzed with two partial correlation analysis in which the need to belong was related to PSRI within the two conditions (i.e., control and mortality-salience prime) while controlling for biological sex, attachment styles (secure, avoidant, and anxious), mood (positive and negative), and DTA. Within the control condition, need to belong and PSRI were significantly correlated: $r(109) = .211$, $p = .026$. Need to belong and PSRI were also correlated within the experimental condition: $r(101) = .343$, $p < .001$. Although the relationship between the need to belong and PSRI was ostensibly stronger in the experimental condition, a follow-up r to z analysis showed that the strength of the relationship between need to belong and PSRI did not significantly differ between the experimental and control conditions: $z = 1.03$, $p = .303$.

TABLE 7.1 Influence of DTA[1] on NTB[2] and PSRI[3]

	NTB			PSRI		
	B	(SE)	p	B	(SE)	p
Intercept						
	3.97	(.52)	< .001	3.70	(.61)	< .001
Control Block						
Sex (1 = female)	.45	(.14)	.002	.49	(.17)	.004
Secure Attachment	.01	(.07)	.937	−.09	(.09)	.311
Avoidant Attachment	−.23	(.06)	< .001	.05	(.07)	.507
Anxious Attachment	.25	(.06)	< .001	−.03	(.07)	.691
Positive Mood	.00	(.06)	.982	.10	(.06)	.133
Negative Mood	.10	(.07)	.138	.15	(.08)	.059
Mortality-Salience Prime	−.02	(.14)	.894	−.21	(.16)	.203
Independent Variable (IV)						
DTA	.03	.06	.641	.15	(.07)	.050
Model Statistics						
	Adj. R^2 = .165, $R^2\Delta$ = .001			Adj. R^2 = .075, $R^2\Delta$ = .016		
	$F\Delta(1, 219)$ = .218			$F\Delta(1, 219)$ = 3.89		
	p = .641			p = .050		

Notes: [1]Death-Thought Accessibility. [2]Need to Belong. [3]Parasocial Relationship Interaction.

Discussion

This study provides preliminary evidence for death-thought accessibility's capacity to elicit parasocial relationship interaction with a mediated performer. DTA did not influence the need to belong, but in both the control and experimental conditions, need to belong and PSRI were significantly correlated. That relationship was stronger in the mortality-salience condition, but the difference was not statistically significant. Ultimately, these findings provide additional construct validation for two propositions: First, DTA elicits relationship striving in terms of PSRI (Mikulincer et al., 2003), and second, PSRI functionally complements interpersonal relationships (Derrick et al., 2009; Knowles, 2007). However, it is also imperative that researchers validate these findings in other contexts and with nonstudent populations.

Implications and Future Research

Consistent with this volume's theme, demonstrating the existential function of PSRI provides an empirical and theoretical foundation for substantially expanding the scope of terror management theory to a rich variety of theoretical and contextual domains. In particular, TMT might be used to better understand the processes of cultivation (Gerbner & Gross, 1976) and entertainment educa-tion (Moyer-Gusé & Nabi, 2010). Additionally, the existential function of PSRI might help researchers better understand how religion defends against DTA and how distal terror management processes might explain, predict, and control social media use.

The capacity of DTA to elicit PSRI should be of particular interest to media effects researchers. Cultivation theorists (Gerbner & Gross, 1976) link television's overrepresentation of violence to viewers' fear of becoming a victim of violent crime. Such feelings of vulnerability might elicit DTA and thus, explain why viewers so readily form parasocial attachments with television performers (see Conway & Rubin, 1991; Kanazawa, 2002). To extend the ecological validity of this study's findings, researchers might investigate DTA as a procedural explana-tion for PSRI with characters appearing in television genres containing scenes of death, like most police procedurals and local television news. In turn, PSRI might provide an additional explanation for cultivation effects. PSRI is already a demonstrated explanation for television's influence on intergroup attitudes (Schiappa et al., 2005) and entertainment education (Moyer-Gusé et al., 2012).

Unfortunately, the lack of broadly applicable and reliable manipulations of PSRI has somewhat inhibited the development of theory and research seeking to explain its influence (Moyer-Gusé & Nabi, 2010). Semmler and colleagues (2015) provide an exception. They used audio-only narration to manipulate PSRI, find-ing that a character using audio-only direct address elicited more PSRI than the same character without audio-only direct address. While useful in audiovisual narratives, audio-only direct address does not translate to nonfictional program-ming, news, or other media (e.g., radio or print). Using validated mortality-salience primes to elicit PSRI offers researchers more flexibility for innovation. Mortality-salience primes could be unobtrusively inserted into a variety of tele-vision genres (e.g., crime stories in television news), television commercials (e.g., public service announcements involving death), or even Internet banner ads (e.g., for a funeral home or for life insurance).

Mortality salience plays an important role in promoting religious adherence (Becker, 1973; Burke, et al., 2010). It might also explain devotion to particular religious persona, like Jesus or the Buddha. Religious texts combine frequent reminders of death with vivid descriptions of religious figures who could be conceptualized as parasocial others. A mechanism of religion's existential func-tion might be explained by adherents striving to form personal relationships with the deities foregrounded in religious doctrines or texts. That hypothesis is con-sistent with contemporary Christianity's emphasis on initiating and maintaining a personal relationship with Jesus. If PSRI with religious deities buffers death awareness, it is possible that religions featuring humanoid-like deities are more rhetorically compelling than religions that do not foreground relatable deities. Indeed, three of the world's major religions (i.e., Islam, Christianity, and Bud-dhism) prominently feature relatable persona, complete with detailed backstories.

Extant research has not examined PSRI with supernatural or religious deities, but Caughy (1984) speculated that such relationships exist between the Ojibway peoples and "thunder gods, fabulous giant monsters, and deceased ancestors" (p. 17). Such relationships are particularly consistent with Giles's (2002) conceptualization of third-order parasocial relationships as "encounters with fantasy or cartoon figures who have no real-life counterpart" (p. 294).

Giles's (2002) broad continuum of social to parasocial others combines with the existential function of those relationships to suggest an expansion of terror management research into the context of computer-mediated communication. Giles (2002) does not limit parasocial interactions to professional media performers or elaborately constructed personas. He includes actual acquaintances, friends, and others with whom one's interactions are mediated. Friends mediated by social media sites are ever present on ubiquitously available computer platforms, making them a potentially powerful source for combating mortality salience. Even "friends" who have long since faded into the background of one's Facebook feed might defend against DTA.

Limitations

The requirements of external validity demand that this study be replicated across a variety of contexts and with nonstudent populations. Those replications should also seek to bolster this study's internal validity by addressing the weak DTA manipulation. It was only marginally significant. The cluttered nature of the experimental situation provides one plausible explanation for that weakness. Student participants completed questionnaires in open classrooms containing myriad signs of symbolic immortality (e.g., T-shirts with religious messages, patriotic logos, and actual people with whom subjects could engage in subtle forms of relationship striving). Replicating this paradigm in more controlled environments and across populations could substantially validate this study's primary conclusion that DTA elicits PSRI.

Unfortunately, DTA was not associated with the more fundamental need to belong. That failure might be explained by a flaw in the questionnaire. Because the need to belong scale serially followed the PSRI scale, subjects might have assuaged their death anxiety with PSRI, making them no different than control subjects on the need to belong scale. That interpretation is consistent with extant findings showing that relationship striving obviates other mechanisms of mortality-salience reduction (Florian et al., 2002).

References

Aristotle. (Trans. 1943). *The politics* (Jowett, Trans.). New York: The Modern Library.

Auter, P. J. (1992). TV that talks back: An experimental validation of a PSI scale. *Journal of Broadcasting and Electronic Media, 36,* 173–182. doi:10.1080/08838159209364165

Auter, P. J., & Moore, R. L. (1993). Buying from a friend: A content analysis of two teleshopping programs. *Journalism Quarterly, 70*, 425–436. doi:10.1177/107769909307000217

Baumeister, R. F., & Leary, M. R. (1995). The need to belong: Desire for interpersonal attachments as a fundamental human motivation. *Psychological Bulletin, 117*, 497–529. doi:10.1037/0033–2909.117.3.497

Becker, E. (1973). *The denial of death.* New York: Free Press.

Berger, P. L., & Luckmann, T. (1966). *The social construction of reality: A treatise in the sociology of knowledge.* Garden City, NY: Doubleday.

Burke, B., Martens, A., & Faucher, E. H. (2010). Two decades of terror management theory: A meta-analysis of mortality salience. *Personality and Social Psychlogy Review, 14*, 155–195. doi:10.1177/1088868309352321

Caughy, J. L. (1984). *Imaginary social worlds.* Lincoln, NE: University of Nebraska Press.

Cohen, J. (1997). Parasocial relations and romantic attraction: Gender and dating status differences. *Journal of Broadcasting and Electronic Media, 41*, 516–529. doi:10.1080/08838159709364424

Cohen, J. (2003). Parasocial breakups: Measuring individual differences in responses to the dissolution of parasocial relationships. *Mass Communication and Society, 6*, 191–202. doi:10.1207/S15327825MCS0602_5

Conway, J. C., & Rubin, A. M. (1991). Psychological predictors of television viewing motivation. *Communication Research, 18*, 443–463. doi:10.1177/009365091018004001

Derrick, J. L., Gabriel, S., & Hugenberg, K. (2009). Social surrogacy: How favored television programs provide the experience of belonging. *Journal of Experimental Social Psychology, 45*, 352–362. doi:10.1016/j.jesp.2008.12.003

Derrick, J. L., Gabriel, S., & Tippen, B. (2008). Parasocial relationships and self-discrepancies: Faux relationships have benefits for low self-esteem individuals. *Personal Relationships, 15*, 261–280. doi:10.1111/j.1475–6811.2008.00197.x

Eyal, K., & Cohen, J. (2006). When good friends say goodbye: A parasocial breakup study. *Journal of Broadcasting & Electronic Media, 50*, 502–523. doi:10.1207/s15506878jobem5003_9

Florian, V., Mikulincer, M., & Hirschberger, G. (2002). The anxiety-buffering function of close relationships: Evidence that relationship commitment is a terror management mechanism *Journal of Personality and Social Psychology, 82*, 527–542. doi:10.1037//0022–3514.82.4.527

Gardner, W. L., & Knowles, M. L. (2008). Love makes you real: Favorite television characters are perceived as 'real' in a social facilitation paradigm. *Social Cognition, 26*, 156–168. doi:10.1521/soco.2008.26.2.156

Gerbner, G., & Gross, L. (1976). Living with television: The violence profile. *Journal of Communication, 26*, 173–199. doi:10.1111/j.1460–2466.1976.tb01397.x

Giles, D. C. (2002). Parasocial interaction: A review of the literature and a model for future research. *Media Psychology, 4*, 279–305. doi:10.1207/S1532785XMEP0403_04

Grow, K. (2013). Walter White laid to rest in 'Breaking Bad' charity funeral: Memorial service raised $17,000 for Albuquerque homeless. *Rolling Stone.* Retrieved from http://www.rollingstone.com/tv/news/walter-white-laid-to-rest-in-breaking-bad-charity-funeral-20131021

Harmon-Jones, E., Simon, L., Greenberg, J., Pyszczynski, T., Solomon, S., & McGregor, H. (1997). Terror management theory and self-esteem: Evidence that increased self-esteem reduces mortality salience effects. *Journal of Personality and Social Psychology, 72*, 24–36. doi:10.1037//0022–3514.72.1.24

Harris, N. (2011). REVEALED: *Royal wedding TV audience closer to 300m than 2bn (because sport, not royalty, reigns).* sportingintelligence. Retrieved from http://www.sportingintelligence. com/2011/05/08/revealed-royal-wedding%E2%80%99s-real-tv-audience-closer-to-300m-than-2bn-because-sport-not-royalty-reigns-080501/

Hartmann, T., Stuke, D., & Daschmann, G. (2008). Positive parasocial relationships with drivers affect suspense in racing sport spectators. *Journal of Media Psychology, 20,* 24–23. doi:10.1027/1864–1105.20.1.24

Higgins, E. T. (1987). Self-discrepancy: A theory relating self and affect. *Psychological Review, 94,* 319–340. doi:10.1037//0033–295X.94.3.319

Horton, D., & Wohl, R. (1956). Mass communication and para-social interaction: Observations on intimacy at a distance. *Psychiatry, 19,* 215–229.

Kanazawa, S. (2002). Bowling with our imaginary friends. *Evolution and Human Behavior, 23,* 167–171. doi:10.1016/S1090–5138(01)00098–8

Knowles, M. L. (2007). *The nature of parasocial relationships.* (Ph.D. Dissertation). Northwestern University, Evanston, IL. (3258551)

Koenig, F., & Lessan, G. (1985). Viewers' relationship to television personalities. *Psychological Reports, 57,* 263–266. doi:10.2466/pr0.1985.57.1.263

Landau, M. J., Solomon, S., Greenberg, J., Cohen, F., Pyszczynski, T., Arndt, J., . . . Cook. A. (2004). Deliver us from evil: The effects of mortality salience and reminders of 9/11 on support for president George W. Bush. *Personality and Social Psychlogy Bulletin, 30,* 1136–1150. doi:10.1177/0146167204267988

Leary, M. R., Kelly, K. M., Cottrell, C. A., & Schreindorfer, L. S. (2013). Construct validity of the need to belong Scale: Mapping the nomological network. *Journal of Personality Assessment.* doi:10.1080/00223891.2013.819511

Maslow, A. H. (1943). A theory of human motivation. *Psychological Review, 50,* 370–396. doi:10.1037/h0054346

Meyrowitz, J. (1994). The life and death of media friends: New genres of intimacy and mourning. In S. J. Drucker & R. S. Cathcart (Eds.), *American heroes in a media age* (pp. 62–81). Cresskill, NJ: Hampton Press, Inc.

Mikulincer, M., & Florian, V. (2000). Exploring individual differences in reactions to mortality salience: Does attachment style regulate terror management mechanisms? *Journal of Personality and Social Psychology, 79,* 260–273. doi:10.1037//0022–3514.79.2.260

Mikulincer, M., Florian, V., & Hirschberger, G. (2003). The existential function of close relationships: Introducing death into the science of love. *Personality and Social Psychology Review, 7,* 20–40. doi:10.1207/S15327957PSPR0701_2

Mikulincer, M., Florian, V., & Tolmacz, R. (1990). Attachment styles and fear of personal death: A case study of affect regulation. *Journal of Personality and Social Psychology, 58,* 273–280. doi:10.1037//0022–3514.58.2.273

Moyer-Gusé, E., Jain, P., & Chung, A. H. (2012). Reinforcement or reactance? Examining the effect of an explicit appeal following an entertainment-education narrative. *Journal of Communication, 62,* 1010–1027. doi:10.1111/j.1460–2466.2012.01680.x

Moyer-Gusé, E., & Nabi, R. L. (2010). Explaining the effects of narrative in an entertainment television program: Overcoming resistance to persuasion. *Human Communication Research, 36,* 26–52. doi:10.1111/j.1468–2958.2009.01367.x

Nordlund, J. (1978). Media interaction. *Communication Research, 5,* 150–175. doi:10.1177/009365027800500202

Perse, E. M., & Rubin, R. B. (1989). Attribution in social and parasocial relationships. *Communication Research, 16,* 59–77. doi:10.1177/009365089016001003

Pyszczynski, T., Greenberg, J., & Solomon, S. (1999). A dual-process model of defense against conscious and unconscious death-related thoughts: An extension of terror management theory. *Psychological Review, 106*, 835–845. doi:10.1037//0033–295X.106.4.835

Rosenblatt, A., Greenberg, J., Solomon, S., Pyszczynski, T., & Lyon, D. (1989). Evidence for terror management theory I: The effects of mortality salience on reactions to those who violate or uphold cultural values. *Journal of Personality and Social Psychology, 57*, 681–690. doi:10.1037//0022–3514.57.4.681

Rowatt, W. C., Cunningham, M. R., & Druen, P. B. (1999). Lying to get a date: The effect of facial attractiveness on the willingness to deceive prospective dating partners. *Journal of Social and Personal Relationships, 16*, 209–233. doi:10.1177/0265407599162005

Rubin, A. M., & Perse, E. M. (1987). Audience activity and soap opera involvement: A uses and effects investigation. *Human Communication Research, 14*, 246–268. doi:10.1111/j.1468–2958.1987.tb00129.x

Rubin, A. M., Perse, E. M., & Powell, R. A. (1985). Loneliness, parasocial, interaction, and local television news viewing. *Human Communication Research, 12*, 155–180. doi:10.1111/j.1468–2958.1985.tb00071.x

Rubin, A. M., & Step, M. M. (2000). Impact of motivation, attraction, and parasocial interaction on talk radio listening. *Journal of Broadcasting & Electronic Media, 44*, 635–654. doi:10.1207/s15506878jobem4404_7

Rubin, R. B., & McHugh, M. P. (1987). Development of parasocial interaction relationships. *Journal of Broadcasting & Electronic Media, 31*, 279–292. doi:10.1080/08838158709386664

Schiappa, E., Gregg, P. B., & Hewes, D. E. (2005). The parasocial contact hypothesis. *Communication Monographs, 72*, 92–115. doi:10.1080/0363775052000342544

Semmler, S. M., Loof, T., & Berke, C. (2015). The influence of audio-only narration on character and narrative engagement. *Communicatin Research Reports, 32*, 54–62. doi:10.1080/08824096.2014.989976

Skok, D. (2009, June 26). *Internet stretched to limit as fans flock for Michael Jackson news*, The Vancouver Sun. Retrieved from http://wayback.archive.org/web/20090703075357/http://www.vancouversun.com/Entertainment/Internet+stretched+limit+fans+flock+Michael+Jackson+news/1736311/story.html

Taubman-Ben-Ari, O., Findler, L., & Mikulincer, M. (2002). The effects of mortality salience on relationship strivings and beliefs: The moderating role of attachment style. *British Journal of Social Psychology, 41*, 419–441. doi:10.1348/014466602760344296

Tsao, J. (1996). Compensatory media use: An exploration of two paradigms. *Communication Studies, 47*, 89–109. doi:10.1080/10510979609368466

Watson, L. A., & Clark, L. A. (1991). *Preliminary manual for the positive and negative affect schedule-expanded form.* Unpublished Manuscript. Southern Methodist University. Dallas, TX.

8

AN EXPERIMENTAL EXAMINATION OF MORTALITY-SALIENCE MANIPULATION TYPE AND LENGTH OF DELAY ON PRESIDENTIAL SUPPORT AND CIVIC ENGAGEMENT

Patrick F. Merle and Jennifer D. Green

The abundance of politically relevant issues pertaining directly or indirectly to death has become a recurrent pattern in local, national, and international media coverage. In 2015, the press was saturated with a multitude of news events evoking a prevalent threat to human lives. Globally televised terrorism, racially charged police violence, Ebola outbreaks, and the practically constant onslaught of weather-related disasters have all indeed contributed to a general heightened sense of mortality. Survey data even indicated that the U.S. population believes defending the country against terrorism constitutes today's top public policy priority for the government (Pew, 2015).

Consistently engulfed in a mediated world featuring ubiquitous menaces to human lives, individuals, as posited by terror management theory (TMT), endorse and strengthen their cultural worldviews to attenuate a feeling of anxiety generated by their subconscious awareness of their own death (Greenberg, Pyszczynski, & Solomon, 1986). To date, the study of such a psychological phenomenon has resulted in more than 400 empirical investigations (Burke, Kosloff, & Landau, 2013; Burke, Martens, & Faucher, 2010; Greenberg, Solomon, & Arndt, 2008). This chapter contributes to this rich scholarship by achieving two objectives: (a) it responds to the call by Burke et al. (2013) to pursue the exploration of relationships between mortality salience (MS) and politically oriented dependent variables, such as presidential support, as well as institutional and interpersonal trust; (b) it elucidates specific methodological details regarding ways to induce mortality salience in individuals, and the length of delay between induction and measurement of the dependent variables.

Most of the research testing MS on political attitudes and behaviors reviewed the support for President George W. Bush in the aftermath of 9/11, leading to what some scholars labeled as the conservative shift hypothesis (Burke et al., 2013;

Jost et al, 2003; Jost, Fitzsimons, & Kay, 2004). The present investigation sought to analyze whether the public would continue to assert an increased approval for a candidate, this time of liberal affiliation, moreover in a context of economic recovery rather than a period of economic recession marked by a global terrorist hunt. Additionally, this study is concerned with variations in MS effects over time. Research previously pointed out the possibility that MS effects may fluctuate as a function of time between MS induction and measurement of the dependent variable (Trafimow & Hughes, 2012). Furthermore, in their meta-analysis, Burke et al. (2013) noted most studies involve one or two short delay tasks, yet little systematic analysis has documented the length of time on these tasks. The present research manipulates time delay as an independent variable to test whether MS effects change over time.

Finally, the chapter concentrates on the effects of MS on trust in political figures and institutional trust as dependent on the induction mode. TMT traditionally inducts MS either by having participants explicitly write about their own deaths or through less explicit routes, and this study examined whether these two induction styles interact with delay length to influence MS effects on the aforementioned variables.

In sum, this chapter presents a 3 (mortality-salience induction mode: control, explicit, or implicit) x 3 (time of delay: 1 minute, 3 minutes, or 5 minutes) between-subjects design to specifically address several methodological concerns as well as extend past MS findings to trust for political figures and institutional trust.

Literature Review

Mortality Salience and Political Attitudes

The investigation of relationships between mortality salience and political attitudes represents a prevalent component in TMT literature (Burke, Kosloff, & Landau, 2013). In a meta-analysis of 31 experiments devoted specifically to the review of citizens' evaluations of political figures and their subsequent intention to vote for candidates as well as their attitudes toward political issues, MS explained 25% of the variance. Furthermore, such effect was found to be stronger than for the seminal relationships with worldview defense and self-esteem (Burke et al., 2013).

Experimental evidence has consistently revealed that mortality salience facilitates the elaboration of negative thoughts and reactions toward people who threaten one's beliefs and worldviews and reinforces support for those perceived as validating similar positions (Greenberg et al, 1990; Rosenblatt et al, 1989). This overarching perspective has been particularly verified in post 9/11 contexts. The experimental work of Pyszczynski et al. (2009) illustrates such scholarship. In their analyses, the authors found Iranian people aware of their own mortality had declared a stronger support for pro-martyrdom attacks against the United States than those in the control condition. In addition, when reminded of death, American citizens holding conservative political views increased their propensity to support military action against people threatening their country. Here, mortality salience led individuals to hold extremist attitudes toward another culture and another group of people, always depicted as threatening in the media. The urge to "hold the anxiety-provoking awareness of mortality at bay" (Burke et al., 2013, p.184–185) led individuals to adjust their responses depending on their perceptions of the threat.

Simple reminders of death seemingly triggered a more aggressive response toward people perceived or described in the media as members of outgroups (Greenberg, Solomon, & Pyszczynski, 1997). Even subtle references to the 9/11 attacks sufficed to generate death-related thoughts and thus increase supportive opinion of a leader whose communication efforts were consistently deployed against terrorism and in defense of the American democracy (Landau et al., 2004). To appease anxiety that can be caused by thinking about dying, individuals express a stronger need for protection and consequently support a leader they perceive as guarantor of their freedoms and privileges. Individuals eager to alleviate death anxiety report specific attitudes and political choices indicative of self-preservation motivations rather than rational decision-making processes and find comfort pledging allegiance to individuals they believe could prolong their survival (Pyszczynski et al., 2006). When MS motivates individuals to further separate themselves from outgroup members and more strongly align with ingroup members, one can easily understand the impact of phrases like "the axis of evil" so often repeated in American news following September 2001.

MS and the Conservative Shift Hypothesis

The hypothesis holds that people with conservative perspectives are more likely to possess worldviews centered on the ideas of stability and security than liberals who can tolerate change more easily (Burke et al., 2013; Jost et al., 2003; Jost, Fitzsimmons, & Kay, 2004). In fact, most of the work published in the area focused on conservative leaders and George Bush in particular in the wake of the 9/11 attacks. Yet, although numerous quantitative evidence reported by Burke et al. (2013) confirmed the conservative shift hypothesis, some scholars believe that MS leads to heightened support for people's preexisting political positions and beliefs, or what might be referred to as a political polarization wherein liberals become more liberal and conservatives, more conservative (Kosloff, Greenberg, Weise, & Solomon, 2010). In fact, an experiment focusing on the prevalence of political ideology of the key figure, manipulating charisma along with political ideology of a hypothetical gubernatorial candidate, showed that under MS, liberals increased their support for the charismatic liberal candidate, and conservative participants increased their support for the charismatic conservative candidate. However, a third possible effect is also viable. Recent investigations conducted during President Obama's first term revealed that the saliency of progressive and liberal values exhibited by the prevailing political party may influence how individuals react to MS (Anson & Zahn, 2011; Vail, Rampy, Arndt, Pope, & Pinel, 2011). Such evidence would suggest some sort of political agenda-setting whereby citizens find themselves in line with the salient political values at the time MS is induced. The data needed to test these competing hypotheses would require pre- and post- MS induction measurements of participants' political party identification and political ideological leaning (i.e., conservative, liberal) to assess changes as a result of MS.

Mortality-Salience Induction Modes

Terror management theorists make the prediction that subconscious thoughts of death can elicit anxiety, which motivates individuals to endorse, or defend, their culture's worldviews and cultural values (Greenberg, Pyszczynski, & Solomon, 1986). Research has shown that when death thoughts have been made conscious for participants, there is no evidence of worldview defense and that only once thoughts of death have been suppressed does worldview defense occur (Greenberg, Pyszczynski, Solomon, Simon, & Breus, 1994).

In Greenberg et al. (1994) participants who thought about their own death showed stronger preferences for pro-American authors and essays than did participants who thought about their own death and imagined that they just learned they had late-stage cancer. The deeper level of processing may have caused conscious thoughts of death to linger longer, which would explain the weaker MS effects for this group. It is possible, therefore, that a longer delay time for these participants would have allowed death thoughts to subside, yielding stronger MS effects. However, because all participants experienced the same time delay, this possibility could not be tested. In fact, as evident in the research reviewed, there is a gap in the literature regarding a systematic examination of MS induction type and length of delay that this chapter explicitly addresses.

There are two meta-analyses that have investigated MS effect sizes across induction modes, delay periods, and a variety of dependent variables. Burke, Martens, and Faucher (2010) reviewed 20 years' worth of MS studies to assess general effect sizes associated with direct effects, moderated effects, and predicted null effects of MS. Burke, Kosloff, and Landau (2013) conducted a meta-analysis on MS effects on political attitudes. Most studies reviewed implemented the Mortality Attitudes Personality Survey (MAPS) as an explicit mortality-salience (EMS) induction. The MAPS is comprised of two open-ended questions that require writing about the physical experience and feelings related to one's own death. Participants are directly asked to think about their own deaths. Implicit MS (IMS) inductions use indirect approaches to eliciting thoughts of death subconsciously. IMS inductions were less common across both meta-analyses, occurring in just 23 of the 164 studies reviewed by Burke et al. (2010) and none of the studies in Burke et al. (2013).

Of the various ways to induce IMS, word tasks have been successful. For instance, participants have been asked to engage in game-like tasks that contain death themes (Hirschberger, 2006; Landau, Kosloff, & Schmeichel, 2009; Zhou, Liu, Chen, & Yu, 2008). Other IMS manipulations include using media representations of death such as stories, images, films, and advertisements (Coolsen & Nelson, 2002; Green & Merle, 2013; Greenberg, Simon, Harmon-Jones, Solomon, Pyszczynski, & Lyon, 1995; Rosenblatt, Greenberg, Solomon, Pyszczynski, & Lyon, 1989; Taubman-Ben-Ari, Florian, & Mikulincer, 2000). Finally, perhaps one of the most clever and ecologically valid ways to induce IMS is by intercepting participants in front of funeral homes or cemeteries (Gailliot, Stillman, Schmeichel, Maner, & Plant, 2008; Jonas, Fritsche, & Greenberg, 2005; Jonas, Schimel, Greenberg, & Pyszczynski, 2002).

There are two compelling reasons to use IMS manipulations. First, they can be more naturalistic than EMS manipulations and therefore bolster ecological validity. Second, because they elicit subconscious rather than conscious thoughts of death, they do not require a dissipation period for MS to take effect. Given these benefits, it is surprising that IMS manipulations have not been used more often in research. Is it possible that one type of induction has stronger MS effects than the other? Hence, the following research question:

> RQ1: Does mortality-salience induction mode influence the strength of worldview defense effects, specifically regarding political attitudes?

Moreover, because EMS manipulations do require a delay period, it is puzzling that there are no systematic investigations of optimal delay periods for this induction type.

Mortality-Salience Delay Periods

As discussed, many TMT studies implement the Mortality Attitudes Personality Survey to induce MS, in which participants explicitly write about what they expect will happen to their bodies as they physically die. This procedure obviously mandates conscious acknowledgment of one's own death, making it an EMS manipulation. TMT posits that explicitly, or consciously, thinking about death should lead to a different set of death defenses, such as by telling ourselves we are likely to live a long, healthy life. Importantly, it is when mortality is salient, but subconscious, that the distal death defenses such as defending a politically charged worldview are theorized to occur (Greenberg, Pyszczynski, & Solomon, 1986). Therefore, when implementing explicit measures of MS, researchers must provide a delay to allow conscious MS to recede to the subconscious level. However, across the studies reviewed by Burke, Martens, and Faucher (2010) there was significant inconsistency in the type and length of delay periods. Some researchers used a single distractor task between induction and measurement, whereas others used two or three. Still other researchers implemented a second independent variable during this time, resulting in inconsistent delays and thusly, questions about whether there is an optimal delay period.

The two reviews by Burke and colleagues (2010, 2013) expose the need for a systematic evaluation of delay times. Therefore, we tested intervals that reflect typical delays in the current literature, namely, 1-, 3-, and 5-minute periods. Moreover, we also examine possible interactive effects of MS induction mode and delay on political attitudes:

RQ2a: Does time delay affect political attitudes?
RQ2b: Do mortality-salience induction mode and time delay interact to influence political attitudes?

Method

Overview

A 3 (mortality-salience manipulation type: control/dental pain, explicit mortality salience, and implicit mortality salience) x 3 (time delay: 1 minute, 3 minutes, or 5 minutes) between-subjects experimental design was implemented. Participants wrote about experiencing either dental pain or their own death, or they unscrambled sentences containing death themes, and then engaged in a word search task for either 1, 3, or 5 minutes before completing items pertaining to presidential support, political interest, civic engagement, institutional trust, and interpersonal trust. The order of these dependent variables was randomized to control for order effects. Participants in the explicit and implicit MS conditions were then debriefed about the MS inductions and the study ended.

Participants

Participants ($N = 305$; age $M = 19.92$, $SD = 1.44$; 68.5% female; 39.3% juniors; 19.3% Hispanic; 81.3% White) were recruited from undergraduate mass communication courses offered at a large Southern university and received extra course credit for participation. The original data file indicated a sample size of 731, however, participants with no data and those who experienced a technical difficulty resulting in inaccurate delay periods were removed from the sample, yielding a sample size of 305.

Measures

Mortality Salience (MS)

The independent variables used in this study have been widely implemented in the TMT literature (Burke, Kasloff, & Landau, 2013; Burke, Martens, & Faucher, 2010). The MAPS was used in approximately 80% of the studies included in the 20-year meta-analysis by Burke et al. (2010) to induce MS. It consists of a control condition and an EMS condition. In the control condition, participants answer the following two questions, "Please briefly describe the emotions that the thought of experiencing dental pain arouses in you," and "Jot down, as specifically as you can, what you think will happen to you physically as you experience dental pain." In the EMS condition, participants respond to the following two questions, "Please briefly describe the emotions that the thought of your own death arouses in you," and "Jot down, as specifically as you can, what you think will happen to you physically as you die and once you are physically dead."

Studies have convincingly shown that the MAPS is an effective procedure for inducing MS (Arndt, Greenberg, & Cook, 2002; Arndt, Greenberg, Solomon, Pyszczynski, & Simon, 1997) and that these effects are not due to changes in affect or physiological arousal (Arndt, Greenberg, & Cook, 2002; Rosenblatt, Greenberg, Solomon, Pyszczynski, & Lyon, 1989). Moreover, the effect sizes for studies that implement this manipulation are considerable. Burke et al. (2010) reported individual effect sizes for 164 MS studies and we used their effect size data to calculate the average effect size for studies with the following characteristics within their review: those that implemented the MAPS and a parallel control writing condition (e.g., dental pain, watching TV, taking exams), and that measured some form of politically charged worldview defense—American patriotism (i.e., national pride; Kazén, Baumann, & Kuhl, 2005), political attitudes, presidential support (Landau, Solomon, Greenberg, Cohen, Pyszczynski, Arndt et al., 2004), voting tendencies for various candidates (Hoyt, Simon, & Reid, 2009), and assessments of authors and essays that either oppose or align with participants' worldviews (Arndt & Greenberg, 1999; Arndt, Greenberg, Solomon, Pyszczynski, & Simon, 1997; Gailliot, Schmeichel, & Maner, 2007; Greenberg, Pyszczynski, Solomon, Simon, & Breus,1994; Harmon-Jones, Simon, Greenberg, Pyszczynski, Solomon, & McGregor, 1997; and McGregor, Gailliot, Vasquez, & Nash, 2007). This totaled 28 individual studies and their respective effect sizes. Effect sizes ranged from .08 to .99 ($M = .43$, $SD = .21$). This value is quite moderate (Ellis, 1999) for effect sizes in the social sciences and strengthens the validity of the MAPS as a procedure for inducing MS and increasing politically charged worldview defense.

Participants in the IMS condition completed a scrambled sentence task shown in past research to elicit MS (Hirschberger, 2006). Respondents are asked to rearrange

23 sentences to form complete and grammatically correct statements. Half of the sentences entail themes of death, "Last night I had a dream about dying," and "I wonder how long I might live," and the other half do not, "I drank five cups of water yesterday."

Dependent Variables

The dependent variable scales were presented in random order and included measures of presidential support, political interest, and civic engagement. Three items borrowed and modified from relevant TMT research (Landau, Solomon, Greenberg, Cohen, Pyszczynski, Arndt, et al., 2004) made up the presidential support index and included, "To what extent are you satisfied (happy) (pleased) with the performance of President Obama?" Response options ranged from 1 *(not at all)* to 7 *(extremely)* ($M = 3.80$, $SD = 1.53$; $\alpha = .96$).

Political interest was measured using five items from the political and social capital literature (Putnam, 2000) including, "I am interested in national politics". Response options ranged from 1 *(not at all)* to 7 *(extremely)* ($M = 4.54$, $SD = 1.53$; $\alpha = .93$).

Civic engagement (Putnam, 2000) was measured using six items including "How likely are you to telephone, write a letter, or visit a government official to express your views on a public issue?" Response options ranged from 1 *(not at all)* to 7 *(extremely*; $M = 4.39$, $SD = 1.12$; $\alpha = .76$). Institutional trust (Putnam, 2000) was measured using three items including, "People in government waste tax-payer's money" (reverse coded). Response options ranged from 1 *(strongly disagree)* to 7 *(strongly agree*; $M = 3.29$, $SD = .70$; $\alpha = .67$). Interpersonal trust (Putnam, 2000) was measured using three items, including "Would you say that most of the time people try to be helpful or that they are mostly looking out for themselves?" Response options ranged from 1 *(not at all)* to 7 *(extremely*; $M = 4.33$, $SD = 1.01$; $\alpha = .60$).

Procedure

Upon providing electronic agreement to take part in the study, participants were immediately randomly assigned to one of the three MS conditions (control group, EMS, or IMS). Participants were then told the next task measured their ability to complete a timed task. For this portion, participants engaged in a word search about the solar system and were randomly assigned to view the word search for either 1, 3, or 5 minutes. Participants were then informed the next task involved reporting their opinions about various forms of political and civic life. Afterward, those randomly assigned to either the EMS condition or IMS conditions were debriefed. All participants were thanked for their time, and the study ended.

Results

Initial tests for gender effects on the five main dependent variables revealed only one statistically significant relationship; men (M = 5.10, SD = 1.29) reported higher political interest than women (M = 4.29, SD = 1.56), t (300) = 4.42, p < .01.

To address whether MS induction type would influence the five measured political attitudes (RQ1), a two-way between-subjects analysis of variance revealed a main effect of MS, F (2,296) = 3.90, p < .05, partial eta squared = .03 on presidential support. A post-hoc Tukey HSD (honest significant differences) analysis further revealed that those in the explicit (M = 3.88, SD = 1.50) as well as implicit (M = 3.99, SD = 1.45) MS conditions reported stronger presidential support than those in the control condition (M = 3.36, SD = 1.64).

RQ2a focused on the effect of time delay on the public's presidential support, assessed with a two-way between-subjects analysis of variance, showed no significant main effect of delay for any of the five dependent variables. To address RQ2b, further review of the data indicated no significant interactions of MS induction and delay on presidential support (F's < .2.00, p's > .42; See Figure 8.1).

Finally, the remaining two-way ANOVAs (analysis of variances) on the other dependent variables—political interest, civic engagement, institutional trust,

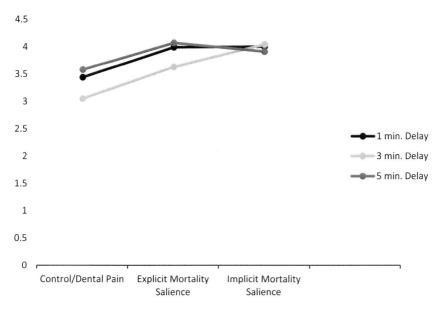

FIGURE 8.1 Effects of Mortality-Salience Induction Mode and Time Delay on Presidential Support

and interpersonal trust—were not significant (F's < 1.86, p's > .13). Overall, MS induction, whether explicit or implicit in nature, demonstrated the only effects on presidential support.

Discussion

The first goal of the present chapter was to examine whether MS induction type (explicit or implicit) would influence the public's political attitude toward the current president. Results indicated the explicit MAPS (Arndt, Greenberg, & Cook, 2002; Arndt, Greenberg, Solomon, Pyszczynski, & Simon, 1997) and the implicit sentence scramble (Hirschberger, 2006) yielded significant effects on political attitudes and more precisely stronger presidential support.

While previous researchers have consistently employed an EMS manipulation, strongly favoring MAPS (Burke et al., 2010; Burke et al., 2013), our analyses indicated that even though implicit and explicit induction types did not significantly differ from one another, a slightly stronger mean was reported for the implicit prime for presidential support. This finding resembles Greenberg, Pyszczynski, Solomon, Simon, and Breus (1994), who also found a stronger MS effect for a less explicitly processed MS induction, and it presents a valuable addition to the existing literature. In the absence of any comparative evidence known to date between induction types, such a result would imply that scholars may select interchangeably an explicit or an implicit MS manipulation, yet data presented here indicate that the formation of death-related sentences from scrambled words could yield a stronger effect in the relationship with political attitudes.

If subconscious mortality salience is what drives the implementation of distal death defenses, and if future work shows that implicit mortality-salience inductions result in more intense distal death defenses, then why use explicit mortality-salience manipulations, which require a period of delay for death consciousness to fade before measuring the effects? Researchers have clearly documented that subconscious mortality salience can be elicited using implicit measures (Coolsen & Nelson, 2002; Gailliot, Stillman, Schmeichel, Maner, & Plant, 2008; Greenberg, Simon, Harmon-Jones, Solomon, Pyszczynski, & Lyon, 1995; Hirschberger, 2006; Taubman-Ben-Ari, Florian, & Mikulincer, 2000), albeit these studies are fewer in number, and thus it is clear that implicit mortality-salience inductions deserve more empirical attention, especially ones that are more naturalistic, such as the use of death-related media content. This conclusion must however remain conditional until further replications establish consistency in similar conditions, that is, an experiment conducted with college students during a positive economic recovery period under a liberal president.

Though the results were not significant, it is peculiar that the control group had more variance in presidential support across delay periods than both MS groups. Control participants experiencing a 3-minute delay had the lowest presidential support of all. If anything, one might expect there to be some potential for psychological processing to vary over the course of 5 minutes for those who have experienced subconscious thoughts of death, but changes seem less likely for the control group. For those in the EMS group, presidential support scores most closely resembled each other at 1 and 5 minutes in time but decreased at 3 minutes. Future work can attempt to untether the intricate processes that might be at play during times of delay while experiencing MS. Moreover, the IMS group appeared to have more consistent responses across delay periods than the EMS group for presidential support and civic engagement. Scores for institutional and interpersonal trust were relatively equal for both types of manipulations across delay periods, and the EMS group reported more consistent responses for political interest at each delay period.

The second goal of the chapter was to advance the literature by testing the effects of delay on presidential support. Participants engaged in a word search for either 1, 3, or 5 minutes. Analyses showed no significant main effects of delay on presidential support. Nor was there a significant interaction between MS induction and delay. The existing inconsistencies of delay in the literature spurred this question to be tested in the current study. Though no statistically significant differences were obtained in this test, future work should consider longer delay periods and perhaps a different delay task.

Finally, this study sought to understand whether certain political measures (political interest, civic engagement, institutional trust, and interpersonal trust) were affected by MS. Results confirmed that mortality salience yields no influence on interpersonal trust, a finding corroborating Green and Merle (2013). This result is also interesting because even though interpersonal trust is included on a popular civic engagement scale (Putnam, 2000), it is the least politically oriented variable that was measured in the study. This could indicate a boundary effect such that MS may not influence individuals' tendency to turn to each other to alleviate MS-induced anxiety. Limited evidence in past studies had shown how in the wake of September 11 people attended church services more regularly (Pyszczynski, Solomon, & Greenberg, 2003), but the paucity of empirical results for MS effects on interpersonal trust across two empirical studies known to date remains puzzling. Even though data previously revealed that individuals experiencing mortality salience reported higher propensity to engage in prosocial behaviors (Ferraro, Shiv, & Bettman, 2005; Hirschberger, Ein-Dor, & Almakias, 2008; Jonas, Schimel, Greenberg, & Pyszczynski, 2002), MS remains of low influence for interpersonal trust. Future work could explore potential explanations for this lack of trust within the confines of other TMT propositions.

Expanding from such findings, future research is also encouraged to explore the relationship with political attitudes and behaviors. Scholars would be advised to examine whether political statements and political coverage dealing with implicit death-related topics continue to yield identical results. Additionally, it may be of interest to ponder whether citizens become slightly desensitized due to the prevalence of fear-induced coverage in the U.S. media. Finally, the strategic communication choices (i.e., word choices, location of events, responses to actions and events) made by candidates and charismatic political figures during election years may also be of value to further investigate such dynamics.

Conclusion

The publication of more than 400 empirical studies in the field of TMT has only left a few stones unturned. Yet, to further advance this research area, this chapter focused specifically on two primordial aspects previously unattended in the scholarship: the influence of MS induction mode and time delay on political attitudes. The main effect of induction (explicit and implicit) certainly corroborates past evidence and justifies the validity of IMS manipulations, rarely used so far. While the absence of time delay effect appears disconcerting, it provides an opportunity for a more meticulous methodological examination of the procedure in place.

References

Anson, J. M., & Zahn, I. (2011). *The effect of mortality salience on political attitudes.* Poster presentation given at Society for Personality and Social Psychology convention. San Antonio, TX (January 27–29).

Arndt, J., & Greenberg, J. (1999). The effects of a self-esteem boost and mortality salience on responses to boost relevant and irrelevant worldview threats. *Personality and Social Psychological Bulletin, 25,* 1331–1341. doi:10.1177/0146167299259001

Arndt, J., Greenberg, J., & Cook, A. (2002). Mortality salience and the spreading activation of worldview-relevant constructs: Exploring the cognitive architecture of terror management. *Journal of Experimental Psychology: General, 131,* 307–324. doi.org/10.1037/0096–3445.131.3.307

Arndt, J., Greenberg, J., Solomon, S., Pyszczynski, T., & Simon, L. (1997). Suppression, accessibility of death-related thoughts, and cultural worldview defense: Exploring the psychodynamics of terror management. *Journal of Personality and Social Psychology, 73,* 5–18. doi.org/10.1037/0022–3514.73.1.5

Burke, B. L., Kosloff, S., & Landau, M. J. (2013). Death goes to the polls: A meta-analysis of mortality salience effects on political attitudes. *Political Psychology, 34,* 183–200. doi:10.1111/pops.12005

Burke, B. L., Martens, A., & Faucher, E. H. (2010). Two decades of terror management theory: A meta-analysis of mortality salience research. *Personality and Social Psychology Review, 14,* 155–195. doi:10.1177/1088868309352321

Coolsen, M. K., & Nelson, L. J. (2002). Desiring and avoiding close romantic attachment in response to mortality salience. *Journal of Death and Dying, 44,* 257–276.

Ellis, P. D. (1999). *Thresholds for interpreting effect sizes.* polyu.edu.hk, Accessed on January 7, 2015.

Ferraro, R., Shiv, B., & Bettman, J. R. (2005). Let us eat and drink, for tomorrow we shall die: Effects of mortality salience and self-esteem on self-regulation in consumer choice. *Journal of Consumer Research, 32,* 65–75. doi:10.1086/429601

Gailliot, M. T., Schmeichel, B. J., & Maner, J. K. (2007). Differentiating the effects of self-control and self-esteem on reactions to mortality salience. *Journal of Experimental Social Psychology, 43*, 894–901. doi:10.1177/0146167208316791

Gailliot, M. T., Stillman, T. F., Schmeichel, B. J., Maner, J. K., & Plant, E. A. (2008). Mortality salience increases adherence to salient norms and values. *Personality and Social Psychology Bulletin, 34*, 993–1003. doi:10.1177/0146167208316791

Green, J. D., & Merle, P. F. (2013). Terror management and civic engagement: An experimental investigation of effects of mortality salience on civic engagement intentions. *Journal of Media Psychology: Theories, Methods, and Applications, 25*, 142–151. doi:10.1027/1864–1105/a000095

Greenberg, J., Pyszczynski, T., & Solomon, S. (1986). The causes and consequences of a need for self-esteem: A terror management theory. In R. F. Baumeister (Ed.), *Public self and private self* (pp. 189–212). New York: Springer Verlag.

Greenberg, J., Pyszczynski, T., Solomon, S., Rosenblatt, A., Veeder, M., Kirkland, S., & Lyon, D. (1990). Evidence for terror management II: The effects of mortality salience on reactions to those who threaten or bolster the cultural worldview. *Journal of Personality and Social Psychology, 58*, 308–318. http://dx.doi.org/10.1037/0022–3514.58.2.308

Greenberg, J., Pyszczynski, T., Solomon, S., Simon, L., & Breus, M. (1994). Role of consciousness and accessibility of death-related thoughts in mortality salience effects. *Journal of Personality and Social Psychology, 67*, 627–637. http://dx.doi.org/10.1037/0022–3514.67.4.627

Greenberg, J., Simon, L., Harmon-Jones, E., Solomon, S., Pyszczynski, T., & Lyon, D. (1995). Testing alternative explanations for mortality effects: Terror management, value accessibility, or worrisome thoughts? *European Journal of Social Psychology, 25*, 417–433. doi:10.1002/ejsp.2420250406

Greenberg, J., Solomon, S., & Arndt, J. (2008). A uniquely human but basic motivation: Terror management. In J. Y. Shah & W. L. Gardner (Eds.), *The handbook of motivation science* (pp. 114–134). New York: Guilford Press.

Greenberg, J., Solomon, S., & Pyszczynski, T. (1997). Terror management theory of self-esteem and social behavior: Empirical assessments and conceptual refinements. In M. P. Zanna (Ed.), *Advances in experimental social psychology* (Vol. 29, pp. 61–139). New York: Academic Press.

Harmon-Jones, E., Simon, L., Greenberg, J., Pyszczynski, T., Solomon, S., & McGregor, H. (1997). Terror management theory and self-esteem: Evidence that increased self-esteem reduces mortality salience effects. *Journal of Personality and Social Psychology, 72*, 24–36. http://dx.doi.org/10.1037/0022–3514.72.1.24

Hirschberger, G. (2006). Terror management and attributions of blame to innocent victims: Reconciling compassionate and defensive responses. *Journal of Personality and Social Psychology, 91*, 832–844. http://dx.doi.org/10.1037/0022–3514.91.5.832

Hirschberger, G., Ein-Dor, T., & Almakias, S. (2008). The self-protective altruist: Terror management and the ambivalent nature of prosocial behavior. *Personality and Social Psychology Bulletin, 34*, 666–678. doi:10.1177/0146167207313933

Hoyt, C., Simon, S., & Reid, L. (2009). Choosing the best (wo)man for the job: The effects of mortality salience, sex, and gender stereotypes on leader evaluations. *Leadership Quarterly, 20*, 233–246. doi:10.1016/j.leaqua.2009.01.016

Jonas, E., Fritsche, I., & Greenberg, J. (2005). Currencies as cultural symbols—An existential psychological perspective on reactions of Germans toward the Euro. *Journal of Economic Psychology, 26*, 129–146. doi:10.1016/j.joep.2004.02.003

Jonas, E., Schimel, J., Greenberg, J., & Pyszczynski, T. (2002). The Scrooge Effect: Evidence that mortality salience increases prosocial attitudes and behavior. *Personality and Social Psychology Bulletin, 28*(10), 1342–1353. doi:10.1177/014616702236834

Jost, J. T., Fitzsimons, G., & Kay, A. C. (2004). The ideological animal. In J. Greenberg, S. L. Koole & T. Pyszczynski (Eds.), *Handbook of experimental existential psychology* (pp. 263–283). New York: Guilford Press.

Jost, J. T., Glaser, J., Kruglanski, A. W., Sulloway, F. J. (2003). Political conservatism as motivated social cognition. *Psychological Bulletin, 129*, 339–375. http://dx.doi.org/10.1037/0033–2909.129.3.339

Kazén, M., Baumann, N., & Kuhl, J. (2005). Self-regulation after mortality salience: National pride feelings of action-oriented German participants. *European Psychologist, 10*, 218–228. doi:10.1027/1016–9040.10.3.xxx

Kosloff, S., Greenberg, J., Weise, D., & Solomon, S. (2010). The effects of mortality salience on political preferences: The roles of charisma and political orientation. *Journal of Experimental Social Psychology, 46*, 139–145. doi:10.1016/j.jesp.2009.09.002

Landau, M. J., Kosloff, S., & Schmeichel, B. (2009). *Perceiving one's actions as meaningful serves a terror management function.* Manuscript in preparation.

Landau, M. J., Solomon, S., Greenberg, J., Cohen, F., Pyszczynski, T., Arndt, J., et al. (2004). Deliver us from evil: The effects of mortality salience and reminders of 9/11 on support for President George W. Bush. *Personality and Social Psychology Bulletin, 30*, 1136–1150. doi:10.1177/0146167204267988

McGregor, I., Gailliot, M. T., Vasquez, N. A., & Nash, K. A. (2007). Ideological and personal zeal reactions to threat among people with high self-esteem: Motivated promotion focus. *Personality and Social Psychology Bulletin, 33*, 1587–1599. doi:10.1177/0146167207306280

Pew. (2015). *Public's policy priorities reflect changing conditions at home and abroad.* Pew Research Center, U.S. Politics & Policy) Retrieved from http://www.people-press.org/2015/01/15/publics-policy-priorities-reflect-changing-conditions-at-home-and-abroad/

Putnam, D. R. (2000). *Bowling alone: The collapse and revival of American community.* New York: MacMillan.

Pyszczynski, T., Abdollahi, A., Solomon, S., Greenberg, J., Cohen, F., & Weise, D. (2006). Mortality salience, martyrdom, and military might: The great Satan versus the axis of evil. *Personality and Social Psychology Bulletin, 32*, 525–537. doi:10.1177/0146167205282157

Pyszczynski, T., Abdollahi, A., Solomon, S., Greenberg, J., Cohen, F., & Weise, D. (2009). Mortality salience, martyrdom, and military might: The great Satan versus the axis of evil. In J. Victoroff, A. W. Kruglanski, J. Victoroff & A. W. Kruglanski (Eds.), *Psychology of terrorism: Classic and contemporary insights* (pp. 281–297). New York, NY: Psychology Press.

Pyszczynski, T., Solomon, S., & Greenberg, J. (2003). In the wake of 9/11: Rising above the terror. In T. Pyszczynski, S. Solomon & J. Greenberg (Eds.), *In the wake of 9/11: The psychology of terror* (pp. 189–198). Washington, DC: American Psychological Association.

Rosenblatt, A., Greenberg, J., Solomon, S., Pyszczynski, T., & Lyon, D. (1989). Evidence for terror management theory I: The effects of mortality salience on reactions to those who violate or uphold cultural values. *Journal of Personality and Social Psychology, 57*, 681–690. http://dx.doi.org/10.1037/0022–3514.57.4.681

Taubman-Ben-Ari, O., Florian, V., & Mikulincer, M. (2000). Does a threat appeal moderate reckless driving? A terror management theory perspective. *Accident Analysis and Prevention, 32*, 1–10. doi:10.1016/S0001–4575(99)00042–1

Trafimow, D., & Hughes, J. H. (2012). Testing the death thought suppression and rebound hypothesis: Death thought accessibility following mortality salience decreases during a delay. *Social Psychology and Personality Science, 3,* 622–629. doi:10.1177/19485506 11432938

Vail, K. E., Rampy, N., Arndt, J., Pope, J. B., & Pinel, E. (2011). *Intolerance of intolerance: Mortality salience, tolerant values, and attitudes toward an anti-Muslim leader.* Unpublished manuscript. University of Missouri-Columbia.

Zhou, X., Liu, J., Chen, C., & Yu, Z. (2008). Do children transcend death? An examination of the terror management function of offspring. *Scandinavian Journal of Psychology, 49,* 413–418. doi:10.1111/j.1467–9450.2008.00665

9

TIME WAITS FOR NO ONE

Mortality Salience and Temporal Agency

Matthew S. McGlone and Nicholas A. Merola

As we grow older, we become increasingly aware of time as a finite resource. Conceiving time as limited rather than unlimited holds important implications for cognition, emotion, and motivation. In particular, Carstensen and her colleagues have demonstrated that perceived time "horizons"—that is, impending and significant changes in life circumstances—influence our selection of goals (Carstensen, Isaacowitz, & Charles, 1999; Fung, Carstensen, & Lutz, 1999). Their findings indicate that when experiential "endings" (graduating from college, leaving home, etc.) become salient, people prefer to pursue emotional goals they can fulfill in the present (spending time with friends and family, engaging in hobbies, etc.) over more instrumental goals with future payoffs (e.g., meeting new people, learning novel skills, etc.). In contrast, people who do not perceive impending life changes assign comparable priority to these goals. The motivational shift induced by contemplating time horizons thus appears to reflect a change in one's sense of control or "agency" with respect to time: When time seems unlimited, we blithely use the present to create a desirable future; when time (as we know it, at least) is running out, the future isn't ours to create, so we focus on the present.

The reported research explored the impact of contemplating the "ultimate" time horizon, death, on "temporal agency" as it is reflected in spontaneous language use. Languages permit different lexical and grammatical choices for describing an event, and by their choices speakers convey different beliefs and attitudes about the event to audiences. One of these choices is the assignment of agency—that is, the ascription of action or change to one or more event-related entities (Dowty, 1991). We use the term *temporal agency* to refer to the manner in which people linguistically assign the capacity for action and change in the passage of time. Previous research has demonstrated the influence of speakers' affective orientation toward an event on their temporal agency assignments. We delineate the concept of temporal agency and review this research in the next section. The subsequent section outlines socioemotional selectivity theory (Carstensen, Isaacowitz, & Charles, 1999) and explains how the motivational mechanisms posited by this theory might manifest themselves in spontaneous discourse about future events. In the final section, we report an experiment.

Time, Affect, and Agency

Like many other abstract concepts, time is linguistically structured by analogical extension from more concrete concepts grounded in physical experience (Lakoff & Johnson, 1980; Miller & Johnson-Laird, 1976). The primary source analog for time is space. The linguistic correspondences between time and space are reflected in the common phrasal lexicon used to denote relations in the two domains (*from Los Angeles to San Francisco/from 9 to 5; the border lies ahead of us/ the future is ahead of us;* etc.). These parallels occur because temporal relations are predicated on a subset of those used for the analysis of spatial location and motion. According to Clark (1973), the applicable subset of spatial relations is determined by conceiving time as a unidimensional, directional, and dynamic entity. Because time is unidimensional, only those spatial terms presupposing one dimension (e.g., *long-short*) also appear in the temporal lexicon, but those presupposing two or more dimensions (e.g., *deep-shallow*) do not. Because time is directional, ordered spatial terms (e.g., *before-after*) have temporal senses, but symmetric terms *(left-right)* do not. We focus here on terms used to convey time's dynamic quality. Numerous terms denoting physical movement are also used to describe the passage of time, as in *The weekend flew by, We're getting close to Thanksgiving,* and so forth.

English and most other languages use two distinct spatial metaphors to encode temporal change (McGlone & Harding, 1998). These metaphors are grounded in our experience of bodily movement, and consequently provide linguistic evidence of time's status as an "embodied" concept (Clark, 1973; Johnson, 1990). To illustrate, compare the assertions *We have passed the deadline* and *The deadline has passed.* These statements differ in two important respects. First, they imply opposite directions of symbolic movement. The former implies a future-bound (past $\rightarrow$ future) direction of temporal passage, but the latter implies a past-bound (past $\leftarrow$ future) direction. Second, the sentences attribute agency—that is, the instrumentality of temporal change—to different entities. The former implies that humans (the referents of *we*) are the agents of temporal change, moving away from inert events in the past and present toward others in the future. In contrast, the latter attributes agency to the event *(deadline)* itself, which has moved from the future beyond present-dwelling human observers into the past. The spatio-temporal relations implied by the human-agent and event-agent metaphors are illustrated in Figure 9.1.

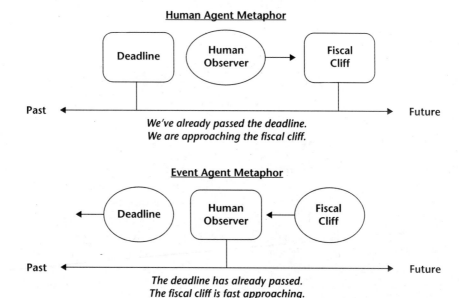

FIGURE 9.1   Two Metaphors of Temporal Passage

As vehicles for conveying temporal sequencing and change, human- and event-agent expressions are functionally equivalent. Thus, *We are approaching the end of the fiscal year* and *The end of the fiscal year is approaching* both convey the same temporal relation (future) between the observer and the event, albeit from different spatiotemporal perspectives. Given their ostensible equivalence, under what circumstances are people inclined to use one type of expression or the other? Research has demonstrated the agentic context in which temporal expressions are encountered can have a significant impact on the ease and manner with which they are comprehended. McGlone and Harding (1998) observed people's comprehension of temporal sentences was facilitated when they were presented in perspectivally consistent blocks (i.e., all human- or event-agent sentences) relative to inconsistent (the two types juxtaposed) blocks. People also used the perspectival information available in these blocks to interpret ambiguous temporal sentences in a contextually consistent manner. For example, when people encountered the ambiguous sentence *The meeting scheduled for next Wednesday has been moved forward two days* in the context of human-agent sentences, most inferred the meeting had been postponed to Friday, consistent with the human-agent entailment directing temporal movement toward the future (see Figure 9.1). In contrast, when this sentence appeared in the context of event-agent sentences, the majority inferred the meeting had been moved earlier in the week to Monday, consistent with the event-agent entailment directing temporal movement toward the past. The influence of linguistic context on temporal thinking is paralleled by spatial context effects documented by Boroditsky and Ramscar (2002), who posed the aforementioned proposition about rescheduling a meeting to people in a variety of situations involving physical movement. When interpreters engaged in forward physical movement themselves (e.g., moving through a lunch line), they preferred the human-agent reading of the proposition; however, when they observed an object moving toward them (e.g., a wheeled chair moving across the room), they preferred the event-agent reading. Taken together, the effects of linguistic and spatial context on temporal language comprehension suggest that the human- and event-agent perspectives are not "dead metaphors" of mere etymological interest, but active cognitive constructs mediating people's thinking about time.

Another contextual factor influencing temporal communication is the speaker's affective orientation toward the event being described (McGlone & Pfiester, 2009). In everyday discourse, people express their feelings about conversational topics in many ways, not just direct declarations like *I'm really into this new job* or *I hate my job*. Sociolinguists have identified a variety of subtle linguistic markers reflecting one's affect, attitude, or stance toward a topic. One such marker is the grammatical passive voice. Communicators opt for passive constructions (e.g., *Louise was helped by John*) over parallel active constructions (e.g., *John helped Louise*) to direct causal attribution away from the thematic agent to the patient (Brown & Fish, 1983). This choice may reflect their attitudes and beliefs about the agent (e.g., John is nurturing) or the patient (e.g., Louise is weak), and in turn may implicitly encourage addressees to form consonant impressions of these parties (LaFrance, Brownell, & Hahn, 1997).

Like grammatical voice, the metaphor one uses to frame temporal passage may constitute a linguistic marker of their affective orientation toward life events. When communicators assign temporal agency to humans *(We're approaching the weekend)* or to events *(The weekend is approaching)*, the assignment reflects different spatial entailments of time's embodied conceptual structure (Clark, 1973). However, affect is also grounded in bodily experience and poses spatial entailments of its own. These entailments are reflected in the etymology of the term *emotion,* which derives from the Latin verb *emovere* denoting "moving out, or migration from one place to another" *(Oxford English Dictionary, 1989)*. According to embodiment theorists, humans' understanding of emotion is predicated on a symbolic relationship between affect and movement, in which we equate positive affect with approach and negative affect with avoidance or passivity (Johnson, 1990; Kovecses, 2000). This relationship is presumed to underlie a variety of behavioral phenomena associated with emotional processing. For example, Cacioppo, Priester, and Berntson (1993) observed that novel pictorial stimuli presented while participants were engaged in arm flexion (a motor action associated with approach) were subsequently evaluated more favorably than stimuli presented during arm extension (associated with avoidance). In recent years, numerous studies employing variants of Cacioppo et al.'s (1993) methodology have demonstrated that approach–avoidance motor actions differentially modulate the affective appraisal of many classes of stimuli, including words, names, faces, and songs (e.g., Niedenthal, Barsalou, Winkielman, Krauth-Gruber, & Ric, 2005).

The motion–emotion link is evident among the various figurative expressions we use to talk about emotional experience (Gibbs, 1994; Kovecses, 2000). Likes and loves are commonly framed in terms of approach (*I'm leaning toward working in the private sector, We've become so close since we started working together*, etc.), while disaffections and detestations are equated with physical withdrawal (*We're far apart on that issue, She pushed me away*, etc.). McGlone and Pfiester (2009) explored the possibility that the conceptual correspondences between motion and emotion influence the way communicators encode the temporal passage of emotionally valenced events. For example, consider the different ways one might talk about a prospective event expected to be pleasant, such as retirement. The human- and event-agent metaphors provide functionally equivalent ways to articulate the retirement's temporal status. However, our desire to encounter pleasant events—that is, the ones we "look forward to"—may predispose us to conceive them in terms of approach, and accordingly attribute temporal agency to ourselves (e.g., *We're getting close to my retirement*). In contrast, our trepidation about experiencing an unpleasant event may incline us to deemphasize our symbolic role in temporal change by instead assigning agency to the event itself (e.g., *The April 15 tax filing deadline is fast approaching*). In this manner, the language we use to encode temporal change may reflect an embodied approach–avoidance affective schema in which communicators symbolically move toward pleasant events but passively observe the arrival of unpleasant ones.

McGlone and Pfiester (2009) report linguistic evidence for this affective schema using different methodologies. In their first study, they searched a large corpus (approximately 14 million words) of written and spoken English for the occurrence of key spatial terms used in a temporal sense (e.g., *come*). Independent coders then examined the immediate discourse context of each identified linguistic token and judged whether the affective valence of the encoded event was positive, negative, or neutral. This analysis indicated that communicators describing temporal passage associated with ostensibly positive events (a wedding anniversary, a noteworthy scientific discovery, etc.) modally characterized themselves as the symbolic locus of temporal change (e.g., *We are coming up on our 10th anniversary; We might be coming to the culminating stage of our search*). In contrast, communicators preferred to encode the passage of negative events (age-related health problems, a projected increase in traffic volume on urban roads, etc.) by assigning the agency of change not to themselves, but to the event (e.g., *When the time comes [that] she can't do things; Average speeds for major arterial roads are expected to decline significantly in coming years*). A similar pattern of agency assignment was observed for temporal expressions employing the other key terms. A second study employed an experimental methodology to explore the motion–emotion link. Participants were asked to describe positive or negative experiences in the recent past. These accounts were then analyzed for the presence of key spatio-temporal terms used in human- and event-agent expressions. These analyses corroborated the correlational findings of the aforementioned corpus study. When recounting positive past experiences, people modally encoded temporal passage using human-agent metaphors. The narratives participants generated for negative events, in contrast, were dominated by event-agent metaphors.

McGlone and Pfiester's (2009) findings suggest the conceptual correspondences between motion and emotion identified by embodiment theorists (Gibbs, 1994; Niedenthal et al., 2005) are operative when people describe and interpret the symbolic motion of temporal passage. Importantly, the operation of these correspondences appears to occur largely outside of awareness. After participants in the aforementioned experiment were informed during debriefing that the researchers were investigating "differences in the way people talk about time when recalling positive and negative experiences," they were then asked to speculate about what these differences might be. Although many hypotheses were offered (e.g., people talk about time as elapsing more quickly for positive than negative events), not one spontaneously generated ideas bearing any resemblance to the notion of temporal agency in focus. Moreover, when the researchers later described the difference between human- and event-agent metaphors and provided examples, the vast majority of participants reported never having noticed the distinction before, and many expressed confusion about how the distinction is drawn.

Temporal agency assignments may reflect not only the affect a speaker associates with a particular past or future event, but also her emotional orientation in the present. McGlone, Ballard, Merola, and McGlynn (2012) explored this issue in a study of electronic correspondence generated by senior executives of the infamous Enron Corporation at important milestones in the company's history. Several studies have mined the Enron email corpus created by the Federal Energy Regulatory Commission during its investigation of the company's collapse. These studies have investigated social networks among employees (e.g., Keila & Skillicorn, 2005), dissemination of proprietary neologisms (Kessler, 2010), and message clustering during critical incidents in the company's downfall (e.g., Berry & Browne, 2005). However, McGlone et al. (2012) focused specifically on metaphoric language used to describe the passage of time by members of Enron's senior management. Using an incident timeline metric suggested by Berry and Browne (2005), they explored the relative frequency of human and event temporal agency assignments in executive correspondence before and after ostensibly positive and negative critical incidents during the 1999–2002 corpus coverage period. Three positive and negative incidents—valenced as such from the perspective of a present-oriented Enron executive with a profit motive—were selected. These events were selected not only for their affective valence but also because they were relatively discrete events that occurred within a single day, thus allowing the researchers to distinguish between correspondence occurring before or after the event with some precision.

This analysis revealed significant, contrasting shifts in temporal agency assignment based on incident valence. When the incidents were positive, executives' use of human-agency assignments (e.g., *Imagine how far we can go with this in just six months!*) increased and event assignments declined; however, when the incidents were negative, event assignments (e.g., *a turning point is fast approaching*) increased and human assignments declined. Interestingly, the shifts in temporal agency assignment observed align better with Berry and Browne's (2005) timeline than with former CEO Jeffrey Skilling's testimony at his 2006 trial about the time course with which he and other senior executives became aware of accounting irregularities and other problems that ultimately led to Enron's downfall. Skilling's testimony was disputed by attorneys for the prosecution, who claimed he and his senior colleagues were aware of these problems far earlier than they claimed. Because temporal agency assignments are typically made outside of conscious awareness, McGlone et al.'s (2012) findings suggest affect-driven temporal agency assignments may constitute a cue to emotional leakage in discourse.

Temporal Perspective, Goals, and Mortality Salience

Socioemotional selectivity theory (SST; Carstensen et al., 1999) proposes that people's orientation toward time influences the goals they pursue. Central to the theory is the acknowledgment that people hold multiple goals, which may be oppositional, and a critical factor in determining which goals to pursue is the salience of time as a limiting factor. Namely, when time is viewed as expansive, goals oriented toward enhancing the future are prioritized. These may include acquiring knowledge and making social contacts. On the other hand, a time-limited view prioritizes goals directed toward emotional connection. Other work on end-of-life perspective has shown orientation toward nonmaterial goals is associated with better mental health outcomes (e.g., Pinquart, Silbereisen, & Froehlich, 2009).

A common source of change in time orientation is aging. Chronological age serves as a constant reminder that "time is running out" (Carstensen et al., 1999). As such, as people age, they shift from goals oriented toward achievement/attainment to goals related to emotional regulation and maintenance. For example, Fredrickson and Carstensen (1990, Study 2) asked participants to evaluate a hypothetical situation in which they could meet and speak with one of three partners for 30 minutes: the author of a book they just read, a new acquaintance whom they appear to have much in common with, or a member of their immediate family. The first two partners represent knowledge and instrumental social contacts, while the family member represents an emotional social contact. An age-related trend emerged, in which older people preferred emotional social contacts, and younger people preferred knowledge and instrumental contact.

Certain life events can also change time orientation. Awareness of deadlines, large life changes, and external threats can raise the salience of time. In Fredrickson and Carstensen's (1990) study, a second group of participants were offered the same hypothetical choice between meeting partners, but the meeting was contextualized as taking place before the participant moved cross-country alone. This ending-oriented context presumably raised young participants' concern with social endings, resulting in more of them desiring to meet a family member and thus pursue an emotional goal. This cognitive reorientation has been replicated in other cultures, and using other situations (e.g., emigration in China; Fung, Carstensen, & Lutz, 1999). For example, Fung and Carstensen (2006) found distinct shifts in goal preference before, immediately after, and four months after the September 11 attack on the World Trade Center. Immediately following the attack, young people showed a significantly greater preference for emotional contact than at the other times. Older adults maintained a steady preference for emotional contact. Similar alterations in perspective were found with respect to the SARS epidemic (Fung & Carstensen, 2006, Study 2). In sum, these studies show that goal orientation changes with time orientation, and that time orientation is influenced by events both external and internal.

More broadly, this perspective is in concordance with research suggesting that aging influences goals (Freund & Ebner, 2005). Young adults orient toward growth goals (e.g., desire to achieve something new), whereas older adults have goals oriented toward maintenance or loss prevention (e.g., staying physically fit; Ebner, Freund, & Baltes, 2006). These goals coincide with an approach–avoidance perspective—a growth goal is an orientation toward approaching the positive, while an avoidance goal is to fend off the negative. Inherent in the shift from approach to avoidance is an acknowledgment that resources may be constrained (Freund & Ebner, 2005) and that goal achievement agency may be reduced (Heckhausen, 1997).

People also go through other changes as they contemplate the approach of end-of-life. According to terror management theory (TMT; Greenberg, Pyszczynski, & Solomon, 1986; Solomon, Greenberg, & Pyszczynski, 1991), the terror humans experience when contemplating death must be managed, resulting in reliance on culture and religion (Solomon et al., 1991), norms (Rosenblatt, Greenberg, Solomon, Pyszczynski, & Lyon, 1989), and avoidance of reminders of our connection with other animals (Goldenburg, Pyszczynski, Greenberg, & Solomon, 2000). When these proximal defenses are threatened, individuals react negatively and defensively (Pyszczynski, Greenberg, & Solomon, 1999).

A key component of TMT is mortality salience. Generally, mortality salience describes an increased awareness of death and dying. Mortality-salience conditions may arise in the ebb and flow of daily life: For example, death awareness has been demonstrated in those standing outside a funeral home versus a few blocks away (Jonas, Schimel, Greenberg, & Pyszczynski, 2002), and by subliminal reminders of the 9/11 terrorist attacks (Landau et al., 2004). In experimental designs, mortality salience is often manipulated with a task asking participants to write down the emotions the thought of their own death arouses, and to write down what will happen to them when they physically die (e.g., Schimel, Simon,

Greenberg, Pyszczynski, Solomon, Waxmonsky, & Arndt, 1999). After under-
going this manipulation, participants become particularly concerned with their
own death or dying. Older people, who face reminders and thoughts of death
and dying, are less and differently influenced by mortality-salience reminders
(Maxfield et al., 2007) and may have alternative means of addressing the fear of
death (Heckhausen, 1997).

Mortality salience serves as a reminder of end-of-life, so it should influence
time orientation in a manner similar to contemplating a time-limited perspective (Fredrickson & Carstensen, 1990) or threats to longevity such as terrorists or SARS (Fung & Carstensen, 2006). As such, it should have a unique and
interesting effect on ascription of spatiotemporal agency by forcing reassessment
of agency to complete goals (Freund & Ebner, 2005). In the reported study,
we expected people asked to contemplate their own mortality would subsequently exhibit evidence in their linguistic behavior of an avoidant perspective
on goal achievement (Ebner, Freund, & Baltes, 2006). Specifically, we expected
mortality salience would temporarily boost people's use of avoidance-oriented
event temporal agency assignments and suppress their use of approach-oriented
human-agency assignments.

Method

Participants

Undergraduates students ($n = 83$) were recruited from communication classes at
a large Southwestern university. The study was conducted using online survey
software that subjects were able to access at their convenience. Due to concerns
regarding the integrity of the mortality-salience manipulation, participants were
presented with the following notice upon accessing the survey: *Please close all other
browser windows and remove distractions. Make sure you have at least 30 uninterrupted
minutes in total to complete this packet. It is very important you complete it in one session.*

Experimental Design and Materials

Participants were randomly assigned to one of two experiential conditions: one
featuring a mortality-salience induction or one featuring a control condition
with a similar writing task. Mortality-salience inductions typically involve asking participants to answer two open-ended questions about death and dying
(e.g., Greenberg et al., 1990). In our experiment, participants in the mortality-
salience condition were given the following instructions, based on DeWall and
Baumeister (2007):

> *Please briefly describe the emotions that the thought of your own death arouses in
> you. Jot down, as specifically as you can, what you think will happen to you as
> you physically die and once you are physically dead.*

Participants in the control condition instead read the following instructions:

> *Please briefly describe the emotions that the thought of dental pain arouses in you* and *Jot down, what you think will happen to you as you experience dental pain*
> (DeWall & Baumeister, 2007).

A minimum of 200 characters was required for each response; participants were instructed to keep writing if they attempted to submit their entry before reaching this minimum.

Following this manipulation, participants completed two distraction tasks. Studies on mortality salience have used puzzles (e.g., Landau et al., 2006) or surveys (e.g., See & Petty, 2006) to distract and delay. Mortality-salience effects are stronger when a distraction and delay occurs between completing the induction task and measuring mortality-salience effects (Greenberg et al., 1994; Pyszczynski et al., 1999). This research suggests time is necessary to avoid proximal defense against mortality salience (e.g., consciously addressing fears and considerations of death; Pyszczynski et al., 1999). In the present study, the first distraction task entailed reading a short story entitled "The Growing Stone"; in the second, participants filled out the positive and negative scales from the PANAS, a commonly used mood assessment tool (Watson, Clark, & Tellegen, 1988). The PANAS subscales ask participants to assess the extent to which they are currently feeling positive (e.g., *proud, strong, excited*) and negative (e.g., *hostile, guilty, nervous*) emotions on a 5-point Likert scale ranging from 1 (*very slightly or not at all*) to 5 (*extremely*).

After the manipulation and distraction tasks, participants were instructed to write a description of events they expected to happen in their lives in the near future. The instructions for this task were written in language neutral with respect to temporal agency:

> *Think about significant events that you expect to occur in your life in the next 6 months. Some of these events will be positive; some of these events will be negative. Describe these events as if you were telling a story; do not simply list the events.*

Participants were given a minimum requirement of 250 words to complete the description task. After this task, they answered a short demographic questionnaire and then were debriefed. On average, participants completed the entire experimental procedure in 22 minutes.

Results

Fifteen of the participants were excluded because they took over 40 minutes to complete the study. We were concerned participants who look longer than this may have paused their participation and resumed it later. Although the mortality-salience induction appears to be robust for some time after the initial induction, the precise duration is unknown (Burke, Martens, & Faucher, 2010), so we chose a cautious estimate. Our final sample was comprised of 68 (48 f) participants (38 in the mortality-salience condition and 30 in the control condition).

Coding

A computerized search function was used to highlight words indicating temporal movement as suggested by McGlone and Pfiester (2009). A pair of coders who were blind to the hypotheses were asked to evaluate each word in context and make two judgments: the valence of the event referenced by the word (positive or negative) and whether the time word was used in a manner that ascribed agency to a human (e.g., *I'm approaching my birthday*) or an event (e.g., *My dentist appointment is coming up*). The words used in this study along with sentence examples are presented in Figure 9.2. Each word was coded in all tenses and forms (e.g., *go* was coded for *go, gone, went, going*). Krippendorff's Alpha was used to assess interrater reliability, and the coder's agreement proved acceptable for both judgments of event valence ($\alpha = .79$) and agency ascription ($\alpha = .86$).

Analysis

Each hit from the computerized search was entered as a case along with its valence and whether it was human or event temporal agency. This resulted in 167 cases for the mortality-salience condition, and 109 cases for the dental pain condition. Chi-square tests of independence were performed to test our hypotheses.

Our first hypothesis predicted participants would assign temporal agency to events when the valence of the event was negative and to humans when the event valence was positive. The co-occurrence of human agency with positive valence and event agency with negative valence was reliably different from chance, X^2 (1, $N = 276$) = 10.31, $p = .001$. As predicted, there were more event- than human-agency assignments for negative events (62.9% vs. 37.1%); for positive events, there were more human- than event-agency assignments (58.1% vs. 41.9%). These findings comports with the broader body of literature on agency ascription in spatiotemporal terms (e.g., McGlone & Pfiester, 2009).

Our second hypothesis predicted participants in the mortality-salience condition would encode proportionally greater numbers of events using event than human agency. The chi-square test for this prediction was significant, X^2 (1, $N = 276$) = 4.83, $p = .034$. As expected, event-agency assignment was more common than human-agency assignment in the mortality-salience condition (58.3% vs. 41.7%). In contrast, the proportion of event- and human-agency assignments in the control condition did not significantly differ, (53.6% vs. 46.4%), $p > .08$

Term	Human-Agent Expressions	Event-Agent Expressions
ahead	*We went ahead with the renovation plan.*	*The renovation plan is ahead of schedule.*
approach	*We are approaching the summer.*	*The summer is approaching.*
begin	*We began the meeting at 3 p.m.*	*The meeting began at 6 p.m.*
behind	*Let's put the matter behind us.*	*All our troubles are behind us.*
close	*We're getting close to kickoff time.*	*Kickoff time is getting closer.*
come	*We have come to the end of the regular season.*	*The playoffs are coming up soon.*
done	*When I'm done with dinner, I'll drive home.*	*When dinner is done, I'll drive home.*
end	*We ended the meeting at 6 p.m.*	*The meeting ended at 6 p.m.*
enter	*We are entering the last month of the fiscal year.*	*The fiscal year is entering its last month.*
finish	*When I've finished dinner, I'll drive home.*	*When dinner is finished, I'll drive home.*
forward	*We are moving forward with the project.*	*The project is moving forward.*
from . . . to/until	*I was in a meeting from 2 to/until 4 p.m.*	*My meeting was from 2 to/until 4 p.m.*
go	*I went through the day feeling tired.*	*As the day went on, I grew tired.*
move	*We are moving quickly through our meeting agenda.*	*The meeting is moving quickly.*
near	*We are nearing the filing date.*	*The filing date is drawing near.*
pass	*We passed the due date on Thursday.*	*The due date passed on Thursday.*
reach	*We have reached the last month of the election season.*	*The election season has reached its last month.*
run	*We are running a few minutes late.*	*The meeting is running a few minutes late.*
start	*We started the fiscal year with a bang.*	*The fiscal year started with a bang.*

FIGURE 9.2 Spatiotemporal Words and Sentence Examples

Analysis of variance on the PANAS was used to check for differences in participant affect between the death and dental pain conditions. The 10-item PANAS negative scale was found to be reliable ($\alpha = .86$) and formed into a composite. No difference between conditions was found; the participants who wrote and thought about death ($M = 2.03$, SD = .74) did not score higher than those who wrote and thought about dental pain ($M = 2.00$, SD = .8), $F (1, 66) = .032$, $p = .858$, *n.s.* A composite from the 10-item PANAS positive scale was also reliable ($\alpha = .87$). Again, no differences between death (M = 2.46, SD = .7) and dental pain (M = 2.35, SD = .85) were detected, ($F (1, 66) = .341$, $p = .561$). As in other mortality-salience research (e.g., Greenberg, Arndt, Simon, Pyszczynski, & Solomon, 2000), participants did not differ significantly between conditions in terms of the negative or positive affect they reported.

Discussion

Humans are the only animals able to contemplate their own mortality. A number of theoretical perspectives describe how increased awareness of death influences cognition. For example, terror management theory (Greenberg et al., 1986; Solomon et al., 1991) provides evidence that awareness of mortality increases reliance on norms and religion, as well as negative reactions toward threats to those cultural buffers against death. Perspectives on aging describe other cognitive changes, such as a reorientation toward emotion-centered goals rather than achievement goals (Carstensen et al., 1999) and reassessment of goal achievement strategies from achievement and growth to maintenance and avoidance (e.g., Freund & Ebner, 2005). The present study investigated whether the awareness of death and subsequent realignment of goals influenced use of the spatiotemporal metaphors in which people frequently describe future events.

We predicted people who were reminded of death would cognitively orient themselves in a manner similar to an older person, and the way in which they assigned agency in future events would reflect this orientation. The results indicated a proportionally greater amount of future events were described using event agency (e.g., *Graduation is coming up*) rather than human agency (e.g., *I'm getting close to graduation*) for participants who completed an induction designed to raise the salience of their own mortality compared to those who completed a different task related to describing dental pain. These results support our predictions, and more generally fit with expectations that cognitive orientation influences spatiotemporal agency ascription.

Other researchers studying situational factors in production and evaluation of spatiotemporal agency have reported results aligned with ours. For instance, McGlone and Harding (1998) observed that when temporal sentences (e.g., *The meeting scheduled for next Wednesday has been moved forward two days*) were presented with other sentences that ascribed agency to either humans or events, comprehension of whether the meeting had been moved closer or further in time was influenced. Similarly, Boroditsky and Ramscar (2002) asked people the same temporal sentence in a variety of situations involving physical movement. When interpreters engaged in forward physical movement themselves (e.g., *moving through a lunch line*), they preferred the human-agent reading of the proposition; however, when they observed an object moving toward them (e.g., *a wheeled chair moving across the room*), they preferred the event-agent reading.

More generally, our findings support previous research demonstrating how affective orientation toward events influences the grammatical agency used in their description. For instance, *We're getting close to summer vacation* is more likely to be uttered than *Summer vacation is getting close* because summer vacation is generally considered a positively valenced event. People metaphorically approach events they are looking forward to and avoid/passively await those they are not. The present study demonstrates the connection between spatiotemporal metaphors and affect is robust. Effects have been found in corpus analysis (e.g., McGlone et al., 2012), experimental work in which participants describe events that have already occurred (e.g., McGlone and Pfiester, 2009), and in the present study, in which participants described events they anticipate occurring in the near future.

A potential challenge to these findings is that the mortality-salience induction created a more negative mood than the dental pain induction. Generalized negative affect would confound the connection between mortality salience and event-agency orientation we predicted, as we would be unable to determine whether it was a time-limited perspective or a negative mood that was responsible for the greater proportion of event-agency assignment. However, as is typical with mortality-salience experiments (e.g., Greenberg, Arndt, Simon, Pyszczynski, & Solomon, 2000), no differences in overall mood were detected between groups of participants. This finding suggests our results were indeed caused by a time-limited perspective induced by increasing death awareness.

Our findings demonstrate that awareness of death is a factor influencing grammatical expressions of efficacy. According to research on aging and goal reappraisal (e.g., Heckhausen, 1997), when people become aware of external limitations on their ability to achieve (such as time), they reorient cognition from an approach–achievement perspective to a maintenance–avoidance perspective. When younger people are reminded of death, either through salient events like the World Trade Center attack, situational reminders such as walking past a funeral home, or the laboratory induction we employed, they adopt a cognitive perspective similar to an older person, and their language use adjusts accordingly.

Our findings are consistent with others demonstrating the psychological distancing induced by mortality salience. Previous studies have explored varied distancing behaviors, such as reduced perceived beauty and negative evaluations of wilderness scenes (Koole & Van den Berg, 2005); reluctance among women to perform breast self-examinations (Goldenberg et al., 2000); negativity toward animals (Beatson & Halloran, 2007); and objectification of the female body (Grabe et al., 2005). Although consistent with previous findings, the current study is one of the few to demonstrate mortality salience–induced distancing in communicative behavior. Communication strategy is an appropriate addition to the set of behaviors serving the terror management theory tenets of (a) adoption of and validation of a cultural worldview, and (b) increasing one's self-esteem by living up to the standards of value prescribed by the worldview. Membership in a language community represents a cultural worldview, as it is to and through the communicative act of language (Ochs & Schieffelin, 1984) we are socialized into our communities (Duranti, 1997). Following linguistic norms such as using indirect reference for affect-laden topics (McCallum & McGlone, 2011) exemplifies living up to value standards that result in self-esteem. The present results hint at a similar self-esteem preserving function of temporal agency assignment: People prefer to assign temporal agency assignment to themselves for events they "look forward to" but abdicate it to negative events they cannot avoid.

References

Beatson, R. M., & Halloran, M. J. (2007). Humans rule! The effects of creatureliness reminders, mortality salience, and self-esteem on attitudes toward animals. *British Journal of Social Psychology, 46*, 619–632. http://dx.doi.org/10.1348/014466606X147753

Berry, M., & Browne, M. (2005). Email surveillance using nonnegative matrix factorization. *Computational and Mathematical Organization Theory, 11*, 249–264. http://dx.doi.org/10.1007/s10588–005–5380–5

Boroditsky, L., & Ramscar, M. (2002). The roles of body and mind in abstract thought. *Psychological Science, 13*, 185–189. http://dx.doi.org/10.1111/1467–9280.00434

Brown, R., & Fish, D. (1983). The psychological causality implicit in language. *Cognition, 14*, 237–273. http://dx.doi.org/10.1016/0010–0277(83)90006–9

Burke, B. L., Martens, A., & Faucher, E. H. (2010). Two decades of terror management theory: A meta-analysis of mortality salience research. *Personality and Social Psychology Review, 14*, 155–195. http://dx.doi.org/10.1177/1088868309352321

Cacioppo, J. T., Priester, J. R., & Bernston, G. G. (1993). Rudimentary determination of attitudes II: Arm flexion and extension have differential effects on attitudes. *Journal of Personality and Social Psychology, 65*, 5–17. http://dx.doi.org/10.1037/00223514.65.1.5

Carstensen, L. L., Isaacowitz, D. M., & Charles, S. T. (1999). Taking time seriously: A theory of socioemotional selectivity. *American Psychologist, 54*(3),165–181. http://dx.doi.org/10.1037/0003–066X.54.3.165

Clark, H. H. (1973). Space, time, semantics, and the child. In T. E. Moore (Ed.), *Cognitive development and the acquisition of language* (pp. 27–63). New York: Academic Press. http://dx.doi.org/10.1111/1467–9230.00134

DeWall, C. N., & Baumeister, R. F. (2007). From terror to joy: Automatic tuning to positive affective information following mortality salience. *Psychological Science, 18*, 984–990. http://dx.doi.org/10.1111/j.1467–9280.2007.02013.x

Dowty, D. (1991). Thematic proto-roles and argument selection. *Language, 67*, 547–619. http://dx.doi.org/10.2307/415037

Duranti, A. (1997). *Linguistic anthropology.* New York: Cambridge University Press. http://dx.doi.org/10.1017/CBO9780511810190

Ebner, N. C., Freund, A. M., & Baltes, P. B. (2006). Developmental changes in personal goal orientation from young to late adulthood: From striving for gains to maintenance and prevention of losses. *Psychology and Aging, 21*, 664–678. http://dx.doi.org/10.1037/0882–7974.21.4.664

Emotion. (1989). In *Oxford English dictionary online* (2nd ed.). Retrieved from http://www.oup.com.

Fredrickson, B. L., & Carstensen, L. L. (1990). Choosing social partners: How old age and anticipated endings make people more selective. *Psychology and Aging, 5*(3), 335–347. http://dx.doi.org/10.1037/0882–7974.5.3.335

Freund, A. M., & Ebner, N. C. (2005). The aging self: Shifting from promoting gains to balancing losses. In W. Greve, K. Rothermund & D. Wentura (Eds.), *The adaptive self: Personal continuity and intentional self-development* (pp. 185–202). New York: Hogrefe. http://dx.doi.org/10.1177/108883832934232

Fung, H. H., & Carstensen, L. L. (2006). Goals change when life's fragility is primed: Lessons learned from older adults, the September 11th attacks and SARS. *Social Cognition, 24*, 248–278. http://dx.doi.org/10.1521/soco.2006.24.3.248

Fung, H. H., Carstensen, L. L., & Lutz, A. M. (1999). Influence of time on social preferences: Implications for life-span development. *Psychology and Aging, 14*, 595–604. http://dx.doi.org/10.1037/0882–7974.14.4.595

Gibbs, R. W., Jr. (1994). *The poetics of mind: Figurative thought, language, and understanding.* Cambridge, UK: Cambridge University Press. http://dx.doi.org/10.1111/j.1467-9280.2007.02013

Goldenberg, J. L., Pyszczynski, T., Greenberg, J., & Solomon, S. (2000). Fleeing the body: A terror management perspective on the problem of human corporeality. *Personality and Social Psychology Review, 4*, 200–218. http://dx.doi.org/10.1207/S15327957PSPR0403_1

Grabe, S., Routledge, C., Cook, A., Andersen, C., & Arndt, J. (2005). In defense of the body: The effect of mortality salience on female body objectification. *Psychology of Women Quarterly, 29*, 33–37. http://dx.doi.org/10.1111/j.1471-6402.2005.00165.x

Greenberg, J., Arndt, J., Simon, L., Pyszczynski, T., & Solomon, S. (2000). Proximal and distal defenses in response to reminders of one's mortality: Evidence of a temporal sequence. *Personality and Social Psychology Bulletin, 26*, 91–99. http://dx.doi.org/10.1177/0146167200261009

Greenberg, J., Pyszczynski, T., & Solomon, S. (1986). The causes and consequences of a need for self-esteem: a terror management theory. In R. F. Baumeister (Ed.), *Public self and private self* (pp. 189–212). New York: Springer-Verlag. http://dx.doi.org/10.1007/978-1-4613-9564-5_10

Greenberg, J., Pyszczynski, T., Solomon, S., Rosenblatt, A., Veeder, M., Kirkland, S., et al. (1990). Evidence for terror management theory II: The effects of mortality salience on reactions to those who threaten or bolster the cultural worldview. *Journal of Personality and Social Psychology, 58*, 308–318. http://dx.doi.org/10.1037/0022-3514.58.2.308

Greenberg, J., Pyszczynski, T., Solomon, S., Simon, L., & Breus, M. (1994). Role of consciousness and accessibility of death-related thoughts in mortality salience effects. *Journal of Personality and Social Psychology, 67*, 627–637. http://dx.doi.org/10.1037/0022-3514.67.4.627

Heckhausen, J. (1997). Developmental regulation across adulthood: Primary and secondary control of age-related changes. *Developmental Psychology, 33*, 176–187. http://dx.doi.org/10.1037/0012-1649.33.1.176

Johnson, M. (1990). *The body in the mind: The bodily basis of meaning, imagination, and reason.* Chicago: University of Chicago Press. http://dx.doi.org/10.2307/431155

Jonas, E., Schimel, J., Greenberg, J., & Pyszczynski, T. (2002). The Scrooge Effect: Evidence that mortality salience increases prosocial attitudes and behavior. *Personality and Social Psychology Bulletin, 28*, 1342–1355. http://dx.doi.org/10.1177/014616702236834

Keila, P. S., & Skillicorn, D. B. (2005). Structure in the Enron email dataset. *Computational and Mathematical Organization Theory, 11*, 183–199. http://dx.doi.org/10.1007/s10588-005-5379-y

Kessler, G. (2010). Virtual business: An Enron email corpus study. *Journal of Pragmatics, 42*, 262–270. http://dx.doi.org/10.1016/j.pragma.2009.05.015

Koole, S. L., & Van den Berg, A. E. (2005). Lost in the wilderness: Terror management, action orientation, and nature evaluation. *Journal of Personality and Social Psychology, 88*, 1014–1028. http://dx.doi.org/10.1037/0022-3514.88.6.1014

Kovecses, Z. (2000). *Metaphor and emotion: Language, culture, and body in human feeling.* New York: Cambridge University Press. http://dx.doi.org/10.1017/CBO9780511816802.023

LaFrance, M., Brownell, H., & Hahn, E. (1997). Interpersonal verbs, gender, and implicit causality. *Social Psychology Quarterly, 60*, 138–152. http://dx.doi.org/10.2307/2787101

Lakoff, G., & Johnson, M. (1980). Conceptual metaphor in everyday language. *The Journal of Philosophy, 77*, 453–486. http://dx.doi.org/10.2307/2025464

Landau, M. J., Goldenberg, J. L., Greenberg, J., Gillath, O., Solomon, S., Cox, C., Martens, A., & Pyszczynski, T. (2006). The siren's call: Terror management and the threat of men's sexual attraction to women. *Journal of Personality and Social Psychology, 90,* 129–146. http://dx.doi.org/10.1037/0022–3514.90.1.129

Landau, M. J., Solomon, S., Greenberg, J., Cohen, F., Pyszczynski, T., Arndt, J., . . . Cook, A. (2004). Deliver us from evil: The Effects of mortality salience and reminders of 9/11 on support for President George W. Bush. *Personality and Social Psychology Bulletin, 30,* 1136–1140. http://dx.doi.org/10.1177/ 0146167204267988

Maxfield, M., Pyszczynski, T., Kluck, B., Cox, C., Greenberg, J., Solomon, S., & Weise, D. (2007). Age-related differences in responses to thoughts of one's own death: Mortality salience and judgments of moral transgressors. *Psychology and Aging, 22,* 343–351. http://dx.doi.org/10.1037/0882–7974.22.2.341

McCallum, N. L., & McGlone, M. S. (2011). Death be not profane: Mortality salience and euphemism use. *Western Journal of Communication, 75,* 565–584. http://dx.doi.org/ 10.1080/10570314.2011.608405

McGlone, M. S., Ballard, D. I., Merola, N. A., & McGlynn, J. (2012). *Time is not on our side: Temporal agency language in the Enron email corpus.* ID360: The Global Forum on Identity, Austin, TX.

McGlone, M. S., & Harding, J. L. (1998). Back (or forward?) to the future: The role of perspective in temporal language comprehension. *Journal of Experimental Psychology: Learning, Memory, and Cognition, 24,* 1211–1223. http://dx.doi.org/10.1037/ 0278–7393.24.5.1211

McGlone, M. S., & Pfiester, R. A. (2009). Does time fly when you're having fun, or do you? Affect, agency, and embodiment in temporal communication. *Journal of Language and Social Psychology, 28,* 3–31. http://dx.doi.org/10.1177/0261927X08325744

Miller, G. A., & Johnson-Laird, P. N. (1976). *Language and perception.* Cambridge, MA: Harvard University Press. http://dx.doi.org/10.1037/0022–3514.88.6.1014

Niedenthal, P. M., Barsalou, L. W., Winkielman, P., Krauth-Gruber, S., & Ric, F. (2005). Embodiment in attitudes, social perception, and emotion. *Personality and Social Psychology Review, 9,* 184–211. http://dx.doi.org/10.1207/s15327957pspr0903_1

Ochs, E., & Schieffelin, B. B. (1984). Language acquisition and socialization: Three developmental stories and their implications. In R. Shweder & R. LeVine (Eds.), *Cultural theory: Essays on mind, self, and emotion* (pp. 470–512). Cambridge, UK: Cambridge University Press. http://dx.doi.org/10.1177/014616702236834

Pinquart, M., Silbereisen, R. K., & Froehlich, C. (2009). Life goals and purpose in life in cancer patients. *Support Care Cancer, 17,* 253–259. http://dx.doi.org/10.1007/ s00520–008–0450–0

Pyszczynski, T., Greenberg, J., & Solomon, S. (1999). A dual-process model of defense against conscious and unconscious death-related thoughts: An extension of terror management theory. *Psychological Review, 106,* 835–845. http://dx.doi.org/10.1037/ 0033–295X.106.4.835

Rosenblatt, A., Greenberg, J., Solomon, S., Pyszczynski, T., & Lyon, D. (1989). Evidence for terror management theory I: The effects of mortality salience on reactions to those who violate or uphold cultural values. *Journal of Personality and Social Psychology, 57,* 681–690. http://dx.doi.org/10.1037/0022–3514.57.4.681

Schimel, J., Simon, L., Greenberg, J., Pyszczynski, T., Solomon, S., Waxmonski, J., & Arndt, J. (1999). Support for a functional perspective on stereotypes: Evidence that mortality salience enhances stereotypic thinking and preferences. *Journal of Personality and Social Psychology, 77,* 905–926. http://dx.doi.org/10.1037/0022–3514.77.5.905

See, Y. H. M., & Petty, R. E. (2006). Effects of mortality salience on evaluation of ingroup and outgroup sources: The impact of pro-versus counterattitudinal positions. *Personality and Social Psychology Bulletin, 32*, 405–416. http://dx.doi.org/10.1177/0146167205282737

Solomon, S., Greenberg, J., & Pyszczynski, T. (1991). A terror management theory of social behavior: The psychological functions of self-esteem and cultural worldviews. In M. P. Zanna (Ed.), *Advances in experimental social psychology* (Vol. 24, pp. 93–159). New York: Academic Press. http://dx.doi.org/10.1016/S0065-2601(08)60328-7

Watson, D., Clark, L. A., & Tellegen, A. (1988). Development and validation of brief measures of positive and negative affect: The PANAS scales. *Journal of Personality and Social Psychology, 54*(6), 1063–1070. http://dx.doi.org/10.1037/0022-3514.54.6.1063

10

"DEATH IS COMING, BUT I'M TOO SCARED TO THINK ABOUT IT"

Defining and Distinguishing the Roles of Death and Fear as Motivators to Cognitive, Affective, and Behavioral Change

Alexander L. Lancaster, Nicholas D. Bowman, and Lindsey A. Harvell

The inescapable reality of death is omnipresent, becoming highlighted at certain times throughout one's life. Perhaps walking into a doctor's office, attending a funeral, or even boarding an airplane can make the fear of death salient among individuals. These death-related thoughts, termed *mortality salience* by Greenberg, Pyszczynski, and Solomon (1986), are a key component of the same authors' terror management theory (TMT). Although the fear of death may be commonly understood as an aversion toward the end of one's life, few definitions exist beyond this understanding. Nyatanga and de Vocht (2006) offered a definition of death anxiety as "an unpleasant emotion of multidimensional concerns that is of an existential origin provoked on contemplation of death of self or others" (p. 413). Common among the terms *mortality salience* and *death anxiety* is the idea that both are negatively valenced emotional states based on the consideration of death. Nonetheless, because the potential for anxiety brought about by death is omnipresent (Pyszczynski, Greenberg, Solomon, Arndt, & Schimel, 2004), it is possible the fear of death is distal in nature, until something happens that makes it salient.

This chapter explores the potential distinctions between the omnipresent, but distal, anxiety of death, and the phasic (i.e., state-based) fear associated with proximal events that could lead to death. To that end, this chapter will include a brief description of TMT (a theory that deals with the omnipresent anxiety about death), a review of relevant literature on fear, and a model that includes elements of TMT, along with a theory of fear more rooted in proximal threats: the extended parallel process model (EPPM; Witte, 1992, 1994). In doing this, the goal is to provide insight into the differences between event-based fear of possible death and the distal, but enduring anxiety associated with mortality. In essence, this chapter proposes a link between state-based fear and trait-based mortality salience.

Terror Management Theory

Greenberg et al.'s (1986) TMT describes individuals' responses to the anxious state brought about by becoming aware of their own mortality. TMT is based largely on Becker's (1962, 1973) proposition that humans' ability to understand death is inevitable leads to a salient fear of mortality. This awareness of death leads individuals to engage in proximal and distal responses, or defenses, as a means of reducing or ameliorating the salient thoughts about death. Taubman-Ben-Ari and Findler (2005) described proximal and distal responses as conscious and unconscious, respectively. Furthermore, as Arndt, Cook, and Routledge (2004) noted, proximal defenses allow individuals to address the death-related issue, such that individuals no longer feel the need to expend further attention or action toward the issue. In short, once proximal responses are activated, individuals can think through the death-related issue and address the emotional response to experiencing mortality salience.

TMT is comprised of four foundational elements: mortality salience, cultural worldviews, self-esteem, and close relationships. Mortality salience is the core element of TMT and refers to an individual's realization that he or she will die. According to TMT, when mortality becomes salient, individuals tend to draw from their cultural worldviews (CWVs) to serve as a buffer of the anxiety experienced when thinking about their inevitable experience of death (Solomon, Greenberg, & Pyszczynski, 2000). CWVs are the second element of TMT and, as Greenberg et al. (1986) noted, can encompass any aspect of an individual's reality, including religion and political party affiliation. Self-esteem, the third element of TMT, functions to buffer the anxiety experienced when mortality is made salient. Individuals with higher self-esteem tend to be better able to work through mortality-salience-induced anxiety than those with lower self-esteem. Similar to self-esteem, close relationships, the fourth component of TMT, serve also as a buffer to the anxiety associated with confronting the reality of death. Together, these TMT elements work such that anxiety can be induced by making mortality salient, and reduced through one or more of the remaining parts of the theory.

In the case of TMT, death awareness, or mortality salience, becomes the driving mechanism that leads individuals to seek the metaphorical security blanket of cultural worldviews and close relationships to overcome the uncomfortable psychological state of anxiety. Previous research guided by TMT has already suggested making mortality salient might influence individuals to save for the future (Zaleskiewicz, Gasiorowska, Kesebir, Luszczynska, & Pyszczynski, 2013), affect attitudes toward immigration (Bassett & Connelly, 2011; Weise, Arciszewski, Verlhiac, Pyszczynski, & Greenberg, 2012), and influence political attitudes (Burke, Kosloff, & Landau, 2013). In line with the theory, the existential anxiety brought about by actively thinking about death can be overcome by holding on to cultural worldviews. An inherent assumption of TMT, however, is these responses are proximal in nature. Common among studies guided by TMT is the use of a written stimulus to arouse the fear of death among participants, a practice introduced by Pyszczynski, Greenberg, and Solomon (1997). Nonetheless, Arndt, Greenberg, Pyszczynski, and Solomon (1997) contended that mortality salience might also be induced through subliminal methods. Extant research, however, has relied primarily on the written stimulus method of inducing mortality salience.

Overall, TMT has been supported by research testing the theory, as evidenced by several extended reviews of the literature (e.g., Greenberg et al., 1997; Solomon et al., 2004), which have concluded that the theory functions as postulated in a variety of contexts. Furthermore, as Burke, Martens, and Faucher (2010) noted, research testing TMT has demonstrated the theory's validity, as its predictions stand supported across cultures and participant groups. Despite this general support of TMT, there remain some concerns regarding the theory. Indeed, some scholars have highlighted potential theoretical limitations and levied critiques of TMT.

TMT has received empirical support, yet it is not without theoretical limitations. For example, Navarrete, Kurzban, Fessler, and Kirkpatrick (2004) argued that TMT assumes the presence of a survival instinct and the theory's adaptive function results in anxiety reduction. Furthermore, Buss (1997) argued TMT focuses solely on internal psychological protection, rather than other adaptive responses. These critiques, and others, stem primarily from the fact that TMT is rooted in the evolutionary biological perspective (Navarrete & Fessler, 2005). It follows, then, in some cases, individuals may experience an event or object that inspires fear, because of the potential for death, without mortality being made salient through written manipulations. This chapter focuses, in part, on this potential distinction between fear of death generated by exposure to some life-threatening event, and mortality salience as induced by heightened awareness through written manipulation.

In this chapter, one goal is to demonstrate that TMT is not a flawed theory, but may at times confuse mortality salience as an enduring state, rather than a phasic state. Indeed, much in the way Navarrete et al. (2004) and Buss (1997) critiqued the solely psychological nature of TMT, this chapter argues the way in which mortality is made salient, in accordance with the theory, may lack ecological validity. In essence, the studies guided by TMT are psychologically valid, but may not be ecologically valid because individuals do not generally write about their own mortality in a nonexperimental condition. At best, this may mean that TMT is somewhat inconsistent with life, and at worst suggests that results found in studies guided by TMT come from the method invariance.

As will be demonstrated, one may not need to use written death thoughts so bluntly to induce mortality salience, and it is likely the fear associated with a potentially deadly event can also lead to mortality salience. In other words, consistent with the natural human tendency to want to guard against death, the threat of mortal injury from some life-threatening event might lead individuals to become death aware in the proximal sense (i.e., in the moment). One goal of this proposed thought is that it may help scholars better understand the link between fear and mortality salience. Although death may be omnipresent, it is possible the proximal fears might be brought about by potential death-inducing incidents, rather than death itself. Before discussing this distinction, the chapter first presents an examination of literature related to fear, fear-based messages, and the theories that have been used to examine these fear appeals.

Fear and Fear Appeals

Fear is a negatively valenced emotional response to some event that introduces a threat into one's immediate future (Easterling & Leventhal, 1989; Witte, 1992). Individuals' experiences of fear tend to draw from two cognitive levels: the semantic (i.e., abstract or conceptual) level and the concrete (i.e., perceptual) level (Easterling & Leventhal, 1989). In other words, individuals respond cognitively to the perception of fear, based on the presence of a cue that activates thoughts about some fearful event. As these authors contended, fear occurs when someone encounters a threat and recognizes it as something that is higher or lower in severity. The emotional response occurs when this threat is activated in one's mind. The recognition of threat and the ensuing emotional response, then, leaves an individual in the maladaptive state of fear.

Witte (1992) used the concepts of fear and threat, and added efficacy (i.e., a cue that leads individuals to consider how effective their response to a fearful situation may be), to form her fear-based message theory, the extended parallel process model. The EPPM, like several theories that preceded it (e.g., the fear-as-acquired drive model [Hovland, Janis, & Kelly, 1953]; the parallel response model [Leventhal, 1970, 1971]; and protection motivation theory [Rogers, 1983]), explains individuals' responses to fear-based messages, in terms of cognitive and affective responses. On a cognitive level, individuals might examine the potential for a person, situation, or object to do them harm, and think about how they should respond. On an affective level, individuals might respond to the uncomfortable state of fear by attempting to assuage the fear without necessarily addressing the initial threat. In the case of death and mortality salience, fear associated with a threat might drive individuals to become aware of their mortality, thereby resulting in an emotional, psychological response. Considering fear is associated with both threatening situations and death, it is possible that theories examining fear-based messages might have a place within research focusing on death and mortality salience. Therefore, it is important to offer a brief examination of fear appeals and the theories that offer explanatory mechanisms for their efficacy.

Fear appeals, as defined by Witte (1992), are "persuasive messages designed to scare people by describing the terrible things that will happen to them if they do not do what the message recommends" (p. 329). The study of fear appeals dates back to the drive models proposed between the early 1950s and 1970. The first of these theories, the fear-as-acquired drive model (Hovland, Janis, & Kelly, 1953), proposed an inverted U-shaped (i.e., curvilinear) relationship between fear and message acceptance. Specifically, the authors proposed a critical point at which an individual would be most likely to accept a fear-based message. This critical point is based on the amount of fearful content within the message, such that if too much fear is aroused, the individual would become progressively less likely to accept the message. Following this first drive model, McGuire's (1968, 1969) two-factor theory retains the curvilinear relationship between fear and message acceptance, but differentiates fear as a cue and a drive. When fear operates as a cue, it interferes with individuals' acceptance or rejection of a message. Conversely, when fear operates as a drive, it motivates individuals to accept the message. In spite of these distinctions, both theories essentially posit a moderate amount of fear is most likely to lead individuals to accept a fear-based message. Both theories also have been rejected after empirical testing (Beck & Frankel, 1981; Rogers, 1983).

In the wake of the drive models, Rogers (1975, 1983) introduced protection motivation theory (PMT) and Sutton (1982) applied subjective expected utility (SEU) theory to fear appeals. Rogers' PMT focuses on a danger control process that occurs as a result of the level of noxiousness and probability of the fearful event occurring. Conversely, Sutton's SEU theory posits three variables work together in a multiplicative fashion to determine an individual's response to a fear appeal: (a) the perceived utility of the threat; (b) the subjective probability that the threat will occur if the target person does not heed the recommended changes in the message; and (c) the subjective probability that the threat will occur if the target person heeds the advice. Research subsequent to these theories has demonstrated flaws in each of the models. Specifically, Sutton and Eiser (1984) found no evidence of the multiplicative function forwarded in SEU, and Witte (1992) noted discrepancies between empirical findings and the PMT model predictions. Witte's EPPM, therefore, continues to be one of the more commonly used theories for fear-based message research.

The EPPM (Witte, 1992, 1994) picks up where previous fear appeals theories left off, positing there are two possible routes that individuals may take when confronted by a fear-based message. These two routes, termed *danger control* and *fear control*, refer to the possible outcomes of a fear appeal message. Whereas danger control is characterized as a cognitive response that addresses the threat levied in the message (usually in accordance with the actions recommended in the appeal), fear control refers to an affective response that quells the emotion of fear but does not address the threatening situation. According to the theory, fear and efficacy drive the potential responses individuals may have when receiving a fear-based message. Fear is the emotional response to the threat highlighted in the message, and efficacy is one's perceived ability to address the fear-inducing threat.

As Witte (1992, 1994) noted, if the fear aroused by the threat is too low, individuals will not have any response to the message because they do not perceive themselves to be at risk of the negative outcomes indicated in the appeal. Conversely, if the message includes a threat that elicits a high level of fear, and individuals do not perceive themselves to have sufficient efficacy to address the threat, they engage in the fear control process. It is the message that arouses a moderate level of fear, among individuals who perceive themselves to have sufficient efficacy to address the threat that is most likely to result in danger control processes. EPPM, like the theories before it, addresses the arousal of fear brought on by some salient threat, and the fears targeted by fear appeal messages may be similar to the existential anxiety discussed in TMT.

Fear and Mortality Salience: How Different Are They?

On the surface, fear may appear to be an all-encompassing emotional response, regardless of the context or situation about which fear is aroused. Indeed, individuals often express the sentiment that they are afraid of death. The question, however, is whether anxiety about death is the same as fear of a situation that might lead to one's death. Specifically, despite the notion that death is omnipresent, and may strike at any moment, fear of eventual death is likely distinct from the proximal fear of a situation that might be deadly. As noted previously, much of the extant TMT research has operated on the assumption that mortality is made salient by having participants write about their future deaths (see Pyszczynski et al., 1997). Nonetheless, it is likely that mortality also can be made salient through events likely to lead to death.

Even when mortality is made salient, as is the case with TMT and associated research, it is perhaps the case that this discomfort is distal in nature, and does not occupy mental space that would make it the subject of constant thought. It follows, then, that fear of death may be activated through a fearful situation that is made salient, rather than simply the thought of eventual death. Although extant research has not studied this potential distinction, some unpublished data suggests that the distinction may exist. Specifically, data from a study by Lancaster, Bowman, and Harvell (2015) recently conducted a study on airline safety, the results of which suggest this distinction between fear and fear of death may exist. This study may hold the first empirical evidence of the conceptual link and distinction between fear associated with the topic of death and fear of events that may lead to death. Therefore, the following section includes an examination of Lancaster and colleagues' study in detail.

Commercial Aviation: Fear of Flying (and Death)

Lancaster et al. (2015) examined the utility of TMT and EPPM in the case of airline safety demonstration videos. Specifically, they predicted that the individuals who are primed to think about their mortality via a fear appeal (i.e., by being told they will die if the airplane they are on crashes), as well as being primed to perceive that they are able to do something to help themselves survive should an airplane crash occur (i.e., paying attention to the safety demonstration video; the efficacy manipulation), would be most likely to pay attention to the safety demonstration video. The researchers chose commercial air travel as a topic because nearly half of the U.S. population suffers from some form of fear of flying (Capafons, Sosa, & Viña, 1999). Despite the fact individuals have upwards of a 70% chance of surviving an airplane crash (Noland, 2007), the perception of the potential for death to occur is likely heightened among passengers when boarding an airplane. Therefore, this study used the purported high probability of dying in an airplane crash as a way of inducing one's mortality salience, rather than having individuals write about their future death. In this way, the study had hoped to use a more ecologically valid induction of mortality salience, in order to test the effect of mortality salience on message attention and recall.

In this study, the researchers used a combination of elements of TMT (i.e., mortality salience) and EPPM (i.e., fear and efficacy) to test whether the fear associated with potentially dying in an airplane crash would influence their recall of the information presented in the safety demonstration video. Recall from the earlier discussion, mortality salience and fear are distinct constructs, and therefore can be manipulated differently while sharing some similarities (i.e., increased fear over an event that also may lead to mortality). Consistent with this idea, Lancaster et al. (2015) hypothesized death-salient participants would have increased recall of the airline safety demonstration video when compared to non–death-salient participants, participants in the high self-efficacy conditions would have greater recall of the information in the video than participants in the low self-efficacy conditions, and self-efficacy would moderate the relationship between mortality salience and recall of the information in the video.

In this study, 192 participants in an online experiment were presented with fabricated reports from the Federal Aviation Administration on bulletins to airline passengers. These bulletins were written to vary the chance of dying while flying with the passenger's ability to respond to an emergency situation, and thereby represented the manipulations of mortality salience and efficacy. After reading one of the four snippets, assigned at random, participants viewed an actual airline safety demonstration video and responded to several measures. Considering the goal of the study was to explore the links between mortality salience and efficacy inductions, and attention paid to the safety demonstration video, the authors employed multiple types of measures, including self-report scales and open response items related to the instructions in the safety demonstration video. Analysis of the data suggested that neither mortality salience nor efficacy had a significant impact on message recall. In fact, very few people were able to accurately recall the information in the safety demonstration video. The results indicated no significant difference in attention paid to the safety demonstration video between individuals who were presented with a mortality-inducing and a non-mortality-inducing message. Furthermore, there were no significant differences between participants who were in the high and low efficacy conditions. These null results, however, are more meaningful than one might consider them to be at first glance.

Lancaster et al.'s (2015) results indicated no significant differences in the outcome of attention to the safety demonstration video. These results, however, suggest that airline passengers might not pay attention to these videos regardless of how they are made to feel about the likelihood of dying should the airplane crash or how efficacious they are made to feel regarding the extent to which they can help themselves in the event of an emergency. Indeed, the vast majority of participants were unable to correctly recall the steps needed to perform vital emergency functions, including opening emergency exits, using supplemental oxygen masks, and donning a life jacket. Because the mortality-salience manipulation failed, it is likely that all participants had some level of mortality salience, as a result of being told that flying on an airplane might lead to their death. This outcome presents a logical starting point for the discussion of the interworking of fear, mortality salience, and efficacy.

Although mortality was not successfully manipulated, some emotional response was. Although the exact emotion cannot be identified, it is known that some participants felt a greater emotional response than others. Specifically, participants in the low efficacy conditions reported a greater emotional response than participants in the high efficacy conditions. From a persuasion perspective (e.g., Witte, 1992, 1994), an emotional response would lead individuals to engage in less cognitive processing. The effect of the emotional response, although outside of the scope of the original study goals, is relevant to the exploration of the manipulation of self-efficacy.

This study was originally designed to explore the effect of mortality salience and efficacy on individuals' processing of airline safety demonstration videos. However, the findings provide evidence for a situation in which efficacy was the driving factor in participants' response to an emotional outcome associated with a life-threatening event. In this case, the authors logically surmised that participants felt an emotional response of fear, as a result of being told that they would likely die in an airplane crash. It was this induction of efficacy that allowed some of these participants to come to terms with that fear, and perceive themselves as able to survive and escape an airplane crash. That participants were not able to recall more information from the safety demonstration video, while disappointing, suggests that there might be other issues associated with attention to safety instructions aboard aircraft. The null effects of this study, however, are meaningful because they represent an ecologically valid outcome: Individuals, overall, do not pay attention to airline safety demonstration videos. At the same time, it is important to highlight the finding that, at the very least, individuals who were made to feel efficacious in surviving the crash perceived they could survive. An explanation of the utility of these results follows, offering some potential extensions of this research.

Extant persuasion research (e.g., Witte, 1992, 1994) suggests individuals can have cognitive or emotional responses to fear-inducing material. In this study, the topic of airplane crashes induced some level of emotional response (likely fear) in all participants, but those who read a message that made them feel efficacious in terms of their ability to survive an airplane crash had less of an emotional response than those who were told they could do nothing to avert the potential of death should they be onboard an airplane that crashed. Thus, future research should use this different manipulation of efficacy, in terms of connecting it with the message. Another extension of this research concerns the manner in which mortality salience is induced. Indeed, Lancaster et al.'s (2015) results suggest that mortality salience might be induced as a result on the emotional fear that is triggered by a life-threatening situation. Considering that previous research guided by TMT (e.g., Harmon-Jones et al., 1997; Rosenblatt, Greenberg, Solomon, Pyszczynski, & Lyon, 1989) has used the two-item manipulation of mortality salience, perhaps alternative means of manipulating mortality salience are not effectively picking up on the presence or absence of this phenomenon. Thus, TMT scholars might consider continuing to refine manipulation checks that pick up on mortality salience.

On a deeper level, the present findings are potentially indicative of broader potentials for the integration of fear and TMT in future research. Specifically, this study did not have a successful manipulation of mortality salience, and participants exhibited no significant differences in message recall based on the death salience conditions. One explanation for this finding is, consistent with arguments earlier in this chapter, that death may be omnipresent but distal in terms of arousing fear. For example, in the present study, participants may have been aware of the potential for death (as a result of aviation disaster), yet their fear of death was not necessarily aroused by making mortality salient. Indeed, the fear may have been associated more strongly with the proximal issue of the potential for death as the result of an airplane crash. Put another way, fear may be the driving mechanism of making mortality salient when events leave individuals confronted with the realization that they might die. Indeed, a potentially deadly event may lead individuals to death salience, but only if fear is activated. Self-efficacy may be key to inducing fear, and by extension, death salience. As a result, individuals may be fearful of events that might lead to death, rather than the idea of death itself, suggesting that fear might be an important predecessor of mortality salience.

Fear as a Means of Inducing Mortality Salience?
An Integrated Model

Overall, Lancaster et al.'s (2015) research indicated that participants had an emotional response to the stimulus materials presented to them in the study. This emotion may have been fear, which is likely because flying and/or crashing in a commercial airplane is a topic that evokes a fearful response. Thus, rather than paying attention to the video as a means of assuaging mortality salience, participants may have responded to the fear associated with dying in a commercial airplane crash. In keeping with this potential distinction between death and fear, forthcoming scholarship will examine this potential distinction between fear of death and fear of events that might lead to death. Whereas TMT posits that individuals will respond in predictable ways to the anxiety associated with realizing they are mortal and will die, an alternative manner of thinking might place mortality salience as the outcome of a threat that activates fear brought about by a situation that may lead to death. Thus, instead of focusing on the anxiety posited to be associated with making the eventuality of death salient, this chapter includes a proposed model of fear and death salience (see Figure 10.1), in which an individual is presented with a threat that leads to death salience through the experience of fear. Much like EPPM, the fear and perceived efficacy influence an adaptive response to the fear.

Fear and mortality salience, being two distinct constructs, may nonetheless coexist, such that the fear of death by a given cause may heighten awareness of mortality. Even though the fear remains caused by some event or occurrence that may lead to one's demise, this fear may trigger death awareness, thereby influencing individuals to respond as a means of guarding against this existential awareness of the potential for impending mortality. Therefore, it is possible that elements of EPPM might fit into a model that also includes mortality salience, and results in adaptive responses to the fear-inducing event. Specifically, this

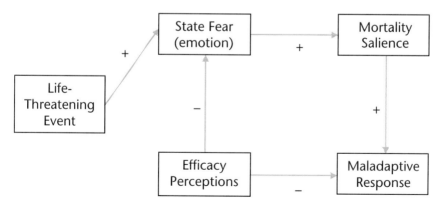

FIGURE 10.1 Proposed Conceptual Model for Fear, Efficacy, Mortality Salience, and Adaptive Responses

model posits that a life-threatening event is positively related to the experience of state fear, conceptualized as an emotional response to the potentially deadly situation. This fear is related positively to mortality-salience induction, which is in turn related to a maladaptive response (i.e., addressing the fear, but not the threat). Efficacy perceptions are negatively related to state fear, as well as negatively related to maladaptive responses.

Overall, the model indicates that the presence of a potentially life-threatening event will induce fear among individuals in the threatening situation. The fear that results from this situation leads to induction of mortality salience, because individuals become aware of the potential for their death to occur due to the situation in which they find themselves (e.g., boarding an airplane). This mortality salience should relate positively to maladaptive responses, because the process is emotional in nature. Furthermore, the assessments of efficacy should be negatively related to maladaptive responses, because feeling efficacious should make individuals believe that they can do something to help themselves get out of the threatening situation.

Concluding Thoughts

This chapter included a primary argument that mortality salience and fear associated with events that have the potential to lead to death are related yet distinct constructs. In the case of individuals confronting events that might lead to their demise, fear may be the contributing factor that leads to mortality becoming salient. Using the example of the airline safety demonstration video study, the chapter also included a case for the distinction between fear and mortality salience. In essence, individuals may be aware that they will someday die, but this fear is likely held in a distal status, out of the realm of thought, until it is activated. Nonetheless, it is a fearful event that activates fear in the mind of individuals who experience the event. This fear, rooted in the possibility of death, activates mortality salience. This model, although hitherto untested, proposes that the integration of elements of TMT and EPPM might be useful in examining mortality-salience induction by means other than self-reflection. Not only might this model aid in conducting research related to mortality-salience induction, but it might serve as an alternative explanation regarding the place of efficacy in this area of research. Indeed, as the title suggests, death may be constantly looming in the background, but people may not begin to think about it until they have experienced some fear-inducing event that could end their lives.

References

Arndt, J., Cook, A., & Routledge, C. (2004). The blueprint of terror management: Understanding the cognitive architecture of psychological defense against the awareness of death. In J. Greenberg, S. L., Koole & T. Pyszczynski (Eds.), *Handbook of experimental existential psychology* (pp. 35–53). New York: Guilford.

Arndt, J., Greenberg, J., Pyszczynski, T., & Solomon, S. (1997). Subliminal exposure to death-related stimuli increases defense of the cultural worldview. *Psychological Science*, *8*, 379–385. doi:10.1111/j.1467–9280.1997.tb00429.x

Bassett, J. F., & Connelly, J. N. (2011). Terror management and reactions to undocumented immigrants: Mortality salience increases aversion to culturally dissimilar others. *The Journal of Social Psychology*, *151*, 117–120. doi:10.1080/00224540903365562

Beck, K. H., & Frankel, A. (1981). A conceptualization of threat communications and protective health behavior. *Social Psychology Quarterly*, *44*, 204–217. doi:10.2307/3033834

Becker, E. (1962). *The birth and death of meaning: A perspective in psychiatry and anthropology.* New York, NY: The Free Press of Glencoe.

Becker, E. (1973). *The denial of death.* New York: Simon & Schuster.

Burke, B. L., Kosloff, S., Landau, M. J. (2013). Death goes to the polls: A meta-analysis of mortality salience effects on political attitudes. *Political Psychology*, *34*, 183–200. doi:10.1111/pops.12005

Burke, B. L., Martens, A., & Faucher, E. H. (2010). Two decades of terror management theory: A meta-analysis of mortality salience research. *Personality and Social Psychology Review*, *14*, 155–195. doi:10.1177/1088868309352321

Buss, D. M. (1997). Human social motivation in evolutionary perspective: Grounding terror management theory. *Psychological Inquiry*, *8*, 22–26. doi:10.1207/s153279 65pli0801_3

Capafons, J. I., Sosa, C. D., & Viña, C. M. (1999). A reattributional training program as a therapeutic strategy for flying phobia. *Journal of Behavior Therapy & Experimental Psychiatry*, *30*, 259–272. doi:10.1016/S0005–7916(99)00028–2

Easterling, D., & Leventhal, H. (1989). The contribution of concrete cognition to emotion: Neutral symptoms as elicitors of worry about cancer. *Journal of Applied Psychology*, *74*, 787–796. doi:10.1037/0021–9010.74.5.787

Greenberg, J., Pyszczynski, T., & Solomon, S. (1986). The causes and consequences of a need for self-esteem: A terror management theory. In R. F. Baumeister (Ed.), *Public self and private self* (pp. 189–212). New York: Springer.

Greenberg, J., Solomon, S., & Pyszczynski, T. (1997). Terror management theory of self-esteem and cultural worldviews. *Advances in Experimental Social Psychology*, *29*, 61–138. doi:10.1016/S0065–2601(08)60016–7

Harmon-Jones, E., Simon, L., Greenberg, J., Pyszczynski, T., Solomon, S., & McGregor, H. (1997). Terror management theory and self-esteem: Evidence that increased self-esteem reduces mortality salience effects. *Journal of Personality and Social Psychology*, *72*, 24–36. doi:10.1037/0022–3514.72.1.24

Hovland, C. I., Janis, I. L., & Kelly, H. H. (1953). *Communication and persuasion: Psychological studies of opinion change.* New Haven, CT: Yale University Press.

Lancaster, A., Bowman, N. D., & Harvell, L. A. (2015, November). *Flying blind to safety: Mortality salience, efficacy, and message recall of airline safety demonstrations.* Presented at the annual meeting of the National Communication Association in Las Vegas, NV.

Leventhal, H. (1970). Findings and theory in the study of fear communications. In L. Berkowitz (Ed.), *Advances in experimental social psychology* (Vol. 5, pp. 119–186). New York: Academic Press.

Leventhal, H. (1971). Fear appeals and persuasion: The differentiation of a motivational construct. *American Journal of Public Health*, *61*, 1208–1224. doi:10.2105/ajph.61.6.1208

McGuire, W. J. (1968). Personality and susceptibility to social influence. In E. Borgatta & W. Lambert (Eds.), *Handbook of personality theory and research* (pp. 1130–1187). Chicago: Rand McNally.

McGuire, W. J. (1969). The nature of attitudes and attitude change. In G. Lindzey & E. Aronson (Eds.), *The handbook of social psychology* (Vol. 3, pp. 136–314). Reading, MA: Addison-Wesley.

Navarrete, C. D., & Fessler, D. M. T. (2005). Normative bias and adaptive challenges: A relational approach to coalitional psychology and a critique of terror management theory. *Evolutionary Psychology, 3,* 297–325. Retrieved from: http://www.epjournal.net/wp-content/uploads/ep03297325.pdf

Navarrete, C. D., Kurzban, R., Fessler, D. M. T., & Kirkpatrick, L. A. (2004). Anxiety and intergroup bias: Terror management or coalitional psychology? *Group Processes & Intergroup Relations, 7,* 370–397. doi:10.1177/1368430204046144

Noland, D. (2007, July). *Safest seat on a plane: PM investigates how to survive a crash.* Popular Mechanics. Retrieved from http://www.popularmechanics.com/technology/aviation/safety/4219452

Nyatanga, B., & de Vocht, H. (2006). Towards a definition of death anxiety. *International Journal of Palliative Nursing, 12,* 410–413. doi:10.12968/ijpn.2006.12.9.21868

Pyszczynski, T., Greenberg, J., & Solomon, S. (1997). Why do we need what we need? A terror management perspective on the roots of human social motivation. *Pyschological Inquiry, 8,* 1–20. doi:10.1207/s15327965pli0801_1

Pyszczynski, T., Greenberg, J., Solomon, S., Arndt, J., & Schimel, J. (2004). Why do people need self-esteem? A theoretical and empirical review. *Psychological Bulletin, 130,* 435–468. doi:10.1037/0033–2909.130.3.435

Rogers, R. W. (1975). A protection motivation theory of fear appeals and attitude change. *Journal of Psychology, 91,* 93–114.

Rogers, R. W. (1983). Cognitive and physiological processes in fear appeals and attitude change: A revised theory of protection motivation. In J. Cacioppo & R. Petty (Eds.), *Social psychophysiology* (pp. 153–176). New York: Guilford.

Rosenblatt, A., Greenberg, J., Solomon, S., Pyszczynski, T., & Lyon, D. (1989). Evidence for terror management theory: I. The effects of mortality salience on reactions to those who violate or uphold cultural values. *Journal of Personality and Social Psychology, 57,* 681–690. doi:10.1037/0022–3514.57.4.681

Solomon, S., Greenberg, J., & Pyszczynski, T. (2000). Pride and prejudice: Fear of death and social behavior. *Current Directions is Psychological Science, 9,* 200–204. doi:10.1111/1467–8721.00094

Solomon, S., Greenberg, J., & Pyszczynski, T. (2004). The cultural animal: Twenty years of terror management theory and research. In J. Greenberg, S. L. Koole & T. Pyszczynski (Eds.), *Handbook of experimental existential psychology* (pp. 13–34). New York: Guilford Press.

Sutton, S. R. (1982). Fear-arousing communications: A critical examination of theory and research. In J. R. Eiser (Ed.), *Social psychology and behavioral medicine* (pp. 303–337). London: Wiley.

Sutton, S. R., & Eiser, J. R. (1984). The effect of fear-arousing communications on cigarette smoking: An expectancy-value approach. *Journal of Behavioral Medicine, 7,* 13–33. doi:10.1007/BF00845345

Taubman-Ben-Ari, O., & Findler, L. (2005). Proximal and distal effects of mortality salience on willingness to engage in health promoting behavior along the life span. *Psychology & Health, 20,* 303–318. doi:10.1080/08870440512331317661

Weise, D. R., Arciszewski, T., Verlhiac, J., Pyszczynski, T., & Greenberg, J. (2012). Terror management and attitudes toward immigrants: Differential effects of mortality salience for low and high right-wing authoritarians. *European Psychologist, 17,* 63–72. doi:10.1027/1016–9040/a000056

Witte, K. (1992). Putting the fear back into fear appeals: The extended parallel process model. *Communication Monographs, 59,* 329–349. doi:10.1080/03637759209376276

Witte, K. (1994). Fear control and danger control: A test of the extended parallel process model (EPPM). *Communication Monographs, 61,* 113–134. doi:10.1080/0363775940 9376328

Zaleskiewicz, T., Gasiorowska, A., Kesebir, P., Luszczynska, A., & Pyszczynski, T. (2013). Money and the fear of death: The symbolic power of money as an existential anxiety buffer. *Journal of Economic Psychology, 36,* 55–67. doi:10.1016/j.joep.2013.02.008

11

GENDER AND TERROR MANAGEMENT THEORY

Stacey A. Passalacqua

The Roman writer Publilius Syrus famously reflected, "As men, we are all equal in the presence of death." What of women, Publilius? Centuries later, gender is frequently referenced in mortality-salience studies. Despite the popularity of its inclusion in research, however, no synthesis of gender and terror management theory (TMT) exists (see Chapter 1 for a review of TMT). This chapter is not intended to be exhaustive—that is, rather than serving as a comprehensive review or meta-analysis of work that has been done thus far in the realm of gender and TMT, several lines of research are selected to illustrate the complex role that gender plays in TMT and the range of effects that mortality salience can have on thoughts about gender and gender-related issues. Lastly, future directions are suggested to advance research in the area of gender and TMT.

Differences in Anxiety

Women consistently self-report higher levels of death anxiety than men, most often assessed via the Death Anxiety Scale (DAS) (Dattel & Neimeyer, 1990; Kastenbaum, 2000; Russac, Gatliff, Reece, & Spottswood, 2007). This phenomenon is not surprising, given that starting roughly around age 6, women have greater general and trait anxiety and higher levels of clinical anxiety than men, with females suffering from almost all types of anxiety disorders at 1.5–2 times the rates of males (Armstrong & Khawaja, 2002; Costa, Terracciano, & McCrae, 2001; McLean & Anderson, 2009; McLean, Asnaani, Litz, & Hoffmann, 2011). McLean and Anderson (2009) identify gender role socialization as a key contributor to the unequal rates of anxiety experienced by men and women. They explain that anxiety is perceived as more compatible with the female gender role than the male gender role, leading to respective tolerance or discouragement that reinforces stereotypes. In terms of coping, females are more encouraged to discuss their emotions, whereas males are expected to gain control of their feelings and engage in problem-solving—these processes further exacerbate differences in anxiety (McLean & Anderson, 2009).

Furthermore, women's death anxiety has been found to fluctuate differently than men's as they age. In a study by Russac and colleagues (2007), levels of death anxiety were at their highest for both men and women in their 20s and declined until women reached their early 50s and experienced a second spike that men did not experience. Death anxiety stabilized at similarly low levels for men and women by age 60 (Russac et al., 2007). Several possible explanations for women's secondary spike in death anxiety are offered. The spike often coincides with the average onset of menopause for women, a life change that "marks the end of a woman's reproductive career, and therefore serves as a stark reminder that she is growing older" (Russac et al., 2007, p. 558). Additionally, Russac and colleagues (2007) suggest that the absence of maternal responsibilities may leave women time to ponder their lives and, consequently, their deaths.

However, the majority of studies that have investigated the degree to which participants perceive death as threatening (most commonly assessed via the Threat Index) have not detected any sex differences (Dattel & Neimeyer, 1990; Russac et al., 2007). Death threat as it operates in the Threat Index can be understood as the extent to which death is seen as incompatible with one's self-concept and existence (Rigdon, Epting, Neimeyer, & Krieger, 1979). That men and women perceive death as equally threatening but women consciously experience (or report to experience) greater anxiety about it was suggested by Burke, Martens, and Faucher (2010) as a possible influence on reactions to mortality salience. Greenberg, Pyszczynski, Solomon, Simon, and Breus (1994) have proposed that expression of negative emotions (such as fear) about death might be responsible for reduced worldview defense. Furthermore, mortality salience inductions are understood to be most effective when thoughts of death have been activated but then fade from conscious awareness (Greenberg et al., 1994). The rationale follows that if women's higher levels of anxiety about death are indicative of greater consciousness of and preoccupation with their mortality, then mortality-salience inductions may operate differently on them, with thoughts of death remaining more accessible and persistent for women than men. However, in their meta-analysis of mortality-salience research, Burke, Martens, and Faucher (2010) found that the overall magnitude of death defenses was not moderated by gender.

Gender in Mortality-Salience Studies

Burke and colleagues (2010) did find gender to be the most frequently used moderator in mortality-salience studies. Gender did not serve as a significant moderator of mortality-salience effects across studies but moderated effects within various individual studies, indicating that men and women may differ in death defense strategies in some contexts but not others (Burke et al., 2010). For example, mortality salience was found in studies to increase men's nationalistic word accessibility and women's relationship word accessibility; male's but not female's attraction to seductive opposite-sex targets; and the degree to which risk was appealing to men but not women. Burke and colleagues (2010) reference numerous studies, however, that produced mixed results or no findings regarding gender differences in mortality-salience responses. Research findings continue to echo those described in Burke's et al.'s (2010) meta-analysis with an assortment of gender differences, mixed results, and no differences among men and women in mortality-salience conditions. Rather than discussing the array of study manipulations that have or have not evoked various death defenses among their male and female participants, the focus henceforth will be on areas of socially significant mortality-salience research in which there have been gender differences or in which the primary issue is clearly concerned with gender.

"Pro-woman" Attitudes

The relationship between gender and death defenses is not unidirectional—gender has been shown to impact death defenses, but death defenses also impact gender-related issues. Fritsche and Jonas (2005) investigated the effect of mortality salience on men's and women's "pro-woman" attitudes, assessed via evaluations of course proposals that included courses promoting women (i.e., courses on gender equity and female leadership). Findings revealed that in the control condition (participants who had been asked about dental pain) there was no difference between male and female evaluations of the proposed pro-woman courses. However, among participants who were asked to reflect on their own deaths, there was a significant sex difference in evaluations of the pro-woman courses—women evaluated the courses more highly, and males provided more negative evaluations. Importantly, evaluations of proposed courses unrelated to gender remained the same in both the control and mortality-salience conditions. These findings are consistent with TMT—espousing positions favorable to one's own group (as women did by positively evaluating pro-woman courses) and derogating positions unfavorable to one's own group (as men did by negatively evaluating pro-woman courses) is a method of worldview defense, a primary anxiety-buffering mechanism in TMT (Fritsche & Jonas, 2005).

Group Identification

Group identification has the potential to bolster self-esteem and thus protect from existential threats; however, when negative aspects of or stereotypes about a member's group are made salient, individuals may engage in decreased group identification to maintain self-esteem. Arndt, Greenberg, Schimel, Pyszczynski, and Solomon (2003) have investigated this phenomenon as it relates to gender and ethnicity. Arndt et al. (2003; Study 1) assessed whether stereotype threat reduced women's ingroup affiliation in the face of mortality salience. They led female participants to believe that they were going to either take the verbal or math portion of the SAT and assessed the degree to which the participants perceived themselves as similar to other women after exposing them to either the control or mortality-salience conditions. Of note, the participants who believed they would take the math exam were asked to indicate their gender and age on the cover page—Spencer, Steele, and Quinn (1999) have shown that reminders of women's gender when they are facing a math test constitute a stereotype threat (as cited in Arndt et al., 2003). Taking the verbal portion of the SAT, on the other hand, represented a low stereotype threat. Those who were in the mortality-salience condition and thought that they would be taking the verbal portion of the SAT exhibited significant identification with other women (assessed via a social projection measure), whereas participants in the mortality-salience condition who thought they would be taking the math portion did not identify with other women any more so than participants in the control group. Notably, in the presence of stereotype threat, the typical group identification evoked by mortality salience is absent.

Individuals hold membership in multiple groups, and the worldviews of these groups do not always align. For example, Americans as a group value individualism and uniqueness, whereas women as a group value inclusion and community—American women thus possess various social identities and, consequently, a multitude of possible motives that might influence their responses to mortality salience (Walsh & Smith, 2007). Walsh and Smith (Study 1) sought to determine whether American college-aged women would be influenced by gender norms of inclusiveness or general cultural norms of uniqueness following mortality-salience induction when primed with either gender identity or self-identity. Findings revealed that in the control group, being primed with gender or self-identity made no difference in the degree to which participants identified with (i.e., felt connected and similar to) other women. However, in the mortality-salience condition, participants primed with gender versus self-identity were significantly more likely to identify with other women. Furthermore, complimentary pens were offered to the participants to test whether they would choose the "unique" pen. The experimenter grabbed five pens out of a clear bag containing an equal mix of green and orange pens (all with black ink); these green and orange were chosen based on past research showing no difference in preference between these colors. With each participant, the experimenter presented a selection of four pens of one color and one pen of the other color. The one pen that differed in color from the other four was considered the unique pen. In the control condition, being primed with gender or self-identity had no effect on pen choice; in the mortality-salience condition, the women primed with gender identity were significantly less likely to choose the unique pen (indicating a desire for inclusiveness) compared to those women who were primed with self-identity (who asserted uniqueness via their choice). Participants' behavior in the face of mortality salience reflected values consistent with the identities that were primed; such findings illustrate that gender cannot be expected to serve as a straightforward predictive variable when individuals occupy multiple social roles, some of which will be more relevant at different times and in different contexts.

Leaders and Gender

Another line of research concerning mortality salience and gender is that of Hoyt, Simon, and Reid (2009), who explored these concepts in relation to preferences for leader gender. Hoyt and colleagues (2009) were interested to see whether ingroup bias or stereotype bias was activated by death-related thoughts when participants' preferences for a male or female leader were assessed. In their first study in which participants were asked to "cast their vote" after reading statements from a fictional male and female political candidate, there was no significant difference in whom men and women voted for; however, in the mortality-salience condition, men strongly preferred the male candidate and women strongly preferred the female candidate, confirming an ingroup bias effect. In Hoyt et al.'s (2009) second study, candidates' descriptions were manipulated to include either communal or agentic characteristics. In the control condition, men and women preferred the candidate of their own sex when the candidate was portrayed as agentic; when the candidate of their own sex was portrayed as communal, participants had no candidate preference. In the mortality-salience condition, however, participant preferences became more complex. Women asked to reflect on their own death preferred the female candidate over the male candidate when she was agentic and he was communal; when the male candidate was agentic and the female candidate was communal, the male candidate was preferred. Men asked to reflect on their own death preferred the male candidate over the female candidate when he was agentic and she was communal; however, when the male candidate was communal and the female candidate was agentic, neither candidate was preferred.

In an effort to further understand the findings of Hoyt et al. (2009), Hoyt, Simon, & Innella (2011) sought to determine whether mortality salience increased the application of leadership stereotypes or whether it affected actual beliefs about what characteristics make for an effective leader, particularly in regard to perceptions of agency and communality. Agency is a stereotypically masculine trait, whereas communality is a stereotypically feminine trait. After participants were prompted to write about an upcoming exam (the control condition) or their own death, they were asked a series of questions to assess their implicit leadership theories. Both male and female participants in the mortality-salience condition rated agentic qualities (e.g., being ambitious, competitive, independent, etc.) as more essential to effective leadership than did male and female participants in the control group; mortality salience had no effect, however, on the degree to which participants rated communal qualities (e.g., being likable, warm, supportive, etc.) as essential to leadership, compared to the control group. In terms of gender differences, women overall rated communal qualities as being more important to leadership than men did. Hoyt et al. (2011) note that their finding about a shift toward more masculine implicit leadership theories in the face of mortality salience has distinct implications in modern society with its multitude of threats to the safety and security of its members. Other research on mortality salience and gender brings with it additional social implications, though of a different variety.

Objectification

Such socially significant research includes the work of Grabe, Routledge, Cook, Andersen, and Arndt (2005), who investigated the effect of mortality salience on objectification of the female body. The objectification of women's bodies is a prominent and pervasive cultural feature in male-dominated societies and is often internalized by female members of these societies. Grabe and colleagues (2005) surmised that "to the extent that the perception of the female body as an object represents a widely endorsed cultural worldview, individuals (both men and women), may be motivated to endorse this belief about women in an effort to gain the security that comes from adopting dominant cultural worldviews" (p. 34). Questionnaires prompted participants to write about either their own death or dental pain and assessed their levels of self-objectification and general objectification of women. Results revealed that female participants reminded of their mortality objectified other females significantly more than did female participants in the control condition. Male participants objectified women similarly in both the mortality salience and control group—Grabe and colleagues (2005) note that this is likely due to the fact that male participants already objectified women at high levels in the control condition. Male participants objectified women roughly twice as much as female participants did in the control condition, but in the mortality-salience condition, there was no significant difference in male and female participants' levels of objectification of women. That is, female participants in the mortality-salience condition objectified women to the same degree that male participants did. Regarding self-objectification, there was no significant difference between male and female participants in the control group, but in the mortality-salience condition, women were significantly more likely to self-objectify. Notably, both women and men for whom their body was a source of self-esteem were more likely to self-objectify when exposed to the mortality-salience manipulation—this finding supports TMT's tenet that individuals seek to bolster self-esteem as a death defense mechanism in mortality-salience conditions.

Objectification of the female body occurs in and perpetuates a sociocultural context of gender inequality and is understood to have serious negative consequences. However, cultural beliefs provide individuals with a sense of order and purpose, and despite their detriment to some members, offer a source of security in the face of existential fears (Grabe et al., 2005). In the case of objectification, "Even though women may prefer not to endorse an objectified woman worldview . . . when they are trying to manage concerns about mortality they may embrace the existential security provided by well-established and widely accepted cultural beliefs about their bodies" (Grabe et al., 2005, p. 36). Societies plagued by poverty and war also tend to feature higher levels of violence against and exploitation of females—the connection between these variables would be worth exploring from a TMT perspective based on Grabe et al.'s (2005) findings.

Goldenberg and Roberts (2004, 2010) have theorized that objectification of the female body, despite its negative consequences, serves the function of reducing the terror of mortality. Women's bodies, particularly because of their reproductive functions (i.e., menstruation, pregnancy, lactation), are considered to be closer to nature and to other animals, which is theorized to be threatening—to be reminded of humans' animal nature is to be reminded that humans, like all living things, will one day die. Viewing an individual as an object (in the case of women, focusing more on their appearance than their personhood) is argued via a TMT perspective to offer separation from "creatureliness" and its accompanying mortality (Goldenberg, Heflick, Vaes, Motyl, & Greenberg, 2009).

Morris, Goldenberg, and Heflick (2014) conducted a series of five studies to examine whether participants (particularly women) would respond to mortality-salience inductions and exposure to reminders of women's reproductive functions with self-objectification. Morris and colleagues (2014) found that this was indeed the case: "Across five studies and three different aspects of female reproductive functioning—pregnancy, menstruation, and breastfeeding—reminders of mortality led women, but not men, to respond in a manner indicative of a more object-like, less human, view of the self" (Morris et al., 2014, p.193). Morris et al. (2014) bring up the concern that there is greater willingness to harm an object, and objectification of women puts them at risk for a multitude of negative outcomes.

Continuing the TMT approach to objectification of females, Morris and Goldenberg (2015) investigated whether women would be considered more attractive under mortality-salience conditions if they were objectified—literally. Male and female participants were asked to reflect on either pain or their own death and then view an advertisement of a sexualized woman merged with an object or an altered version of the image that separated the woman from the object. The two versions of objectification advertisements shown to participants were a woman in a bikini merged with a beer bottle and a woman who was part of a calendar. The control versions of the aforementioned advertisements were, respectively, a woman on a plain background next to a beer bottle and a woman holding a calendar. Questions about the attractiveness of the woman in the advertisement followed. Morris and Goldenberg (2015) found that men in the mortality-salience condition rated the model in the advertisement as more attractive when she was objectified compared to when she was separate from an object; conversely, men in the control condition rated the model as more attractive when she was separated from the object compared to when she was objectified. There were no significant effects found for women.

Conclusion

One clear pattern that arises from the data on gender and TMT seems to be that death defenses frequently involve thoughts or behavior based on gender stereotypes and traditional beliefs about gender. A selection of studies has been addressed here as illustrations of this phenomenon, but a meta-analysis focusing on this point would do much to advance work in the area. Stereotypical thoughts and behavior, on the part of men and women in mortality-salience conditions, contribute to ideology that is hegemonic and limiting for both genders. Whether death defenses stem from such ideas as male leaders being best, or from beliefs that women's reproductive functions make them animalistic, the perpetuation of such mind-sets benefits no one, despite the supposed utility of related defenses to reduce the terror of mortality. Unfortunately, to alter subconscious processes at work in TMT would be challenging enough in and of itself; beyond that, worldviews and sources of self-esteem based on these worldviews are culturally embedded and have been internalized by members, making change a worthwhile but hefty challenge.

Researchers possess demographic data that allow them to cleanly divide male and female participants into distinct categories for comparison, making gender the most commonly analyzed moderator in mortality-salience studies (Burke et al., 2010). However, gender cannot independently predict responses to mortality salience, though in particular conditions and if a particular identity is made salient, being male or female can increase the likelihood that a participant will react in a particular manner in an experimental condition. Many of the findings from research on gender and TMT are intriguing, precisely because they raise more questions than they do provide answers. TMT offers a unique perspective on issues such as the objectification of women, ideas about and endorsement of leaders, sexuality, risky behavior, and much more. Rather than simply continuing to catalog gender-related morality salience responses in this or that context, it is important to justify the inclusion of gender in the larger framework of TMT, to identify patterns in the existing research, begin seriously theorizing, and address finding implications more fully if we are to advance our understanding in this realm. To be clear, oversimplifying gender in TMT would be a gross injustice; this call is one to recognize the complexity at the intersection of these concepts and to begin thinking critically about the twists and turns of these knots rather than attempting to untangle that which cannot and should not be untangled.

References

Armstrong, K. A., & Khawaja, N. G. (2002). Gender differences in anxiety: An investigation of the symptoms, cognitions, and sensitivity towards anxiety in a nonclinical population. *Behavior and Cognitive Psychology, 30,* 227–231. doi:10.1017/S1352465802002114

Arndt, J., Greenberg, J., Schimel, J., Pyszczynski, T., & Solomon, S. (2003). To belong or not to belong, that is the question: Terror management and identification with gender and ethnicity. *Journal of Personality and Social Psychology, 83*(1), 26–43. doi:10.1037//0022-3514.83.1.26

Burke, B. L., Martens, A., & Faucher, E. H. (2010). Two decades of terror management theory: A meta-analysis of mortality salience research. *Personality and Social Psychology Review, 14*(2), 155–195. doi:10.1177/1088868309352321

Costa, P. T., Jr., Terracciano, A., & McCrae, R. R. (2001). Gender differences in personality traits across cultures: Robust and surprising findings. *Journal of Personality and Social Psychology, 81*(2), 322–331. doi:10.1037//0022-3514.81.2.322

Dattel, A. R., & Neimeyer, R. A. (1990). Sex differences in death anxiety: Testing the emotional expression hypothesis. *Death Studies, 14,* 1–11. doi:10.1080/07481189008252341

Fritsche, I., & Jonas, E. (2005). Gender conflict and worldview defence. *British Journal of Social Psychology, 44,* 571–581. doi:10.1348/014466605X27423

Goldenberg, J., Heflick, N., Vaes, J., Motyl, M., & Greenberg, J. (2009). Of mice and men, and objectified women: A terror management account of infrahumanization. *Group Processes & Intergroup Relationship, 12*(6), 763–776. doi:10.1177/1368430209340569

Goldenberg, J. L., & Roberts, T. A. (2004). The beast within the beauty: An existential perspective on the objectification and condemnation of women. In J. Greenberg, S. L. Koole & T. Pyszczynski (Eds.), *Handbook of experimental existential psychology* (pp. 71–85). New York: Guilford Press.

Goldenberg, J. L., & Roberts, T. A. (2010). The birthmark: An existential account of why women are objectified. In R. Calogero, S. Tantleff-Dunn & J. K. Thompson (Eds.), *The objectification of women: Innovative directions in research and practice* (pp. 77–100). Washington, DC: American Psychological Association.

Grabe, S., Routledge, C., Cook, A., Andersen, C., & Arndt, J. (2005). In defense of the body: The effect of mortality salience on female body objectification. *Psychology of Women Quarterly, 29,* 33–37. doi:10.1111/j.1471–6402.2005.00165.x

Greenberg, J., Pyszczynski, T., Solomon, S., Simon, L., & Breus, M. (1994). Role of consciousness and accessibility of death-related thoughts in mortality salience effects. *Journal of Personality and Social Psychology, 67*(4), 627–637. doi:10.1037/0022-3514.67.4.627

Hoyt, C. L., Simon, S., & Innella, A. N. (2011). Taking a turn toward the masculine: The impact of mortality salience on implicit leadership theories. *Basic and Applied Social Psychology, 33*(4), 374. doi:10.1080/01973533.2011.614173

Hoyt, C. L., Simon, S., & Reid, L. (2009). Choosing the best (wo)man for the job: The effects of mortality salience, sex and gender stereotypes on leader evaluations. *Leadership Quarterly, 20,* 233–246. doi:10.1016/j.leaqua.2009.01.016

Kastenbaum, R. (2000). *The psychology of death* (3rd ed.). New York: Springer.

McLean, C. P., & Anderson, E. R. (2009). Brave men and timid women? A review of the gender differences in fear and anxiety. *Clinical Psychology Review, 29,* 496–505. doi:10.1016/j.cpr.2009.05.003

McLean, C. P., Asnaani, A., Litz, B. T., & Hoffmann, S. G. (2011). Gender differences in anxiety disorders: Prevalence, course of illness, comorbidity and burden of illness. *Journal of Psychiatric Research, 45,* 1027–1035. doi:10.1016/j.jpsychires.2011.03.006

Morris, K. L., & Goldenberg, J. (2015). Objects become her: The role of mortality salience on men's attraction to literally objectified women. *Journal of Experimental Social Psychology, 56,* 69–72. doi:10.1016/j.jesp.2014.09.005

Morris, K. L., Goldenberg, J. L., & Heflick, N. A. (2014). Trio of terror (pregnancy, menstruation, and breastfeeding): An existential function of literal self-objectification among women. *Journal of Personality and Social Psychology, 107*(1), 181–198. doi:10.1037/a0036493

Rigdon, M. A., Epting, F. R., Neimeyer, R. A., & Krieger, S. R. (1979). The threat index: A research report. *Death Education, 3,* 245–270. doi:10.1080/07481187908252956

Russac, R. J., Gatliff, C., Reece, M., & Spottswood, D. (2007). Death anxiety across the adult years: An examination of age and gender effects. *Death Studies, 31,* 549–561. doi:10.1080/07481180701356936

Spencer, S. J., Steele, C. M., & Quinn, D. M. (1999). Stereotype threat and women's math performance. *Journal of Experimental Social Psychology, 35,* 4–28. doi:10.1006/jesp.1998.1373

Walsh, P. E., & Smith, J. L. (2007). Opposing standards within the cultural worldview: Terror management and American women's desire for uniqueness versus inclusiveness. *Psychology of Women Quarterly, 31,* 103–113. doi:10.1111/j.1471–6402.2007.00335.x

12

USING PERSUASION TO SAVE LIVES

A Counterattack Plan for Suicide, Substance Abuse, and Psychological Distress Prevention

Michael J. Sherratt, Grant C. Corser, and Hilary Monson

Prior to the War on Terrorism, the United States Army had a lower rate of suicide and substance abuse than the general public (Kuehn, 2009). However, in 2008 the U.S. Army suicide rate surpassed the U.S. civilian rate and continued to escalate (Department of Defense, 2010, 2011). The change in the suicide rate among soldiers who are actively in the U.S. Army is alarming. Equally alarming is a recent report issued by the U.S. Department of Veteran's Affairs that estimates a suicide rate of 22 U.S. veterans per day (Kemp & Bossarte, 2012). One factor that appears to be influencing this rate of suicide increase is the reluctance of military personnel to participate in mental health services. This reluctance to seek mental health services is not new (Christian, Stivers, & Sammons, 2009; Moore, 2011); however, seeking mental health services during periods of active combat, and during times of war may be especially important. In fact, it is estimated that less than 10% of military personnel with issues relating to mental health participate in mental health services (Hoge et al., 2006). Among the remaining 90% of U.S. soldiers with mental health challenges, it is believed they do their best to conceal, ignore, or try to overcome their psychological disparity on their own.

Programs such as Ask Care Escort (ACE), Applied Suicide Intervention Skills Training (ASIST), and many official briefs have given soldiers efficacy in suicide and substance abuse intervention with their fellow soldiers. Currently, these efforts to overcome the loss of life and dysfunction because of suicide and substance abuse have in many ways been addressed as separate elements. However, these well intentioned educational briefs have not been well received by military personnel and colloquially are known as *death by PowerPoint* to the soldiers they are trying to influence (Jobes, 2013). In 2009, the United States Army implemented a resiliency training program as part of the Comprehensive Soldier and Family Fitness program (Lester, Harms, Herian, Krasikova, & Beal, 2011). This program does appear to be successful in decreasing substance abuse (Harms, Herian, Krasikova, Vanhove, & Lester, 2013). One explanation for this program's success is the mortality-salience differences between the treatment and the control groups. This is addressed later in this chapter. The current resiliency training program can become even more successful if it exploits the extant principles of terror management theory (TMT; Greenberg, Pyszczynski, & Solomon,1986) to reduce negative stigmas associated with mental health services.

The literature is replete with studies that evidence a negative stigma associated with seeking mental health services. This stigma presents an especially strong resistance among military personnel and reduces their seeking mental health services (Britt et al., 2011; Corrigan, 2004; Hoge et al., 2004). In general, people are reluctant to admit they have mental health deficiencies and are reluctant to seek mental health services (Mak, Poon, Pun, & Cheung, 2007). This is supported by a misconception tendency to attribute mental health shortcomings to one's self (Mak et al., 2007). This tendency may be exacerbated in military culture, wherein weakness is not tolerated and continual strengthening is honored. This might account for and explain the development of the negative stigma associated with seeking mental health services because issues of mental health are perceived as antithetical to being "mentally tough." This stigma barrier is so strong that Jobes (2013) is skeptical that it will ever be overcome and postulates that the magnitude of suicide in the military is so great that unconventional and innovative approaches need to be applied in order to decrease the existing problems.

Combat exposure has been shown to be a major element in suicide among military personnel (Anestis, Bryan, Cornette, & Joiner, 2009; Selby et al., 2010). However, upon deeper analysis of this relationship, it is possible that it is not the combat exposure contributing to the suicide rate of the military, but the post hoc consequences of combat exposure. Bryan and colleagues (2013) found that combat exposure is not directly related to suicide. They suggested that combat increases the *downstream* factors in the same way child abuse increases problems in adulthood. A study by Bryan and Rudd (as cited in Bryan, Hernandez, Allison, & Clemans, 2013), which was conducted with actively suicidal soldiers, demonstrated no correlation between combat exposure and suicide attempts or suicide attempt lethality; instead, nondeployment stressors and traumas were associated with suicide attempts. In fact, in both the 2010 and 2011 Department of Defense suicide reports, it is reported that the majority of suicides by military personnel have been among those who were not deployed (Department of Defense, 2010, 2011).

Thus, it appears that focusing solely on preventing *combat*-related issues such as suicide and substance abuse issues might be counterproductive. It appears that prevention focus should be on what Bryan and colleagues (2013) refer to as the downstream factors, specifically as they relate to post-traumatic stress disorder (PTSD), substance abuse, depression, and relationship strain. Other studies show stigma being the major cause of soldiers not seeking help (Britt et al., 2011;

162 Michael J. Sherratt et al.

Corrigan, 2004; Hoge et al., 2004). In other words, the focus needs to be on decreasing the stigma of seeking mental health services to overcome the downstream factors instead of focusing on preventing these issues.

It should be noted that this brief is not designed to extinguish the mental health stigma through a means of tolerance development. That is, it is not intended to promote a sense of vulnerability nor is it loss-framed in its focus on preventing undesirable behaviors such as suicide and substance abuse. Moreover, it is designed to promote an intrinsic motivation within the individual soldier to strive for mental health fitness and strive to become mentally stronger, even if by means of seeking help from mental health professionals. Unlike previous and current briefs, the structure of this brief is *not* inconsistent with values and beliefs of the U.S. military.

This brief employs extant knowledge of decades of research on TMT (Greenberg, Pyszczynski, & Solomon, 1986). Specifically, one of TMT's fundamental postulates is that humans possess an innate defense mechanism that maintains psychological equilibrium once one has been faced with reminders of one's mortality. Apparently, even fathoming one's mortality can trigger mechanisms of defense to combat the knowledge of imminent demise. In other words, the structure of the brief will produce a magnification and validation of the beliefs and values that the soldiers already hold by applying the knowledge gained from over 400 studies that support TMT's validity.

Terror Management Theory

TMT is a robust theory that explains how humans maintain psychological equilibrium despite the knowledge that they will someday die. It also explains how humans cope with events that elicit mortality salience (MS). According to Burke, Martens, and Faucher (2010), TMT was developed to account for why individuals have a common need to create meaning and possess self-esteem. Greenberg and colleagues (1997) proposed that the ability for individuals to anticipate what is yet to come (i.e., contemplate the future), along with the human dimension to self-reflect, results in an individual's knowledge of mortality and an emotional display of anxiety and terror. Many researchers have proposed two distinct psychological mechanisms that humans engage in to manage the existential terror that is experienced because of these cognitive capacities (Greenberg, Pyszczynski, & Solomon, 1997). First, humans engage in behavior and cognitive efforts intended to confirm their cultural worldview. This allows the person to create meaning and manipulate an understanding of the world in such a way as to gain a reasonable sense of value and a sense of symbolic immortality. The second means of terror management involves behavioral and cognitive efforts that allow current life standards that are set by the individual's society and culture to be defined in such a way that an individual feels he or she is a person of value. In other words, a person is able to increase self-esteem. These two actions maintain psychological equanimity in humans after being confronted with reminders of their own mortality (Greenberg, Pyszcynski, & Solomon, 1997).

Research indicates that defenses of death anxiety can occur at proximal or distal levels. The proximal defense level is a psychological mechanism that suppresses death thoughts from conscious awareness (Arndt, Cook, & Routledge, 2004; Greenburg, Pyszczynski, Solomon, Simon, & Breus, 1994). The typical method of measuring the activation of proximal defense is by administering a word completion exercise immediately after the death salient manipulation. During the word completion exercise the participants are asked to complete word fragments. These word fragments can have multiple completions that give insight to the participants' conscious awareness. The typical mortality-salience paradigm measures about six words that could be completed to indicate accessibility of death-related thoughts. For example, COFF_ _ could be completed as COFFEE or COFFIN. Studies have shown that mortality-salient groups complete statistically less death completions than the control group. The theory maintains that after a death salient event, humans suppress the thought of death. So, when they are given the word completions, the death-related words have been suppressed resulting in participants completing the words with non-death-related words. It appears that if participants are given a distraction after the initial MS event, they then react with a distal defense against the death-related anxiety.

The distal defense is characterized as possessing a hyper-regard for one's cultural worldview (CWV) beliefs. Examples include phenomena such as a desire for stiffer penalties for non CWV compliance (Arndt, Cook, & Routledge, 2004; Greenberg, Pyszczynski, Solomon, Simon, & Breus, 1994), a greater desire to engage in dangerous behavior (if that behavior is culturally valued; Taubman-Ben-Ari, 2004), influences on political preferences (Cohen, Solomon, Maxfield, Pyszczynski, & Greenberg, 2004; Weise et al., 2008), and men's sexual attraction to women (Landau et al., 2006). To ensure a distal defense is activated, individuals must be subjected to some type of cognitive distraction after the death salience event for at least 2 minutes, with the optimal distraction interval being 7 to 20 minutes (Burke, Martens, & Faucher, 2010). An alternate method is to engage in a task that requires a high enough cognitive load to inhibit the death-thought suppression (Arndt, Greenberg, Solomon, Pyszczynski, and Simon, 1997).

One objection to using TMT theory to persuade military personnel is that they might have developed some type of resistance or inoculation to death-related content, especially during time of active deployment in war zones. However, Van den Berg and Soeters (2009) conducted a study that looked at differences between Dutch soldiers who were deployed to Iraq compared with Dutch soldiers who were in garrison. The soldiers in Iraq used less death completion words than the soldiers in garrison, which would be constant with TMT's prediction that people suppress death thoughts after mortality salience. Consistent with theories of distal defense,

Van den Berg and Soeters found that soldiers who were deployed to Iraq and under a high mortality threat were more likely to endorse their CWV than those who were in garrison (see also Dechesne, Van den Berg, & Soeters, 2007).

Military Cultural Worldview

In military culture, one of the most highly regarded cultural values is strength (Christian, Stivers, & Sammons, 2009; Moore, 2011). The concept of strength refers to one's capacity to meaningfully contribute to collective military operations while maintaining a sense of self-reliance and a lack of being vulnerable. From the soldier's perspective, strength contributes to purpose of life and self-esteem, and ensures a greater chance of combat survival and mission success (Moore, 2011). An additional part of the military CWV is trusting in the strength of fellow soldiers. This is sometimes collectively known as the concept of "Mission First" in the creed "Mission First, Soldiers Always." Mission first refers to the primacy of the mission, while "Soldiers Always" refers to the leaders' responsibilities to insure the well-being of the soldiers under their command. "Mission First, Soldiers Always" is bolstered by the belief that in addition to one's own sense of strength, others must also possess strength. Again, from a soldier's perspective, if one's military associate (a.k.a. battle buddy) is strong, this contributes to the greater good of the military and contributes to soldier's beliefs that lives are being protected. This value of strength and unit cohesion enhances the psychological stability of the individual soldier and the soldiers within the unit (Freeman & Freeman, 2009). A high level of physical and psychological strength provides the individual with confidence to overcome adversity in battle where losing means capture, maiming, or death of self or battle buddy.

Consistent with the military CWV of strength is the concept of mental toughness. To underscore the value of mental toughness among military personnel, mental toughness is among the evaluative criteria that can be included in each soldier's yearly written evaluation (Department of the Army, 2014). This evaluation becomes a permanent part of a soldier's military record. This creates a challenge for soldiers and other military personnel. On the one hand, the military values a person being aggressive and enduring. On the other hand, it is more and more recognized that at times, military personnel and soldiers need to express inadequacy or a need for help to ultimately contribute to mental toughness. Collectively, this expression or expressed need of help appears to be discouraged and stigmatized (Petrovich, 2012).

This stigma may be upheld by justifiable anxiety that if military personnel are diagnosed with a qualifying level of a mental disorder, it will inhibit their deployment qualifications and they will be discharged from the military (Castro, Hayes, & Keane, 2011). The further up the hierarchical chain of command a person is, the more he or she may suffer from what Moore (2011) calls the "double stigma" (p. 15). Senior military personnel face the difficult dilemma of coping with both the potential negative stigma that junior members of the military face for admitting the need for help, and senior military personnel must cope with the potential negative stigma of being perceived as weak to the individuals they lead. That is, to perpetuate the culture of strength, senior military personnel are often not allowed, culturally, to express any vulnerability (e.g., a need for mental health services).

When overcoming the negative mental health seeking stigma in the military, there are two principle issues to consider. First, by its very nature and purpose, the military has many aspects of its culture that are markedly different than civilian culture. Second, death salience is a prevalent occurrence in the military. Congruent with TMT, these issues appear to perpetually strengthen military CWVs. For example, military training includes frequent instruction on things such as how to tourniquet a person's blown-off limb before the individual bleeds out; treating a sucking chest wound, to enable respiration; and calling a medevac request. Among the most difficult frequent trainings is to learn to whom first aid should be administered in a combat setting. To survive, soldiers are taught under what circumstance they must deny first aid to someone who has little to no hope of surviving during the tumult of a mass casualty event. The degree to which a person is subjected to this type of death salience is dependent on their military occupational specialty (MOS); however, regardless of the MOS, everyone in the military is subjected to high levels of death salience. From a TMT perspective, the level and frequency of MS helps to explain why the CWV of the military is robust and difficult to change.

Rationale for Implementation

Most briefs and programs run counter to the military CWV; in contrast, the brief proposed in this chapter seeks to overcome the resistance faced by military personnel to seek mental health services. Specifically, the brief outlined herein employs principles outlined in TMT and exploits soldiers' existing attitudes of complete strength. This brief is intended to trigger the military CWV attitude of being strong and exhibiting strength in all aspects of one's military operations. There exists ample research demonstrating developmental processes in military training. For example, studies have demonstrated that improvement of social fitness builds resilience within the military (Cacioppo, Reis, and Zautra, 2011). Also, Cacioppo and colleagues (2011) have demonstrated that military personnel who have developed meaningful relationships with others tend to be more resistant to developing PTSD. It appears this can also occur outside of a military context (Lyons, 2009; Maack, Lyons, Connolly, & Ritter, 2011). Because resilience to PTSD is also affected by one's precombat mental health, the cohesion of the military unit while in combat, and how much the soldier feels a part of that unit (Freeman & Freeman, 2009; Meichenbaum, 2011), it can be inferred that a shift to a psychological fitness paradigm to seek mental health services will improve significant relationships, military interpersonal relationships, the development of functionality, and overcoming precombat mental health challenges among military personnel. Most important to the military, however, would be the increased resilience to the negative consequences of combat.

The brief outlined in this chapter is designed to provide an unconventional and innovative method of addressing the issues of suicide and substance abuse among military personnel. Its intent is to help soldiers overcome the stigma of seeking mental health services in a manner that is conducive to the extant strength mind-set of the military. This method is consistent with Bates and colleagues (2010) and Jobes (2013), who focused on psychological fitness instead of applying a prevention attitude to decrease the undesirable occurrences of suicide and substance abuse. Further, it is proposed that this brief will build resilience to other nonbattle injuries such as depression and PTSD. The brief could also serve as an introduction to the current military resiliency training program.

Viewing the current military resiliency training program through a TMT lens may explain both why there are successful components of the program and ways in which the program can be improved. Others have conducted research on the current resilience training programs (Harms, Herian, Krasikova, Vanhove, & Lester, 2013; Lester, Harms, Herian, Krasikova, & Beal, 2011). In their research, the four units in the treatment condition received resiliency training from an abbreviated version of the current Comprehensive Soldier and Family Fitness (CSF2) resiliency training, and a control group received a different type of resiliency training. The treatment group demonstrated a significant change in only 5 out of the 19 areas measured. Although when age was accounted for, researchers found 11 of the 19 areas showing a significant change for the age group of 18 to 24 years old. However, what cannot be accounted for in these studies (Harms, Herian, Krasikova, Vanhove, & Lester, 2013; Lester, Harms, Herian, Krasikova, & Beal, 2011) were differences in MS experiences due to nonequivalent deployment periods. This could be a confounding variable. From a TMT perspective, it raises the question of whether it was the MS that actually was responsible for the differences observed, and if the results would be stronger if the data were analyzed with MS experiences as a variable.

Taken all together, there is ample justification to consider a TMT-based brief to compliment the current resiliency training. The current CSF2 training could be more effective because of its potential to decrease negative stigmas associated with developing current mental fitness and increase soldiers' intrinsic motivation to participate in resiliency training.

TMT Grounded Mental Fitness Brief

In this section the basic instructions and an outline of the TMT grounded mental fitness brief are provided to those who would be involved in its implementation. The first section, labeled *Leadership Brief,* is intended for those in leadership positions (e.g, commissioned and noncommissioned officers) to provide them with important information. The subsequent sections, labeled *Stages 1 through 4,* are intended to inform those delivering the mental fitness brief to military personnel.

The personal connection (Gass & Seiter, 2011) with soldiers is one key element of this mental fitness briefing program. Each mental fitness briefing should occur at a company level, or lower, which means it should be delivered to about 100 people or fewer. This number of personnel is desirable because it maximizes interpersonal connections among those participating. Another benefit to delivering this brief to 100 or fewer people at a time is to personalize the importance of mental fitness strengthening to their specific MOS, which is easier to achieve in groups of this size. Finally, delivery at the company level is desirable because different companies may have different MOSs and strategic functions.

Leadership Brief

The first stage of the program will consist of a Pre-Mental Health Fitness Brief with military personnel whose rank is E-6 or higher, prior to the main Mental Health Fitness Brief delivered to the whole company. In order for this briefing to be effective, those in leadership positions should demonstrate strong support and advocacy of the mental health fitness program. This is important because as prior research has demonstrated, when those in leadership positions set an expectation of help-seeking, instead of a negative mental health stigma, the suicide ideation and behaviors significantly lowered as compared to a group whose leadership maintained the negative stigma attitude (e.g., Warner et al., 2011).

The leadership brief will also be beneficial to persuade leadership by priming military CWV perspectives prior to the MS procedure. The E-6 and above leadership will be soldiers who have been in the military for a longer period of time than soldiers of a lower rank. It is conceivable that those with a higher rank will have a more solidified military CWV, and this military CWV might carry with it a higher negative stigma level of seeking mental health help. Arndt, Greenberg, and Cook (2002) found that when a CWV value was primed in the participants before the MS procedure, the prime determined the CWV used to defend against death anxiety.

Stage 1 of Mental Fitness Brief

Once the military CWV prime has been established during the leadership brief, the TMT Grounded Mental Fitness Brief will begin with the introduction of the MS event. This will be accomplished by showing a "HOOHA" style video, which will include as its content depictions of violent combat with individuals firing weapons and artillery. It will also include tanks firing and planes blowing-up objects. Throughout the clip, images and video will show psychologically fit (strong) soldiers evacuating wounded and dead soldiers after being hit by the enemy. It will emphasize using psychological fitness to overcome the situation. This clip would constitute the MS event. After the video, the person giving the brief should explain the importance of the mental fitness the soldiers displayed in the HOOHA video. This should be coupled with explanations of physical fitness and strength. It is important to couple together aspects of mental fitness with aspects of physical fitness and strength to encourage the reduction of mental health seeking negative stigma. Next, the presenter should pose the question, "How many other professions are equal to the military in combined mental and physical abilities?" This is meant to be a rhetorical question, and the purpose of this question is to cause those participating in the brief a moment's reflection and to transition away from the clip.

Stage 2: A Distraction Task

After the rhetorical question, the presenter will introduce Stage 2, which consists of a self-introduction. In this self-introduction it is important that the presenter establish credibility and rapport with the company being briefed by demonstrating their common similarities. Credibility can be established by describing qualifications such as education and experiences (Gass & Seiter, 2011). Rapport can be established if the presenter appears to share similar values and demeanor with those in the company (Gass & Seiter, 2011). This introduction also serves as a distractor task, research indicates that for CWV gravitation to occur, a non-death-related distraction should occupy about 7 to 20 minutes of time after the MS procedure (e.g., Burke, Martens, & Faucher, 2010). Thus, this introduction should be within a similar time frame.

Stage 3: Strengthening Military CWV After MS

Before entering Stage 3 briefing, the presenter must be equipped with knowledge about the company to whom the briefing is being presented. This will promote company specific CWV gravitation and serve as the bolstering function of MS defense. For example, if being given to an artillery unit, the instructor should ask questions such as, "How important is having the ability to make sound, split-second decisions during an artillery raid?" and "As a combat leader, is your ability to handle your gun section's non-combat-related issues, such as mental weakness or problems at home, as important as knowing the capacities of your Howitzer?" "Will both of these affect your mission accomplishment?" Next, allow for some discussion to take place. As the discussion continues, the presenter should ask, "Is it possible to increase our mental fitness the same way we increase our physical fitness?" and "Should we all be working on our mental fitness?" Lastly, the presenter may then explain that the needs of the mind are no different than the need to increase physical fitness.

Stage 4: Increasing Mental Fitness

In this stage the presenter should brief military personnel on specific ways of increasing mental fitness. It is the responsibility of the presenter to provide accurate methods of increasing mental health fitness.[1] At a minimum, the presenter should cover topics explaining neurological functioning during combat operations, show how mental health professionals can assist soldiers in becoming mentally stronger, and dispel some of the myths of therapy.

Discussion

Similar to physical development, or being trained on new equipment, the psychological well-being of a soldier needs development and training. This proposed TMT Grounded Mental Fitness Brief is based on empirically derived principles, and is intended to develop the concept of mental fitness as a critical aspect of combat readiness. In addition to affording combat readiness among soldiers, this brief is also intended to reduce the negative stigma associated with seeking mental health services. This is primarily accomplished by augmenting a military CWV with the belief that mental fitness is as necessary as physical fitness. It is important for military personnel to be resilient to multiple threats. Resilience can be developed as a natural learning consequence or with the aid of mental health professionals (Meichenbaum, 2011; Ungar & Lerner, 2008). It is possible that military personnel who accept and use mental health services may be able to reduce the threat or severity of potential traumatic events. Further, if this brief is followed properly, there remains the possibility that some potentially traumatic events could contribute to *post-traumatic growth*, which has been demonstrated to be inversely related to suicide ideation (Gallaway, 2011).

The processing and treatment of a traumatic event can help individuals process later challenges in life (Prati & Pietrantoni, 2009; Ungar & Lerner, 2008). The suicide, substance abuse, and psychological struggles soldiers face should be continually addressed by military personnel and improved upon so these warriors can positively reintegrate back into civilian life. Many briefs and programs are designed to directly address suicide ideation and substance abuse. However, some studies (e.g., Britt et al., 2011; Corrigan, 2004; Hoge et al., 2004) have indicated that the negative stigma associated with seeking mental health services is the most influential factor in keeping soldiers from seeking these services. Changing this cultural value of seeking mental fitness to become a better soldier and person should help to lower suicide ideation substance abuse and other psychological challenges. Although the principles outlined in this brief are grounded in empirical findings, further research is necessary to assess the validity of these postulates.

This proposed brief has no intention of eliminating the current CSF2 resilience program, but has the potential to increase its effectiveness because of the aforementioned benefits. This TMT-based brief applies extant principles to decrease the stigma among military personnel in seeking mental health services. Soldiers do not respond well to weakness tolerance; conversely, they are intentionally trained to take the fight to the enemy and be aggressive against adversity. This program magnifies these fostered characteristics; in fact, it entices soldiers to strive to become holistically stronger and change the process of preventing suicide, substance abuse, and psychological issues from a defensive plan to an all-out offensive.

Note

1. It is beyond the scope of this chapter to provide mental conditioning techniques. The presenter is encouraged to research the most current theories of increasing mental fitness.

References

Anestis, M. D., Bryan, C. J., Cornette, M. M., & Joiner, T. E. (2009). Understanding Suicidal Behavior in the military: An evaluation of Joiner's interpersonal—psychological theory of suicidal behavior in two case studies of active duty post-deployers. *Journal of Mental Health Counseling, 31*, 60–75.

Arndt, J., Cook, A., & Routledge, C. (2004). The blueprint of terror management: Understanding the cognitive architecture of psychological defense against the awareness of death. In J. Greenberg, S. L. Koole & T. Pyszczynski (Eds.), *Handbook of Existential Psychology*. [Kindle Reader version]. Retrieved from http://www.amazon.com/Kindle-eBooks

Arndt, J., Greenberg, J., & Cook, A. (2002). Mortality salience and the spreading activation of worldview-relevant constructs: Exploring the cognitive architecture of Terror Management. *Journal of Experimnetal Psychology, 131*, 307–324. doi:10.1037//0096–3445.131.3.307

Arndt, J., Greenberg, J., Solomon, S., Pyszczynski, T., & Simon, L. (1997). Suppression, accessibility of death-related thoughts, and cultural worldview defense: Exploring the psychodynamic of Terror Management. *Journal of Personality and Social Psychology, 73*, 5–18.

Bates, M. J., Bowles, S., Hammermeister, J., Stokes, C., Pinder, E., Moore, M., . . ., & Burbelo, G. (2010). Psychological fitness. *Military Medicine, 175*, 21–38.

Britt, T. W., Bennett, E. A., Crabtree, M., Haugh, C., Oliver, K., McFadden, A., & Pury, C. L. S. (2011). The theory of planned behavior and reserve component veteran treatment seeking. *Military Psychology, 23*, 82–96. doi:10.1080/08995605.2011.534417

Bryan, C. J., Hernandez, A. M., Allison, S., & Clemans, T. (2013). Combat exposure and suicide risk in two samples of military personnel. *Journal of Clinical Psychology, 69*, 64–77. doi:10.1002/jclp.21932

Burke, B. L., Martens, A., & Faucher, E. H. (2010). Two decades of terror management theory: A meta-analysis of mortality salience research. *Personality and Social Psychology Review, 14*(2), 155–195.

Cacioppo, J. T., Reis, H. T., & Zautra, A. J. (2011). Social Resilience. *American Psychologist, 66*, 43–51. doi:10.1037/a0021419

Castro, F., Hayes, J. P., & Keane, T. M. (2011). Issues in assessment of PTSD in military personnel. In B. A. Moore & W. E. Penk (Eds.), *Treating PTSD in military personnel, a clinical handbook* (pp. 23–41). [Kindle Reader version]. Retrieved from http://www.amazon.com/Kindle-eBooks

Christian, J. R., Stivers, J. R., & Sammons, M. T. (2009). Training to the warrior ethos: Implications for clinicians treating military members and their familes. In S. M. Freeman, B. A. Moore & A. Freeman (Eds.), *Living and surviving in harm's way* (pp. 27–49). New York, NY: Taylor & Francis Group.

Cohen, F., Solomon, S., Maxfield, M., Pyszezynski, T., & Greenberg, J. (2004). Fatal attraction: The effects of mortality salience on evaluations of charismatic, task-oriented, and relationship-oriented leaders. *American Psychological Society, 15,* 846–851.

Corrigan, P. (2004). How stigma interferes with mental health care. *American Psychologist, 59,* 614–625.

Dechesne, M., Van den Berg, C. E., & Soeters, J. (2007). International military collaboration under threat, a field study in Kabul. *Conflict Management and Peace Science, 24,* 25–36.

Department of the Army, DA PAM 623–3. (March 2014)

Department of Defense. (2010). Department of Defense Suicide Event Report. Retrieved from http://www.armyg1.army.mil/hr/suicide/docs/DoDSER_2010_Annual_Report.pdf

Department of Defense. (2011). Department of Defense Suicide Event Report. Retrieved from http://timemilitary.files.wordpress.com/2013/01/exsum_dodser_2011_annual_report.pdf

Freeman, A., & Freeman, S. M. (2009). Vulnerability factors: Raising and lowering the threshold for response. In S. M. Freeman, B. A. Moore & A. Freeman (Eds.), *Living and surviving in harm's way* (pp. 107–122). New York: Taylor & Francis Group.

Gallaway, M. R. (2011). The association between deployment-related posttraumatic growth among U.S. army soldiers and negative behavioral health conditions. *Journal of Clinical Psychology, 67*(12), 1151–116. doi:10.1002/jclp.20837

Gass, R. H., & Seiter, J. S. (2011). *Persuasion, social influence, and compliance gaining* (4th ed., pp. 73–140). London: Pearson Education, Inc.

Greenberg, J., Pyszczynski, J., & Solomon, S. (1986). The causes and consequences of a need for self-esteem: A terror management theory. In R. F. Baumeister (Ed.), *Public self and private self* (pp. 189–212). New York: Springer-Vering.

Greenberg, J., Pyszczynski, T., & Solomon, S. (1997). Terror management theory of self-esteem and cultural worldviews: Empirical assessments and conceptual refinements. *Advances in Experimental Social Psychology, 29,* 61–141.

Greenberg, J., Pyszczynski, T., Solomon, S., Simon, L., & Breus, M. (1994). Role of consciousness and accessibility of death-related thoughts in mortality salience effects. *Journal of Personality and Social Psychology, 67,* 627–637.

Harms, P. D., Herian, M. N., Krasikova, D. V., Vanhove, A., & Lester, P. B. (2013). *The comprehensive soldier and family fitness program evaluation report #4: Evaluation of resilience training and mental and behavioral health outcomes.* Retrieved from Army Fit website: https://armyfit.army.mil/MRT/Secured/Documents/Reference/Tech%20Report%204%20-%208APR13%20PM%20FINAL%20FOR%20PUBLICATION.pdf

Hoge, C. W., Auchterlonie, J. L., & Milliken, C. S. (2006). Mental health problems, use of mental health services and attrition from military service after returning from deployments to Iraq or Afghanistan. *Journal of the American Medical Association, 295,* 1023–1032.

Hoge, C. W., Castro, C. A., Messer, S. C., McGurk, D., Cotting, D. I., & Koffman, R. L. (2004). Combat duty in Iraq and Afghanistan, mental health problems, and barriers to care. *The New England Journal of Medicine, 351*(1), 13–22.

Jobes, D. A. (2013). Commentary on "suicide among soldiers: A review of psychosocial risk and protective factors". *Psychiatry, 76*(2), 126–131.

Kemp, J., & Bossarte, R. (2012). *Suicide data report, 2012*. Retrieved from U.S. Department of Veteran's Affairs website: www.va.gov/opa/docs/Suicide-Data-Report-2012-final.pdf

Kuehn, B. M. (2009). Soldier suicide rates continue to rise: Military, scientists work to stem the tide. *Journal of the American Medical Association, 301*, 1112–1113.

Landau, M. J., Goldenberg, J. L., Greenberg, J., Gillath, O., Solomon, S., Cox, C., Martens, A., & Pyszczynski, T. (2006). The siren's call: Terror management and the threat of men's sexual attraction to women. *Journal of Personality and Social Psychology, 90*, 129–146. doi:10.1037/0022–3514.90.1.129

Lester, P. B., Harms, P. D., Herian, M. N., Krasikova, D. V., & Beal, S. J. (2011). *The comprehensive soldier fitness program evaluation report #3: Longitudinal analysis of the impact of master resilience training on self-reported resilience and psychological health data.* Retrieved Army Fit website: https://armyfit.army.mil/MRT/Secured/Documents/Reference/Comprehensive%20Soldier%20Fitness%20-%20Technical%20Report%203%20(Efficacy%20of%20CSF).pdf

Lyons, J. A. (2009). Intimate relationships and the military. In S. Freeman, B. Moore & A. Freeman (Eds.), *Living and surviving in harm's way* (pp. 371–393). New York: Taylor & Francis Group.

Maack, D. J., Lyons, J. A., Connolly, K. M., & Ritter, M. (2011). Couples and family therapy. In B. A. Moore & W. E. Penk (Eds.), *Treating PTSD in military personnel, a clinical handbook* (pp. 141–154). [Kindle Reader version]. Retrieved from http://www.amazon.com/Kindle-eBooks

Mak, W. S., Poon, C. M., Pun, L. K., & Cheung, S. (2007). Meta-analysis of stigma and mental health. *Social Science & Medicine, 65*(2), 245–261. doi:10.1016/j.socscimed.2007.03.015

Meichenbaum, D. (2011). Resiliency building as a means to prevent PTSD and related adjustment problems in military personnel. In B. A. Moore & W. E. Penk (Eds.), *Treating PTSD in military personnel, a clinical handbook* (pp. 325–344). [Kindle Reader version]. Retrieved from http://www.amazon.com/Kindle-eBooks

Moore, B. A. (2011). Understanding and working within the military culture. In B. A. Moore & W. E. Penk (Eds.), *Treating PTSD in military personnel, a clinical handbook* (pp. 9–22). [Kindle Reader version]. Retrieved from http://www.amazon.com/Kindle-eBooks

Petrovich, J. (2012). Culturally competent social work practice with Veterans: An overview of the U.S. Military. *Journal of Human Behavior in the Social Environment, 22*, 863–874. doi:10.108/10911359.2012.707927

Prati, G., & Pietrantoni, L. (2009). Optimism, social support, and coping strategies as factors contributing to posttraumatic growth: A meta-analysis. *Journal of Loss & Trauma, 14*(5), 364–388. doi:10.1080/15325020902724271

Selby, E. A., Anestis, M. D., Bender, T. W., Ribiero, J. D., Nock, M. K., Rudd, M. D., . . ., & Joiner, T. E. (2010). Overcoming the fear of lethal injury: Evaluating suicidal behavior in the militay through the lens of the interpersonal-psychological theory of suicide. *Clinical Psychology Review, 30*, 298–307.

Taubman-Ben-Ari, O. (2004). Risk taking in adolescence: "To be or not to be" is not really the question. In J. Greenberg, S. L. Koole & T. Pyszczynski (Eds.), *Handbook of Existential Psychology* (pp. 104–121). [Kindle Reader version]. Retrieved from http://www.amazon.com/Kindle-eBooks

Ungar, M., & Lerner, R. M. (2008). Introduction to a special issue of research in human development: Resilience and positive development across the life span: A view of the issues. *Research In Human Development, 5*, 135–138. doi:10.1080/15427600802273961

Van den Berg, C., & Soeters, J. (2009). Self-perceptions of soldiers under threat: A field study of the influence of death threat on soldiers. *Military Psychology, 21*, S16-S30. doi:10.1080/08995600903249081

Warner, C. H., Appenzeller, G. N., Parker, J. R., Warner, C., Diebold, C. J., & Grieger, T. (2011). Suicide prevention in a deployed military unit. *Psychiatry, 74*, 127–141.

Weise, D. R., Pyszezynski, T., Cox, C. R., Arndt, J., Greenberg, J., Solomon, S., & Kosloff, S. (2008). Interpersonal politics: The role of terror management and attachment processes in shaping political preferences. *Association for Psychological Science, 19*, 448–455.

13

RUNNING IN WHILE RUNNING OUT

First Responders Communication During Traumatic Events

Dariela Rodriguez, Theodore A. Avtgis, and Corey Jay Liberman

When both natural and manmade disasters occur, there is an incredible amount of uncertainty-reducing and sense-making behavior that people engage in. Whether in reference to the victim or others who are potentially susceptible to the threat, such processing and resulting behavior have an impact on the degree of resiliency for the victims as well as the entire community. This is best illustrated in the dramatic increase in research looking at resiliency. According to Bonanno (2004), resiliency can be considered the ability of adults who are exposed to isolated events that have the potential to be highly disruptive (e.g., causing death or life-threatening situations) to recover and adjust to a traumatic experience. This allows them to remain somewhat stable and display high levels of psychological and physical functioning after the traumatic event. Terror management theory (TMT) works to predict and explain how individuals, and in the case of the current chapter, first responders and emergency personnel in particular, are able to compartmentalize the potential of death and still carry on the task set forth.

First Responders

While existing literature and research have been mostly focused on the victims of traumatic events, since the terror attacks on the World Trade Center on September 11, 2001, there has been a dramatic increase in resources being expended on public safety resources and personnel. Given the nature of the day-to-day routines involved in the various first responder careers, one has to question, what are the cumulative effects of experiencing serial traumatic events and impact on psychological and physical functioning? First responders can be defined as those people who are first on the scene to assist citizens through a crisis situation (First Responders, 2013). Such roles include police, fire, emergency medical services, military, and civilian personnel to name but a few. In the course of an average shift, a first responder is constantly under the potentiality of not only responding to traumatic events but also becoming a possible victim of such events. Events involving children, mass casualties, and acts of natural and manmade disasters are just a few of the myriad trauma experiences that can be experienced on a day-to-day basis. Further, most of the first responder positions do not have very high levels of financial compensation. For example, according to the U.S. Bureau of Labor Statistics (2015), there are approximately 98,500 police, fire, and ambulance dispatchers in the United States earning a median annual salary of $36,300. This begs the question, in light of limited financial compensation, what are the primary motivations for such a career choice?

According to Benedek, Fullerton, and Ursano (2007), first responder proximity to the crisis event, duration, and intensity of exposure to the event were the most significant predictors of physical and mental well-being. It should be noted that most research has focused on pathologies or negative outcomes associated with first responder effects as a result of incident exposure such as burnout (Alexander & Klein, 2001; Figley, 1998), traumatic stress (Marmar, Weiss, Metzler, Delucchi, Best, & Wentworth, 1999; Ursano, Fullerton, Tzu-Cheg, & Bhartiya, 1995; Wagner, Heinrichs, & Eklert, 1998), lasting loss of compassion (Figley & Stamm, 1999), and secondary traumatic stress (Figley, 1995) with little to no research focusing on positive or prosocial outcomes (see, for example, Pietrantoni & Prati, 2008). The goal of this chapter hopes to use TMT as a means for identifying possible motivating factors responsible for people engaging in first responder related behavior and the accompanying cognitions associated with that behavior. More specifically, we will apply TMT's dimensions of self-esteem, worldview, and self-efficacy to first responders.

Terror Management Theory

Terror management theory works to explain what happens to individuals when the possibility of death or serious injury becomes salient and when the possibility of death generates significant cognitions and fears (Greenberg & Arndt, 2011). Essentially, the theory seeks to answer the questions of what do people do in the face of death or serious illness. Individuals have natural fight or flight instincts built into their psychological and physiological processes (Greenberg & Arndt, 2011). Such processes are engaged in the face of either real or anticipated danger. TMT expands this concept to ask what happens when people know death or serious injury can be a logical outcome as a result of behaviors they engage in? It also attempts to explain the psychological processes that come from the need to rationalize their subsequent behavioral strategies (Greenberg & Arndt, 2011).

Jeff Greenberg, Sheldon Solomon, and Tom Pyszczynski first developed TMT as an attempt to shore up what they believed was unaddressed in the field of psychology. More specifically, they explored the reasoning and decision-making processes of people when they are faced with death or serious injury as a possible outcome associated with their behavioral choices (Greenberg & Arndt, 2011). TMT looks to two factors that influence the three assumptions of the theory: self-esteem and social worldview (Greenberg & Arndt, 2011; Greenberg, Pyszczynski, Solomon, Rosenblatt, Veeder, Kirkland, & Lyon, 1990; Harmon-Jones, Simon, Greenberg, Pyszczynski, Solomon, & McGregor, 1997). *Self-esteem* is defined as self-perceptions and other-perceptions of an individual comprising a summative evaluation of self-worth (Greenberg & Arndt, 2011; Schmeichel, Gailliot, Filardo, McGregor, Gitter, & Baumeister, 2009). *Worldview* is the "set of beliefs about the nature of reality shared by groups of individuals that provides meaning, order, permanence, stability, and the promise of literal and/or symbolic immortality to those who live up to the standards of value set by the worldview" (Harmon-Jones et al., 1997, p. 24). Self-esteem is often influenced by, and can influence, the worldview a person ascribes to. Not living up to the standards of these worldviews can result in a negative self-perception, which, in turn, can cause a person to experience higher levels of anxiety than they would otherwise normally experience (Harmon-Jones et al., 1997). This is explained as the anxiety-buffer hypothesis of TMT.

Self-Efficacy and TMT

One of strongest indicators of reduced levels of distress, however distress is conceptualized, is self-efficacy (Gibbs, 1989; McCammon, Durham, Jackson-Allison, & Williamson, 1988). According to Bandura (1997), efficacy is a person's belief that he or she has the requisite skill or ability to enact a measure of control over one's environment and the events that occur within that environment. For example, self-efficacy has been associated with low levels of traumatic stress and depression in firefighters (Heinrichs, Wagner, Schoch, Soravia, Hellhammer, & Ehlert, 2005; Regehr, Hill, & Glancy, 2000; Regehr, Hill, Knott, & Sault, 2003).

In a study of 961 first responders, Pietrantoni and Prati (2008) found that emergency rescue personnel in what is considered "high-risk" occupations assessed the impact of community, collective efficacy, and self-efficacy on compassion fatigue, burnout syndrome, and compassion satisfaction. Results indicated that high levels of self-efficacy predicted decreased compassion fatigue, burnout, and collective efficacy, and increased a sense of community. The authors concluded that self-esteem plays a central role in the mental health and well-being of first responders.

In light of these data, coupled with the fact that most first responder careers do not pay lucrative monetary salaries, one must look to other factors that result in career choices that require people to consistently put themselves at risk of serious injury or death as a requisite part of their job description in efforts to assist in rescuing and restoring a sense of security to complete strangers. This willingness to put oneself in serial exposure to serious injury or death may have some underpinnings in personality traits, societal influences, and/or neurobiology. This willingness to knowingly risk one's life is often in contrast to the general sense of self-preservation instilled in human beings. The contributions to self-esteem and cultural worldview as put forth by TMT could serve as an important explanatory element as to the role that self-efficacy plays in the motivation of first responders behavior.

There is an inherent human desire for people to want to live forever. In pursuit of this desire, people have looked to everything from medical technology to diet and exercise, as well as supplements that are all designed to keep a person healthy and improve the quality of life. As a means of preserving a posthumous legacy, individuals have sought iconic stature of celebrity or heroism to ensure a positive impact on society consistent with the person, and society's, worldview. These avoidance behaviors have often been attempted to be explained through the use of terror management theory.

According to TMT, when death- or serious-harm-related fears are experienced, and mortality becomes a salient factor in a person's cognitive processes, people will rely on their worldview and self-esteem to make sense of the fears generated by the possibility of death; if a person's self-esteem is congruent with their cultural worldview. Anxiety regarding mortality salience is greatly reduced, resulting in greater sense making and coping skills. However, if either of these "buffers" are threatened or are incongruent, leading to lower levels of sense making and coping skills, mortality will become more salient (Burke, Martens, & Faucher, 2010; Greenberg & Arndt, 2011; Pyszczynski, Greenberg, & Solomon, 1999).

Self-Esteem

As stated before, one's self-esteem is often built upon two factors both drawn from the concept of an individual's cultural worldview (Pyszczynski et al., 1999; Schmeichel et al., 2009). These are explicit and implicit self-esteem (Pyszczynski et al., 1999; Schmeichel et al., 2009). *Explicit self-esteem* describes a person's self-perception of whether he or she is meeting the standards of the worldview the person subscribes to (Greenberg et al., 1990; Rosenblatt, Greenberg, Solomon, Pyszczynski, & Lyon, 1989). The assessment of an individual agreeing or disagreeing with his or her own inherent sense of self-perception is often referred to as *implicit self-esteem* (Greenberg et al., 1990; Rosenblatt, Greenberg, Solomon, Pyszczynski, & Lyon, 1989). When either self-esteem is challenged, the natural reaction is to develop arguments advocating how a person has upheld his or her worldview or to note that other people have failed to provide, via behavioral choices, to align with the worldview (Greenberg et al., 1990; Rosenblatt et al., 1989). Such arguments serve to persuade others into thinking that a person's behavior is positively correlated with others who share the same worldview, thus creating an ingroup connection while simultaneously putting other people who do not share the same worldview in the outgroup. This is seen as a means of self-preservation (Greenberg et al., 1990; Rosenblatt et al., 1989). Using this line of reason, the ingroup member is trying to rationalize him- or herself as more worthy of "surviving" either physically or figuratively the potential danger than other people. In the figurative sense, this can help an individual establish him- or herself as a "hero" of sorts, thereby ensuring a legacy should death or serious injury occur.

Worldview

One's worldview is comprised of the individual's perception of the rules and regulations set forth by members of the society or group he or she identifies with (Burke et al., 2010; Pyszczynski et al., 1999). Though these views can be, and are, shared by multiple members of society, the degree to which people are perceived to live up to these values and beliefs is based on subjective interpretation. Because living up to worldview expectancies is perceptual in nature, they are neither objective nor tangible. However, such expectancies can affect a person's psychological and physiological well-being in ways that could be construed as objective and tangible. For example, saying prayers or performing a ritualized routine before entering a crisis situation can alter the cognitions associated with potential death or serious injury in ways that reduce anxiety and increase cognitions of nobility, heroism, and righteousness. If an individual is less afraid of death and can think clearly in the face of danger, he or she is more likely to have a positive outcome than one who cannot react.

In the world of first responders, the prevailing worldview assumes that people who choose such careers are considered heroes. When considering fire fighters, police officers, and military, to name but a few, the understanding is often that these men and women sacrifice everything for complete strangers. With this understanding comes the realization for members of the first responder community that failure is not an option. The belief, and sometime overly exaggerated belief, in the skill and efficacy of both themselves and their teams reduces the anxiety associated with potentially catastrophic outcomes.

Self-Efficacy

Self-efficacy is defined as the belief in one's task completion ability based on performance-based outcomes (Bandura, 1977). In the first responder professions, which are typically team based, self-efficacy is often developed as part of participation in the task with other like-minded people. For example, as firefighters experience success in training and in actual crisis situations, they will not only develop more skill as firefighters but will develop further trust in the skill sets of others, as well. They will develop a stronger sense of self-efficacy through this increase in team efficacy. Whether perceptual or real, the increase in self and other efficacy influences the resultant behavior.

In the movie *Jarhead* set during the first Gulf War, viewers see a scene where the main characters, members of the United States Marine Corp, first arrive in the Persian Gulf and are being briefed for their mission. The commanding officer was showing the Marines images of the torture that the people of Kuwait were being subjected to through the use of chemical warfare by then-dictator Saddam Hussein. The goal of this briefing was to get the Marines to believe that they are fighting for the freedom of America by freeing the people of Kuwait. The whole speech boils down to one idea, that the sacrifice of one's life will bring democracy, freedom, and self-determination to the people of Kuwait (an American cultural worldview); subsequently, the death of any of the troops will result in a hero legacy due to sacrifice in pursuit of these western ideals.

If this speech were being given to most members of the civilian population, the end result would most likely not be met with the overall enthusiasm that it was met with in this particular scene in the film. The passion felt by the Marines is built on the aforementioned worldview, but also the incredibly high sense of self-efficacy that the Marines, when compared to the average citizenry, have in their ability to execute the task at hand.

Verbal Persuasion

Efficacy is not only present in the understanding of one's individual skill, but also in the trust of his or her team's proficiency in task completion. Both individual and team efficacy is developed through factors such as verbal persuasion, psychological states, emotional arousal, and even vicarious experience (Bandura, 1977, 1997). Each of these factors can be linked to a stronger sense of self-esteem, and the influence that self-esteem has cognitive, affective, and behavioral dimensions described in terror management theory.

The first factor of verbal persuasion is often present even before individuals are part of first responder teams. The mass media, social reverence, and hero status that society often affords to first responders are all influences that many in these roles attribute to their decision to pursue such careers. Positive feedback, based on informational instruction and performance-based praise, are all aspects of verbal persuasion that would also influence self-esteem in positive ways (Bandura, 1977, 1997).

Psychological States

Self and team efficacy have a direct influence on the psychological state of the individuals and the team as a whole (Bandura, 1977, 1997). The trust that is built through success can have positive psychological effects between members of the group and within each individual member resulting in increased self and team efficacy. Trust in a team is based on the perception of success (Bandura, 1977, 1997). This collective perception is comprised of individual perceptions that people have of the team. This collective perception of success and perceived high ability levels are often the basis for positive self-esteem that influences motivation. This motivation is also directly connected to both psychological and physiological arousal (Bandura, 1977, 1997).

Vicarious Experiences

Training modules are utilized to model the experiences within the lives of first responders to help prepare them for situations in the field. For example, computer simulations or other types of "witnessing" through the experiences of others are types of ways people are psychologically and physiology enculturated into expectancies for behavioral strategies when confronting a crisis situation. Another type of influence is live modeling, which allows participants to gain a sense of the experience to help alleviate anxieties and negative thoughts that could result in negative behavioral choices when actually encountering a real crisis situation (Bandura 1977, 1997). Such training provides the individual the opportunity to hone his or her skills, as well as learn how well each member of the team would do in any given situation (Bandura 1977, 1997). Taken as a whole, all of these elements serve to provide the first responder with cognitive, affective, and behavioral choices that can be considered "best practices."

Running In

According to statistics, there were 1,140,750 active firefighters in the United States in 2013 ("U.S. Fire Department Profile," 2014). Of this total, 353,600 were professional firefighters and 786,150 served as volunteers. Given the number of individuals active in departments throughout the country, one's perception of the death toll in this extremely dangerous profession would most likely be greater than the actual death toll of 22 reported in 2012 (*U.S. Fire Administration*, 2013). This number, 22, could influence how people interpret the probability of death or serious injury associated with the profession. Contributing to this is the fact that this number includes training deaths or those in which training could have contributed (i.e., heart attack within days of a training run). Because of this, the perception of the possibility of death could be reduced considerably by building confidence within the ranks of the first responders and supporting the connection between self-efficacy (built through training) and self-esteem (developed through self-efficacy), which are both aspects of TMT. It is the confidence instilled through experience and knowledge that allows first responders to run in and face death while all others are running out.

The concept of an individual willing to risk his or her life for complete strangers is often the definition many have of a hero. The image of a firefighter or police officer rescuing people from danger is often conjured up when the word *hero* is used. The reason we consider these men and women heroes lies in the fact that when we see a rescue situation depicted in the media, we see people recoiling and fleeing from danger while simultaneously first responders are actively engaging the dangerous situation without the appearance of any trepidation. They are perceived as doing what they are trained to do, which is to resolve chaotic situations and mitigate any possible danger in whatever form it may take. However, through the explanation and application of TMT and its resultant concepts of efficacy, self-esteem, and social worldview, we still have the question of why an individual would select a career that clearly has increased risks of death or serious injury. He or she is able to do so due to particular cognitive, affective, and behavioral strategies that serve to mitigate the perceived susceptibility of death or serious injury as well as how one interprets such susceptibility.

Conclusion

The trust that one has in his or her ability, as well as the abilities of his or her teammates, is what allows these individuals to look in the face of death or serious injury and find a reason to continue on with the job at hand. In Western culture, people in first responder positions are looked at like heroes; the knowledge that not every being is capable of mentally or physically making the choice to sacrifice his or her life for another or risk serious injury is the cornerstone of the perception, or worldview. That is, first responder careers are viewed as careers of respect and honor.

As stated before, the view of these careers as heroic is one that our society perpetuates through stories beginning from early childhood. Fire trucks on clothing, plastic fire hats, trips to see the fire house and police department, and images of the military winning wars for the United States are all assimilating tactics targeted at developing and perpetuating such a worldview. Because of this, those who usually take it upon themselves to commit to a first responder career often do so with the understanding that it is a noble profession and one that holds the highest level of responsibility as it involves making decisions that will determine the life and/or death of others. The training that is inherent in the development of first responder careers helps to make this worldview a reality; these men and women become the heroes they have always heard about. The sense of self-efficacy as well as the self-esteem that is afforded by the worldview, the training, and enacting the hero lifestyle, as stated in TMT, will mitigate fear of death and serious injury and serve as a motivator to the behavioral choices of first responders when encountering crisis situations.

References

Alexander, D. A., & Klein, S. (2001). Ambulance personnel and critical incidents: Impact of accident and emergency work on mental health and emotional well-being. *British Journal of Psychiatry, 178*, 76–81. doi:10.1192/bjp.178.1.76

Bandura, A. (1977). Self-efficacy: Towards a unifying theory of behavioral change. *Psychological Review, 84*, 191–215. http://dx.doi.org/10.1037/0033–295X.84.2.191

Bandura, A. (1997). *Self efficacy: The exercise of control.* New York: Freeman.

Benedek, D. M., Fullerton, C., & Ursano, R. J. (2007). First responders: Mental health consequences of natural and human-made disasters for public health and public safety workers. *Annual Review of Public Health, 28*, 55–68. doi:10.1146/annurev.publhealth.28.021406.144037

Bonanno, G. A. (2004). Loss, trauma, and human resilience: Have we underestimated the human capacity to thrive after extremely aversive events? *American Psychologist, 59*, 20–28. http://dx.doi.org/10.1037/0003–066X.59.1.20

Burke, L. B., Martens, A., & Faucher, E. H. (2010). Two decades of terror management theory: A meta-analysis or mortality salience research. *Personality and Social Psychology Review, 14*(2), 155–195. doi:10.1177/1088868309352321

Figley, C. R. (1995). Compassion fatigue as secondary traumatic stress disorder. An overview. In C. R. Figley (Ed.), *Compassion fatigue* (pp. 1–20). New York: Brunner Mazel.

Figley, C. R. (1998). Burnout as systemic traumatic stress: A model for helping traumatized family members. In C. R. Figley (Ed.), *Burnout in families: The systemic costs of caring* (pp. 15–28). Boca Raton, FL: CRC Press.

Figley, C. R., & Stamm, B. H. (1999). Secondary traumatic stress: Self-care issues for clinicians, researchers and educators (2nd ed.). In C. R. Figley (Ed.), *Compassion fatigue* (pp. 3–28). Lutherville, MD: Sidran Press.

First Responders.gov. (2013). *United States homeland security.* Retrieved from http://www.firstresponder.gov/pages/Default.aspx

Gibbs, M. S. (1989). Factors in the victim that mediate between disaster and psychopathology: A review. *Journal of Traumatic Stress, 2*, 489–514. doi:10.1002/jts.2490020411

Greenberg, J., & Arndt, J. (2011). Terror management theory. *Handbook of Theories of Social Psychology, 1*, 398–415.

Greenberg, J., Pyszczynski, T., Solomon, S., Rosenblatt, A., Veeder, M., Kirkland, S., & Lyon, D. (1990). Evidence for the terror management theory II: The effects of mortality who threaten or bolster the cultural worldview, *Journal of Personality and Social Psychology, 58*(2), 308–318. http://dx.doi.org/10.1037/0022–3514.58.2.308

Harmon-Jones, E., Simon, L., Greenberg, J., Pyszczynski, T., Solomon, S., & McGregor, H. (1997). Terror management theory and self-esteem: Evidence that increases self-esteem reduced mortality-salience effects. *Journal of Personality and Social Psychology, 72*(1), 24–36. http://dx.doi.org/10.1037/0022–3514.72.1.24

Heinrichs, M., Wagner, D., Schoch, W., Soravia, L., Hellhammer, D., & Ehlert, U. (2005). Predicting posttraumatic stress symptoms from pretraumatic risk factors: A 2-year prospective follow up study in firefighters. *American Journal of Psychiatry, 162*, 2276–2786. http://dx.doi.org/10.1176/appi.ajp.162.12.2276

Marmar, C. R., Weiss, D. S., Metzler, T. J., Delucchi, K. L., Best, S. R., & Wentworth, K. A. (1999). Longitudinal course and predictors of continuing distress following critical incident exposure in emergency services personnel. *The Journal of Nervous and Mental Disease, 187*, 15–22.

McCammon, S., Durham, T., Jackson-Allison, E., & Williamson, J. (1988). Emergency workers' cognitive appraisal and coping with traumatic events. *Journal of Traumatic Stress, 1*, 353–372.

Pietrantoni, L., & Prati, G. (2008). Resilience among first responders. *African Health Sciences, 8*, S14-S20.

Pyszczynski, T., Greenburg, J., & Solomon, S. (1999). A dual-process model of defense against conscious and unconscious death-related thoughts: an extension of terror management theory. *Psychological Review, 106*(4), 835–845. http://dx.doi.org/10.1037/0033–295X.106.4.835

Regehr, C., Hill, J., & Glancy, G. D. (2000). Individual predictors of traumatic reactions in firefighters. *The Journal of Nervous and Mental Disease, 188*, 333–339.

Regehr, C., Hill, J., Knott, T., & Sault, B. (2003). Social support, self-efficacy and trauma in new recruits and experienced firefighters. *Stress & Health, 19*, 189–193. doi:10.1002/smi.974

Rosenblatt, A., Greenburg, J., Solomon, S., Pyszczynski, T., & Lyon, D. (1989). Evidence for terror management theory I: The effects of mortality salience on cultural values. *Journal of Personality and Social Psychology, 57*(4), 681–690. http://dx.doi.org/10.1037/0022–3514.57.4.681

Schmeichel, B. J., Gailliot, M. T., Filardo, E. A., McGregor, I., Gitter, S., & Baumeister, R. F. (2009). Terror management theory and self-esteem revisted: The roles of implicit and self-esteem in mortality salience effects. *Journal of Personality and Social Psychology, 96*(5), 1077–1087. http://dx.doi.org/10.1037/a0015091

Ursano, R. J., Fullerton, C. S., Tzu-Cheg, K., & Bhartiya, V. R. (1995). Longitudinal assessment of posttraumatic stress disorder and depression after exposure to traumatic death. *Journal of Nervous and Mental Disease, 183*, 36–42.

U.S. Bureau of Labor Statistics. (2015). *Police, fire, and ambulance dispatchers*. Retrieved from www.bls.gov/ooh/office-and-administrative-support/police-fire-and-ambulance-dispatchers.htm

U.S. fire administration: Firefighter fatalities in the United States in 2012. (2013). Retrieved from www.usfa/fema.gov/downloads/pdf/publications/ff_fat12.pdf

U.S. fire department profile. (2014). Retrieved from www.nfpa.org/research/reports-and-statistics/the-fire-service/administration/us-fire-department-profile

Wagner, D., Heinrichs, M., & Eklert, U. (1998). Prevalence of symptoms of posttraumatic stress disorder in German professional firefighters. *American Journal of Psychiatry, 155*, 1727–1732.

14

TMT IN LAS

Lessons From a Terror Management Field Experiment at Las Vegas McCarran International Airport

Lindsey A. Harvell, Tyler F. Stillman, Gwendelyn S. Nisbett, Kyle Cranney, and Amber L. Schow

For the past two decades, academics conducting terror management theory (TMT) research have focused their experiments primarily in laboratories. In some ways, this is an ideal form for TMT research, since the research often requires a highly controlled environment. However, only having lab experiment data can hinder generalizability. With the increasing interdisciplinary nature of TMT research, scholars are attempting to conduct research that is more applied. The best parts of laboratory TMT research and field research can be combined in field experiments. The current chapter reviews one such field experiment conducted by the authors with the hope that the lessons we learned will be of use to likeminded researchers.

Field experiments can be supplemental to laboratory experiments. The majority of past TMT literature focuses on the effects of existential awareness in laboratories. However, very little TMT research addresses what happens when one is death aware *outside* of the laboratory. Therefore, field experiments are beneficial to TMT research in three main ways. First, TMT field experiments allow us to examine TMT in a less controlled setting. We can see what happens when real-world variables are present. Second, by conducting experiments in the "real world" we can generalize better and gain a more thorough understanding as to how certain variables would affect actual individuals in everyday situations. Third, we gain a better understanding for how natural death awareness (i.e., not artificially produced) is affecting people in their everyday lives.

While field experiments offer an applied look into the effects of existential awareness, TMT field experiments can be tricky. This chapter examines the process of conducting a TMT experiment. The field experiment described here is one that was completed at Las Vegas McCarran International Airport (LAS) in March 2014. This project shows the difficulties that TMT field experiments produce as well as the theoretical insight gained from using this method. Ultimately, TMT field experiments are a useful tool to give a deeper theoretical understanding of TMT.

Terror Management Theory

Terror management theory (Pyszczynski, Greenberg, & Solomon, 1997) is the social psychological study of the predictable attitudes and behaviors associated with existential anxiety. The theory builds on the work of Ernest Becker (1973), positing that death primes and subsequent anxiety instigate people to seek out relief. TMT grew out of a desire to apply social psychological methodological rigor to more macro-level explorations of existential thought; thus TMT is a motivational theory interested in explaining why people do what they do.

TMT is influenced by existential philosophy and evolutionary biology. Humans evolved with a high level of intelligence and the ability to self-reflect—in a sense, people can project themselves into the future (Solomon, Greenberg, Schimel, Arndt, & Pyszczynski, 2004). High intelligence was an adaptive advantage over other animals because humans had a keener ability to exploit resources and form partnerships with other humans. The downside to such high intelligence was the existential anxiety that comes with knowing you are going to die. Mortality is such an overwhelming concept, pondering it would inhibit almost any other cognitive or affective activity (Greenberg et al., 1990). Thus, people developed defenses against existential anxiety through developing a cultural worldview defense and bolstering their self-esteem (Pyszczynski et al., 1997) and relying on close relationships (Mikulincer, Florian, & Hirschberger, 2003).

The major components of TMT include the mortality-salience hypothesis, cultural worldview defense, and self-esteem. Mortality salience posits that pondering one's own death leads to anxiety. People seek out a relief to this anxiety by relying on their cultural worldview (CWV), which is built on things like religion, family, and culture (Pyszczynski et al., 1997). Self-esteem level also works as a palliative for existential anxiety. CWV and self-esteem work together. When people have purpose and meaning in life and are living up to dictates of their CWV, then self-esteem increases. A higher self-esteem is linked to a greater ability to deal with existential anxiety (Pyszczynski et al., 2005). Close personal relationships work hand in hand with CWV and self-esteem to bolster anxiety defenses (Florian, Mikulincer, & Hirschberger, 2002). The need to bolster CWV has been linked with more negative evaluations of outgroup cultures and people (Solomon et al., 2000).

People have two mechanisms to deal with the terror of death: proximal defense and distal defense (Arndt, Cook, & Routledge, 2004). The proximal defense mechanism is immediate after the onset of death anxiety. People tend to change the subject and put thoughts of death out of their minds. Distal defense occurs after a delay period. It is manifested when thoughts of death are outside of focal awareness. Mortality is salient in that thoughts of death are cued up or primed just under the surface; this causes existential anxiety.

Much of TMT research is conducted in lab settings with tight controls on mortality-salience manipulations and distal defense delays. In lab experiments, mortality salience is manipulated through having participants write about their own death followed by a distracter task in order to provide enough delay to bring about distal defense.

TMT research tends to focus on distal defense and the associated psychological coping strategies (CWV, self-esteem bolstering, and relying on close relationships). Previous research suggests 10–15 minutes is the prime delay amount (Burke et al., 2010). In a field experiment, this delay period is not viable. For this particular study, passengers at LAS were recruited and given the manipulation and subsequent survey in one phase. Thus, this study focuses on the proximal defense mechanism as opposed to distal defense.

Terror Management Theory and Field Experiments

Field experiments can be defined as components that represent a natural setting (Harrison & List, 2004). For TMT, these most often would be framed laboratory experiments with participants from the field. Because many things are at play, you must have a firm grasp on what is being controlled and the extraneous "noise" in the field from which you are collecting (Harrison & List, 2004).

Field experiments meet all of the characteristics of true experiments, but are conducted in a natural setting (Singleton & Straits, 2010). These experiments can take and have taken place anywhere; elevators (Latane & Dabbs, 1975), department stores and their parking lots (Forgas, Dunn, & Granland, 2008), and subways (Piliavin & Piliavan, 1972), to name a few. Field experiments pose interesting internal and external validity issues. Internal validity (the ability to claim causal relationships) tends to be middle of the road or high depending on the situation with field experiments, but extremely high with laboratory experiments (Roe & Just, 2009). On the other hand, external validity (the ability to generalize the relationships found in a study to other situations) tends to be midlevel to high with field experiments, but extremely low for laboratory experiments. Hence one sacrifices a little bit in terms of causal inference in order to achieve greater external reliability.

While field experiments offer researchers fairly decent to good internal and external validity, there are some pitfalls to choosing this methodology. First, there is not as much experimental control available for field experiments when compared to their laboratory counterparts due to their natural setting (Singleton & Straits, 2010). For this reason, field experiments are often held at a lower standard or a higher standard depending on what kind of validity the researcher is striving for (Harrison, 2005). Second, sometimes it is not possible to have a true control group, so field experiments often make it harder to determine if there are systematic differences between the experimental groups (Singleton & Straits, 2010). Third, the manipulation of the independent variable may be less controlled and more open to interpretation therefore making data analysis interpretation more difficult (Singleton & Straits, 2010). Last, there can be legal and ethical issues with field experiments (Singleton & Straits, 2010). Most often with TMT, these ethical issues arise with possible psychological harm in the field. Additionally, there are times in field experiments where you may not be able to acquire consent prior to participation in the study (Singleton & Straits, 2010). For these reasons, field experiments should be approached with extreme caution.

TMT field experiments are often more complex than your average experiment. Due to the manipulation, time delays, and manipulation check, it is imperative the researcher is fairly meticulous about how the experimental survey is completed. Because of this level of difficulty, and the only recent emergence of applied interdisciplinary TMT research, TMT field experiments are rare. There is one TMT field experiment to date that investigated the impact of mortality salience and self-esteem on smokers' compliance with antismoking messages anchored in a variety of health and social themes (Martin & Kamins, 2008). This study was conducted in a shopping mall, and significant effects were found. Additionally there was no mention of any field experiment difficulties. This was the first hint that field experiments and TMT could work. Because this field experiment was shown to work in a small scale, we decided to embark on a TMT field experiment on a much larger scale at Las Vegas McCarran International Airport.

Las Vegas McCarran International Airport Field Experiment

This TMT field experiment took place during March 2014 at Las Vegas McCarran International Airport. We wanted to get a well-rounded passenger participant list (all geographical locations and all socioeconomic statuses), and for that reason all domestic and international gates were accessed. We began in the low-end carrier (e.g., Spirit, AirTran, etc.) gates and worked our way to the midlevel carrier (Southwest), to high-level domestic (e.g., Delta, United, American, Virgin America), and to international (e.g., Virgin Atlantic, Condor, etc.). This allowed for the most diverse sample possible. We received participants representing all geographical locations within the United States as well as the international locations of Canada, France, Germany, United Kingdom, Switzerland, and Australia. Data collection took place in one day over the course of 7 hours. Two faculty members and two graduate students were present for data collection.

Planning

The planning for a TMT field experiment in such a high-security location takes a lot of preplanning and negotiation between the lead researcher, the airport administration, and Homeland Security. The first thing the principle investigator did was to contact LAS administration. This occurred in October 2013 and continued through November 2013. This included many phone calls and emails explaining the purpose and why LAS. When conducting research at such a high-security facility, this was the hardest part of the process. However, we finally gained preliminary approval (pending background checks) in November 2013.

The lead researcher's next task was to screen graduate students and choose the best for this kind of research. Ultimately, the principle investigator chose graduate students who were currently employed by airplane-related companies. One graduate student is employed by Syberjet and the other is employed by SkyWest Airlines. These graduate students were chosen because of their interest in and experience with airports. In the months leading up to the March 2014 data collection, the researchers focused on obtaining Institutional Review Board approval (granted January 2014). In February 2014, the four researchers' names were submitted for Homeland Security background checks, a requirement to conduct research inside the security gates without a ticket. In the meantime, funding was obtained from the School of Business for travel and the Department of Communication at a small Western university for the cost of candy.

Implementation

Data collection took place at LAS 3 days prior to most spring breaks and 1 day before Malaysian Airlines Flight 370 went missing; therefore, the missing airliner did not affect the data. This project not only examined the utility of TMT field experiments; it also examined how flight anxiety/death awareness affects consumerism behaviors within an airport and how flight anxiety works in place of death awareness in experiments. Participants were randomly assigned into one of two conditions, experimental and control. The experimental conditions were asked to describe in detail what their main fears or anxieties are about air travel. The control conditions were asked to describe in detail their overall experience while spending time in LAS. This allowed us to give some feedback to LAS about what their passengers were thinking and feeling through our control conditions.

Prior to arriving at the airport, the surveys were ordered as every other one, experimental and control, to ensure random assignment into conditions. Once arriving at the airport, we were greeted by the public relations division of LAS. Because we were required to be escorted while inside security, that division was responsible for escorting us. Every 2 hours we were escorted by a new individual from that department. Once our badges were assigned, we were brought through a less stringent security process (due to our background checks). We began our data collection journey at the A gates, which services the low-budget carriers. Passenger participants were obtained from Spirit Airlines and AirTran Airlines. From there we continued to the B and C gates, which mainly service Southwest Airlines. After a short break for lunch, D gates were accessed, servicing the high-end domestic carriers (e.g., Delta, United, American). We ended the day in the

E gates, which service the international carriers. We were able to collect data during a Virgin Atlantic Airlines layover as well as a Condor Airlines layover. Once the international gates were exhausted, we turned in our badges and left the airport with a total of 167 surveys from passenger participants.

LAS Field Experiment Problems

Part of the novelty of this TMT field experiment is (a) TMT field experiments have rarely been done and (b) the high-security nature of an international airport makes this TMT field experiment particularly worthy of discussion. One of the more exciting aspects of this study was to see what occurred while in the field. We were particularly interested in what occurred despite the advanced planning and attention to detail. No experiment is perfect and with that being said, we did run in to some problems while completing data collection at LAS. These problems are important to address and discuss in order to not only provide information for data collection of TMT field experiments but also to provide insight in to conducting these field experiments in a high-security area, such as an international airport.

The first problem that became apparent at the beginning was telling passenger participants to complete the survey in order. During previous studies in the lab, the lead researcher always observed participants completing the survey in order. However, at the beginning of data collection we noticed many passenger participants were not completing the survey in order. Because of TMT's death manipulation and death-thought accessibility measure (manipulation check), the surveys must be completed in order or you will not get the desired effects. Once the researchers realized this occurred, we started telling passenger participants to complete the survey in order. Those surveys that were not completed in order were thrown out ($N = 6$).

The second problem that we noticed early on was the strong desire for passenger participants to talk to one another while taking the survey. This is one constraint to conducting field experiments in general. In a lab setting, the desire to talk to other participants would be low to nonexistent. If participants did talk in a lab setting, the researcher would be able to quickly fix the problem. However, when conducting experiments in the field, especially an airport, it is not easy to control discussions among passenger participants and other passengers. Because two different surveys were randomly distributed, this did cause some confusion in passenger participants. However, once they checked to see that theirs were different, it seemed to work as a deterrent from discussing their survey with other passenger participants, therefore working in our favor.

The next set of problems concerns actually finding passenger participants willing to complete the study. As you can imagine, international airports are busy places, and LAS is no exception. During the morning data collection, it was apparent that some researchers were better at getting people to respond than others. Once one passenger participant said no, the rest of the passenger participants surrounding them also said no. Therefore, receiving a no was detrimental for data collection in that particular gate area. Because of this, in the afternoon one researcher quit recruiting and focused on keeping all of the surveys together and keeping a running count for how many passenger participants were in each condition. The next problem we ran into was that passengers headed to some geographical locations were more apt to complete the surveys than others. This was important to note to the researchers so that we didn't have a large amount from one particular geographical area; that all geographical areas were represented. We noticed passenger participants from Little Rock, Arkansas, and Oklahoma City, Oklahoma were the most eager to complete surveys. However, Kansas City, Missouri, passengers outright refused to participate. Our international passenger participants were also willing to complete surveys. It is important to note that when collecting data from international passenger participants, it was important to engage in a conversation with them first to ensure they could speak English well enough to complete the survey. Due to LAS's "unique" culture, the researchers needed to ensure passenger participants were not intoxicated while completing the survey. This also required pre-conversations prior to handing out the survey. Last, gambling may have played a role in whether passenger participants were willing to take part in the study. Because gambling is unique to LAS, it provides other options for activities while waiting for a flight. Therefore, we may have missed some passenger participants because they chose to gamble while waiting for their flight rather than waiting in the waiting area. Furthermore, those passengers choosing to wait in the private airline lounges also were not an option for participants.

With these issues, it seems fair to state this was not a true random sample. However, we can ensure there was random assignment into experimental conditions. When conducting research with field experiments, you run the risk of not getting every type of participant you would like. But, with the advanced planning and the presence in every gate area in LAS, we ensured the most diverse sample possible. Because of this we do feel it is representative of the population of passengers flying through LAS on an everyday basis. These problems help lay the groundwork for future TMT field experiments. While there were some problems with this field experiment, it provides interesting insight to what it is like to complete a TMT field experiment. Additionally, we feel there is a future in TMT research for field experiments and would like to call for more to be completed.

Future of TMT Field Experiments

We have argued that there are benefits and costs associated with laboratory research and field experiments. In particular, laboratory experiments allow strong causal inference, whereas field experiments are conducive to strong external validity. For instance, when past research has investigated the effects of mortality salience on adherence to cultural norms, researchers included traditional methods of inducing mortality salience (i.e., write about what will happen after your death) as well as taking advantage of a cemetery to induce mortality salience (Gailliot, Stillman, Schmeichel, Maner, & Plant, 2008). Rather than recommend one approach or another, we hope that in the future, researchers will conduct complementary laboratory and field experiments.

Given the bulk of empirical evidence for mortality salience comes from laboratory research (Burke, Martens, & Faucher, 2010), we consider the need to support laboratory findings with field research as especially important for mortality salience. Indeed, our intention in writing this chapter is that other likeminded researchers will benefit from the field experiment approach we took at McCarran International Airport. However, given the numerous difficulties we experienced in conducting this research, it may be that field experiments of the future are better conducted in cemeteries as opposed to airports.

References

Arndt, J., Cook, A., & Routledge, C. (2004). The blueprint of terror management: understanding the cognitive architecture of psychological defense against the awareness of death. In J. Greenberg, S. L. Koole & T. Pyszczynski (Eds.), *Handbook of experimental existential psychology* (pp. 35–53). New York: Guilford.

Becker, E. (1973). *The denial of death.* New York: Free Press.

Burke, B. L., Martens, A., & Faucher, E. H. (2010). Two decades of terror management theory: A meta-analysis of mortality salience research. *Personality and Social Psychology Review, 14,* 155–195.

Florian, V., Mikulincer, M., & Hirschberger, G. (2002). The anxiety-buffering function of close relationships: Evidence that relationship commitment acts as a terror management mechanism. *Journal of Personality and Social Psychology, 82*(4), 527–542. doi:10.1027//0022.3514.82.4.527

Forgas, J. P., Dunn, E., & Granland, S. (2008). Are you being served . . . ? An unobtrusive experiment of affective influences on helping in a department store. *European Journal of Social Psychology, 38*(2), 333–342. doi:10.1002/ejsp.455

Gailliot, M. T., Stillman, T. F., Schmeichel, B. J., Maner, J. K., & Plant, E. A. (2008). Mortality salience increases adherence to salient norms and values. *Personality and Social Psychology Bulletin, 34*(7), 993–1003.

Greenberg, J., Pyszczynski, T., Solomon, S., Rosenblatt, A., Veeder, M., Kirkland, S., & Lyon, D. (1990). Evidence for terror mangement theory II: The effects of mortality salience on reactions to those who threaten or bolster the cultural worldview. *Journal of Personality and Social Psychology, 58*(2), 308–318.

Harrison, G. W. (2005). Field experiments and control. In G. W. Harrison, J. Carpenter & J. A. List (Eds.), *Field experiments in economics (Research in experimental economics, Volume 10)* (pp. 17–50). Bigley, UK: Emerald Group Publishing Limited.

Harrison, G. W., & List, J. A. (2004). Field experiments. *Journal of Economic Literature, XLII,* 1009–1055.

Latane, B., & Dabbs, J. M. (1975). Sex, group size, and helping in three cities. *Sociometry, 38,* 180–194.

Martin, I. M., & Kamins, M. (2008). Relationships can disappear in a puff of smoke: A test of terror management theory and risk perceptions on smoking behavior. *Journal of Consumer Behaviors, 7,* 14–28.

Mikulincer, M., Florian, V., & Hirschberger, G. (2003). The existential function of close relationships: Introducing death into the science of love. *Personality and Social Psychology Review, 7*, 20–40. doi:http://dx.doi.org/10.1207%2FS15327957PSPR0701_2

Piliavin, J. A., & Piliavin, I. M. (1972). Effect of blood on reactions to a victim. *Journal of Personality and Social Psychology, 23*(3), 353–361. doi:10.1037/h0033166

Pyszczynski, T., Greenberg, J., & Solomon, S. (1997). Why do we need what we need? A terror management perspective on the roots of human social motivation. *Psychological Inquiry, 8*, 1–20.

Pyszczynski, T., Greenberg, J., & Solomon, S. (2005). The machine in the ghost: A dual process model of defense against conscious and unconscious death related thought. In J. Forgas, W. P. Kipling & S. M. Laham (Eds.), *Social motivation: Conscious and unconscious processes* (pp. 40–54). New York: Cambridge University Press.

Roe, B. E., & Just, D. R. (2009). Internal and external validity in economics research: Tradeoffs between experiments, field experiments, natural experiments, and field data. *American Journal of Agricultural Economics, 91*(5), 1266–1271.

Singleton, R., & Straits, B. (2010). *Approaches to social research* (5th ed.). New York: Oxford University Press.

Solomon, S., Greenberg, J., & Pyszczynski, T. (2000). Pride and prejudice: Fear of death and social behavior. *Current Directions is Psychological Science, 9*, 200–204. doi:10.1111/1467–8721.00094

Solomon, S., Greenberg, J., Schimel, J., Arndt, J., & Pyszczynski, T. (2004). Human awareness of mortality and the evolution of culture. In M. Schaller & C. S. Crandall (Eds.), *The psychological foundations of culture* (pp. 15–40). Mahwah, NJ: Lawrence Erlbaum Associates.

15

CULTURAL UNIVERSALS AND DIFFERENCES IN DEALING WITH DEATH

Young Chin Park and Tom Pyszczynski

Terror management theory (TMT; Solomon, Greenberg, & Pyszczynski, 1991; Pyszczynski, Solomon, & Greenberg, 2015) posits that one of the most important functions of human culture is to provide meanings and values that help people assuage the potential for anxiety that results from their awareness of the inevitability of death. From this perspective, the cultural meaning systems that contemporary humans use to derive security are the products of a long process of human innovation, debate, and revision that occurred gradually—and sometimes rapidly—over the course of human history as our ancestors became aware of death and used their sophisticated intellectual capacities to invent beliefs and values that helped them control their death-related fears. Although TMT addresses many other aspects of human behavior and experience, at its core, it is a theory of culture. It posits that although different groups of people, living in different times and places, developed different meaning systems, managing the potential for existential terror is a universal human need that all cultures must address, albeit sometimes in very different ways. This chapter will explore the commonalities and differences in the ways that cultures address the problem of death.

Terror Management Theory

TMT (Solomon et al., 1991, 2015) starts with a consideration of how human beings are both similar to and different from all other animals. Like other animals, humans are born with an innate proclivity for self-preservation and continued existence. But human beings have evolved cognitive capacities that are far more sophisticated than what is found in any other species. Human beings are capable of symbolic thought and language, auto-noetic thought that makes it possible to project oneself in time and recall past events and imagine future ones that have not yet experienced, and self-awareness, the ability to step back and conceive of oneself as a unique being, distinct from all others. These abilities are highly adaptive and play important roles in the human self-regulatory system, (Carver & Scheier, 1981, 2000) that provides our species with the flexibility in behavior necessary to adapt to and prosper in diverse and rapidly changing ecological niches. However, they also give rise to a major problem that changed the nature of our species. Our sophisticated intelligence makes us aware of the inevitability of our own death, and that death can come at any time for a multitude of reasons, none of which are particularly appealing. The juxtaposition of this awareness of the inevitability of death with our innate propensity for continued survival produces the potential for paralyzing terror that would be highly aversive and likely to undermine the goal-directed behavior necessary to our survival.

To cope with this terror, our ancestors used their sophisticated cognitive capacities to invent ways of understanding the world that give meaning, purpose, and significance to their lives; provide standards for valued behavior; and encompass preexisting belief systems that provide hope of either literally or symbolically transcending death. Ideas that helped our ancestors cope with their awareness of death were thus especially appealing, likely to be shared with others, and eventually institutionalized as cultural knowledge. Thus, awareness of death transformed the way our ancestors used their intelligence to interpret their experiences to create the world of meaning in which they lived, which provided the basis upon which later generations built to create the world of meaning in which humankind currently lives.

Literal immortality is provided by cultural beliefs that life continues in some form after physical death. Although the specific content of these beliefs varies, all cultures promote the existence of some form of afterlife, whether it be in the form of a heavenly paradise, an ongoing cycle of reincarnation, a blending of consciousness with one's ancestors, or a multitude of other ways in which life is believed to continue after physical death. Elaborate details of the nature of these afterlives are provided in sacred texts, such as the Bible, the Quran, and the Tibetan Book of the Dead. Spiritual beings or deities that have the power to control life and function as gatekeepers to the afterlife are also found in virtually all cultures. Some ancient cultures, such as those found in Egypt, China, and Meso-America, devoted enormous portions of their economies to build necropolises that served as gateways to the afterlife for their dead that continue to exist and fascinate visitors thousands of years after their last residents vanished. Although there is some debate as to whether the earliest hunter-gather cultures had afterlife beliefs (e.g., Norenzayan et al., 2014; Wright, 2009), from the perspective of TMT, such beliefs would be expected to develop gradually over time and place as early humans struggled to come to grips with the awareness of their mortality. It appears that there was considerable cross-cultural pollination of immortality beliefs, with later belief systems often building on previous ones, as, for example, in the roots of many Jewish, Christian, and Muslim beliefs in earlier Zoroastrian ideas, or in some ideas adapted by Buddhism finding precedence in Taoism, Confucism Jainism, and Hinduism.

Over the past several hundred years, science and philosophy provided new ways of understanding nature that undermined beliefs in literal immortality among some people in some parts of the world. Nonetheless, recent international surveys suggest that only 23% of people worldwide believe that one ceases to exist after physical death, ranging from a low of 2% in Indonesia to a high of 40% in South Korea and Spain (only 11% of Americans reported believing that life ceases after physical death; Ipsos, 2011). The rise of scientific worldviews has also encouraged renewed efforts to use scientific means to defeat death, in the form of technologies that are hoped to radically increase the length of the human lifespan and make immortality a practical possibility (e.g., de Grey, 2005; Kurzweil, 2001). Hope for scientific ways of extending the human lifespan may begin providing another means of coping with the problem of death, which may be especially appealing to those who do not believe in spiritual forms of afterlife.

All cultures, even modern ones that eschew belief in literal immortality, also provide the hope of symbolic immortality, the possibility of transcending death by being part of something greater than oneself that continues on into eternity. By being part of a family, ethnic group, religion, nation, political party, corporation, or profession, one is able to continue on by virtue of the continued prospering of the groups with which one identifies. This symbolic form of immortality is enhanced when we make valued contributions to these groups, leaving marks such as monuments, fortunes, new ideas, works of art, music, literature, or science. Thus symbolic immortality is attained by conceiving of oneself as a valuable participant in a meaningful universe—which is the essence of self-esteem. TMT posits people protect themselves from the ever-present potential for anxiety that results from their awareness of the inevitability of death by maintaining self-esteem and faith in their cultural worldviews.

Self-esteem and cultural worldviews attain the capacity to protect people from anxiety through the socialization process, in which the protection from distress provided by attachment to parents or other primary caretakers is transferred to these two psychological entities as a shield against the anxiety that arises from awareness of the inevitability of death. As Bowlby (1970) and other attachments theorists (e.g., Shaver & Mikulincer, 2002) suggest, affectional bonds between parent and child, initiated through comforting physical contact in the earliest days of life, function to relieve children's distress when their needs are not being met or their continued existence is threatened. This comfort and protection quickly becomes associated with parental love, which becomes the child's primary basis for security. As children mature and their capacities increase, displays of parental affection become increasingly contingent on their increasingly competent behavior, such that being a good little boy or girl becomes associated with parental affection and protection.

Because of their own socialization into the culture's worldview, parents are especially pleased and affectionate when their children exemplify cultural values and less so when they fall short of them. As verbal abilities and the capacity for increasingly abstract thought emerge, the parents and other significant others add to this protection by teaching children the cultural worldview, which usually includes concepts of deities or a supernatural world that provides protection on a grander scale to those who believe in and live up to the culture's values. As children become aware of the inevitability of death and there are things from which their parents cannot protect them, this protection becomes increasingly transferred to the culture and its spiritual concepts, which usually include hope guides for how to transcend death in the afterlife. In this way, children become enculturated into the beliefs and values of their culture as the sources of meaning and value they use as a shield against the potential anxiety. This suggests that cultural differences in parenting practices and style should be associated with cultural differences in how people cope with the problem of death—a hypothesis that, to our knowledge, has not yet been directly tested.

Thus, from the perspective of TMT, awareness of death and vulnerability is a universal human problem that is addressed differently by different cultures. The incredible diversity of cultural beliefs and values that have existed over the course of history, and that continue to exist across the diverse regions of the planet, show this problem can be addressed in many different ways. From the perspective of TMT, the common feature that cuts across the time and space that separates these diverse cultures is that construing oneself as a valuable participant in a meaningful universe provides protection from anxiety rooted in the existential contradiction of wanting to live, but knowing that one must someday die.

Empirical Assessments of TMT Hypotheses

Empirical support for TMT comes from studies testing variations and combinations of three basic hypotheses (for recent reviews, see Greenberg, Vail, & Pyszczynski, 2014; Kesebir & Pyszczynski, 2011). Studies testing the *anxiety-buffer hypothesis* have shown that increasing self-esteem makes people less prone to subjectively experienced anxiety, physiological arousal, and anxiety-related behavior (for a review, see Pyszczynski, Greenberg, Solomon, Arndt, & Schimel, 2004). Studies testing the *mortality-salience (MS) hypothesis* have shown that reminders of death increase the tendency to cling to one's worldview, embrace those who support it and reject those who challenge it, and strive harder to bolster one's self-worth (for a meta-analytic review, see Burke, Martens, and Faucher (2010). Studies testing the *death-thought accessibility (DTA) hypothesis* have shown that threats to self-esteem, worldview, or close attachments increase the accessibility of death-related thoughts while boosts to any of these psychological entities reduce DTA (for a review, see Hayes, Schimel, Arndt, & Faucher, 2010). Research has also combined these hypotheses in various ways, showing, for example, that boosting self-esteem, affirming one's worldview, or thinking about close attachment figures eliminates defensive responses to MS and that the same conditions that increase DTA also increase the pursuit of faith in one's worldview, self-esteem, and close attachments (Arndt, Cook, & Routledge, 2004).

Support for these basic TMT hypotheses has been provided by well over 500 experiments conducted in over 30 countries the world over. Although most of these studies were conducted with participants from Western cultures (Burke et al., 2010) in the United States, Canada, and Europe, a substantial number were conducted in the Middle East and North Africa (Israel, Palestine, Iran, Ivory Coast, Turkey) and Asia (Japan, Korea, China, Hong Kong, Tibet, India), and a few were conducted with bicultural individuals (e.g., bicultural Aboriginal Australians, Asian Americans). Nonetheless, Martin and van den Bos (2014, p. 50) recently argued TMT "trivializes culture" and glosses over important cultural differences. They note, for example, that there is some evidence MS effects tend to be less consistent and of smaller magnitude in non-Western cultures and several studies in non-Western cultures have failed to find any effects of MS at all. They note Burke et al's (2010) meta-analysis found MS affected Americans significantly more than Europeans, Israelis, or Asians, and suggest non-Americans may not show terror management defenses to the same degree as Americans. In addition, Yen and Cheng (2010) conducted a meta-analysis of 24 experiments in East Asian cultures and concluded the average effect size of worldview defense was not significantly different from zero (p. 189).

Although it may be that findings from TMT research thus far have been more consistent in American and Western cultures than in other regions, this does not imply TMT is less applicable to non-Western cultures. First, it is important to note theory-consistent effects of death reminders have emerged in *all* cultures in which TMT hypotheses have been tested. It is also important to realize cultural differences in responses to death are *exactly* what TMT predicts, given that cultures vary in the ways in which they address the universal human problem of mortality. It should also not be surprising that, at this point in the development of research on these issues, results are more consistent in studies of Western cultures. Although intended to illuminate both universal features of the human condition and cultural differences in how people deal with these issues, TMT was developed by American psychologists and inspired most directly by previous theorizing within the Western intellectual tradition (e.g., Ernest Becker, Otto Rank, Soren Kierkegaard, Sigmund Freud). Perhaps most importantly, the research paradigms developed to test TMT hypotheses were developed and initially tested within the context of Western culture, most notably the United States near the end of the 20th century. Thus the implicit assumptions about human nature that formed the backdrop for these programs of research were undoubtedly shaped by the cultural backgrounds of those designing this research. So although we acknowledge the possibility of cultural biases and short-sightedness in the reasoning that led to these programs of research and encourage the development of new paradigms for studying these issues that build from non-Western perspectives, the important question for cultural researchers is whether findings from paradigms that originated within any given culture generalize to other cultures, and if not, what is responsible for these differences.

Research on Cultural Similarities and Differences in Terror Management Processes

We turn now to a critical assessment of similarities and differences in how people from different cultures deal with their awareness of death. TMT posits that death is a universal human problem that people cope with by deploying their cultural worldviews, self-esteem, and close attachments. TMT also posits that the specific ways in which people deal with awareness of death depends on the cultural worldviews they have internalized to provide solace in the fact of this knowledge. How well does the research available to date fit this analysis? And what additional questions need to be asked to enhance our understanding of cultural universals and differences in dealing with death?

Literal Immortality, Symbolic Immortality, and Cultural Worldview Defense

Numerous studies have shown that thoughts of death (i.e., mortality salience) motivate people to think and behave in ways that validate and support their culture's shared meaning systems that provide the hope of literal and symbolic immortality. Research has found that MS increased American participants' belief in an afterlife (e.g., Osarchuk & Tatz, 1973; Schoenrade, 1989) and Canadian participants' faith in gods and supernatural powers, including those not part of their own culture's teachings (Norenzayan & Hansen, 2006). This latter finding that MS increased faith in supernatural powers not part of one's own cultural tradition is intriguing. Although it is possible this suggests that death concerns lead people of faith to align with deities not part of their worldview, we suspect these findings more likely reflect a sense that the different deities embraced by different cultures reflect the same underlying spiritual powers that are experienced differently depending on one's cultural background. It may also be that the existence of any spiritual entities increases the plausibility of the existence of one's own, and that these findings reflect an indirect bolstering of one's own faith.

Research has also shown that MS increases attitudes and behaviors aimed at providing symbolic immortality. For example, MS makes Americans more interested in fame in the form of having a star named after them (Greenberg et al., 2010), greater attraction to artwork by celebrities (Greenberg et al., 2010), and less worried that a plane will crash when a celebrity is a passenger on it

(Kesebir & Chiu, 2008). MS also increases the appeal of money and material objects, another source of symbolic immortality, in the United States and Poland (e.g., Kasser & Sheldon, 2000; Zaleskiewicz, Gasiorowska, Kesebir, Luszczynska, & Pyszczynski, 2013). For example, MS has been shown to increase estimates of one's future income among Americans and estimates of the size of currency notes among Poles. Even very subtle ads for a university's Day of the Dead celebration increased web surfers' willingness to spend money on luxury goods (Chopik & Edelstein, 2014). Thinking about spending or saving money decreases the accessibility of death-related thoughts among Americans and Poles, although thoughts of savings are more effective in this regard, perhaps because savings preserves one's fortune (Zaleskiewicz et al., 2013). Of course, many cultures, especially religious ones, discourage the pursuit of material wealth in favor of spiritual pursuits. In such cases, MS would be expected to reduce the appeal of material goals. Consistent with this reasoning, research has shown that existentially threatening life events reduced the desire for material goods among Hong Chinese Christians but not among atheists (Hui, Chan, Lau, Cheung, & Mok, 2014).

Other research has shown that MS affects attitudes toward another common source of symbolic immortality—having children—in the United States, the Netherlands, Germany, and China (e.g., Fritsche et al., 2007; Wisman & Goldenberg, 2005) and that these effects are sensitive to specific features of the cultural context. For example, an initial study conducted in the Netherlands showed that reminders of death increased the desire for children among men but not women. Follow-up studies showed the null effect among women was due to ambivalence related to the conflict between parenting and career experiences by many contemporary Western women; MS increased the desire for children among women when they were previously primed with information about the compatibility of parenting and careers. Research conducted in Germany showed that MS increased the desire for offspring and the accessibility of thoughts related to children among both men and women, and that priming thoughts of children reduced DTA (Fritsche et al., 2007). Further support for the role of offspring in promoting symbolic immortality comes from research showing that MS increased the desire to name one's offspring after oneself (Vicary, 2011). Research in China shows that viewing images of baby animals reduced death-thought accessibility, and that Chinese participants who read news reports of the death of babies predicted shorter life expectancies for themselves than people who read about death in general (Zhou, Lei, Marley, & Chen 2009). MS also increased Chinese disapproval of their government's birth control policy (Zhou, Liu, Chen, & Yu, 2008). These findings likely reflect the value of promoting the future of the group by producing more children.

From the perspective of TMT, maintaining faith in one's worldview and self-esteem are essential requirements for being remembered by others and thus are important pathways to symbolic immortality. Thus, research shows that

MS promotes more positive reactions to those who validate one's worldviews and more negative reactions to those who violate or challenge it (Greenberg et al., 1990), harsher judgments for social transgressors (Abdollahi, 2006; Florian & Mikulincer, 1997), and increased stereotyping (Schimel et al., 1999) and nationalistic identity (Greenberg et al., 1994), which provides additional evidence of the role of death concerns in promoting symbolic immortality striving through ingroup identity. These findings come from studies conducted in the United States, Canada, the Netherlands, Germany, France, Poland, Italy, Spain, the United Kingdom, the Ivory Coast, Israel, Palestine, and Iran.

It appears the effects of death reminders on diverse forms of worldview supportive behavior are not related to the person's specific thoughts or emotional reactions to the problem of death. The vast majority of these studies have assessed such affective responses and found no correlation between the strength of emotional and defensive responses. About 10 years ago, the senior author began corresponding with Iranian psychologist Adbollhossein Abdollahi, who wrote to discuss the fact that many students in his classes at a Muslim university in Iran reported they did not fear death and actually hoped it would come soon so as to hasten their transition to paradise. We discussed differences in the way Iranian and American cultures approached death, including the traditional practice of Iranians praying while holding their burial shrouds purchased during their pilgrimage to Mecca, and of men crawling down into their already-dug-out graves to pray. Despite the far greater openness to death found in Iranian culture, Abdollahi (2006) replicated five separate types of MS effects in field and laboratory studies in Iran, including findings of MS increasing punishment for a person who violates cultural values, increasing charitable giving to a beggar, and increasing negative attitudes toward outgroups. These findings suggest that defensive responses to MS are not specific to cultures that outwardly sanitize, euphemize, or otherwise hide death from public view.

These typical forms of worldview defense have also been observed in MS studies conducted in Asian cultures. Japanese undergraduates become more critical toward an anti-Japan essay writer when reminded of their own death (Heine, Harihara, & Niiya, 2002). Hong Kong Chinese students evaluated a pro–Hong Kong essay author in a more positive way and allocated more job vacancies to members of their ingroup after MS relative to a control group, (Tam, Chiu, & Lau, 2007). Similarly, non-Buddhist South Koreans gave more negative evaluations to a person who criticized Korea and were more supportive of government policies aimed at protecting South Korea from North Korea after being reminded of their mortality (Park & Pyszczynski, 2015). However, Ma-Kellams and Blascovich (2011) found that MS increased European American students negative attitudes toward prostitution and blaming of innocent victims but had the opposite effect on Asian Americans, leading to decreased derogation of prostitutes and increased sympathetic attitudes toward innocent victims. Despite the occasional inconsistent result, the finding that MS affects attitudes and behavior relevant to one's cultural worldview is highly robust and consistent across diverse cultures. Findings of cultural differences in how thoughts of death affect these attitudes are intriguing and call for additional research and conceptual analysis of how these responses relate to the cultures in question.

Self-Esteem

There is also a large body of evidence supporting the TMT proposition that the motivation to maintain self-esteem is rooted in the protection from anxiety that it provides. Boosting self-esteem makes people less prone to anxiety and anxiety-related behavior; reminders of death increase diverse forms of self-esteem striving; threats to self-esteem increase DTA; and boosts to self-esteem reduce DTA and eliminate the effect of MS on worldview defense (for a review, see Pyszczynski, Greenberg, Solomon, Arndt, & Schimel, 2004). Research shows the types of behaviors that MS motivates people to pursue in order to bolster their self-esteem vary depending on the particular cultural standards to which they are committed. For example, those whose self-esteem is contingent on their driving ability drive faster and perform more risky maneuvers on a driving simulator; those who value physical strength exert more force when squeezing a hand dynamometer; those who value physical fitness increase their intentions to spend time at the gym; those who place great value of physical appearance report more monitoring of their appearance and increased intentions to have sex. None of these tendencies are increased by MS among people who place less value on these particular sources of self-worth.

Given that cultures vary in the extent to which they value different behavior and characteristics, it follows that there will be cultural variability in the domains of self-esteem upon which people rely for protection from existential fear. Cultural psychologists have long noted that cultures vary considerably in how they construe the self, its relation to the group, and the types of behavior and attitudes regarding the self that are valued and discouraged (e.g., Markus & Kitayama, 1991; Triandis, 1989). Cultural psychologists argue that the cognitive, emotional, and motivational elements of the self-system are cultural constructions and that the nature of the self varies greatly depending on one's culture. Far and away the most widely discussed and researched cultural difference in selfhood is whether the self is construed primarily as an independent being in which one's uniqueness and individualism is emphasized, or an interdependent being, in which one's relations and connections to others is are emphasized.

Western cultures, especially those in Europe and North America, conceive of the self as an independent and autonomous entity, distinct from all others. Geertz (1975) described the Western individualistic conception of self as one in which the person is viewed as "a bounded, unique, more or less integrated motivational and cognitive universe, a dynamic center of awareness, emotion, judgment, and action organized into a distinctive whole and set contrastively both against other such wholes and against a social and natural background" (p. 48). From this perspective, independence, uniqueness, autonomy, and expressing one's own unique essence are highly valued. The Western value of individual excellence promotes a more competitive approach to life and less veiled expressions of selfishness and egotism

Although Western concept of self recognizes the value of relating to and connecting with others, this is usually construed as an effective way of controlling others so that one's own needs are met.

In contrast, many other cultures, especially those in East and Central Asia, Africa, and parts of the Middle East and South America, emphasize the interdependent and interconnected nature of self, in which one is defined largely in terms of one's relations with others. As Markus and Kitayama (1991) describe it, "Experiencing interdependence entails seeing oneself as part of an encompassing social relationship and recognizing that one's behavior is determined, contingent on, and, to a large extent organized by what the actor perceives to be the thoughts, feelings, and actions of others in the relationship," in which people are "more connected and less differentiated from others" and "motivated to find a way to fit in with relevant others, to fulfill and create obligation, and in general to become part of various interpersonal relationships" (p. 227). Cultures that promote an interdependent self place greater value on connectedness, communion, and cooperation with others, thus encouraging an interdependent self-concept. To maintain social ties, such cultures value cooperativeness, humility, modesty, and self-effacement as ways of promoting interpersonal harmony (Heine, Lehman, Markus, & Kitayama, 1999).

These cultural differences in the way the self is construed suggest that people from individualistic and interdependent cultures would differ in the ways they use self-esteem to cope with the problem of death. Some have argued the pursuit of self-esteem is a Western affectation not found in interdependent cultures (e.g., Heine, Lehman, Markus, & Kitayama, 1999), because people in East Asian interdependent cultures typically do not show the self-serving biases and self-aggrandizement typically taken as indicators of self-esteem striving in Western individualistic cultures. We think this view entails adopting an overly narrow Western understanding of self-esteem. Instead, we agree with theorists who view the divergent self-related behavior of people from individualist and interdependent cultures as distinct ways of living up to their culture's values regarding appropriate and valued behavior (e.g., Sedikides, Gaertner, & Toguchi (2003)). Indeed, the TMT definition of self-esteem as the sense that one is living up to the standards of value prescribed by one's cultural worldview explicitly links self-esteem to cultural values. Thus, a person embedded in a culture that values individualism and standing out from others would seek self-esteem by boldly demonstrating how he or she towers above others on valued dimensions, while a person embedded in a culture that values interpersonal harmony would seek self-esteem by seeking interpersonal harmony, deferring to others, and humbly avoiding implying that he or she stands out from or is better than other group members.

Studies of the effect of MS on self-esteem-related behavior in East Asian cultures sometimes document differences from what is typically found in parallel research in Western cultures. By and large, the findings from this research are what would be expected given the interdependent nature of East Asian cultures that value interpersonal harmony and humility (but there are some notable exceptions, to be discussed later).

Wakimoto (2006) found that Japanese students who were strongly enculturated to the Japanese interdependent worldview responded to MS by viewing their success more negatively and rating themselves in a self-effacing manner, in accordance with the interdependent cultural value of modesty and humility. However, MS decreased these tendencies among those less enculturated to the Japanese worldview, thus producing responses more in line with the typical individualistic mode of self-esteem maintenance. A follow-up study replicated this effect and showed that MS increased expectations of positive responses from friends for one's self-effacing attributions (Wakimoto, 2009). Further evidence of the role of interpersonal connections in terror management processes among Japanese students is provided by studies showing that viewing positive interactions with friends as closer in time is associated with greater satisfaction with one's relationships and that MS leads participants to view such positive interactions between themselves and friends as closer in time (Wakimoto, 2011).

Research also documents many other ways that death reminders increase the tendency of East Asians to associate the self with their ingroup. For example, Watanabe and Karasawa (2012) found that MS led Japanese participants to make faster judgments in a self-ingroup matching task but did not affect their speed on a self-outgroup matching task. In a related vein, MS increased Hong Kong Chinese participants' preference for others who praised their nation over those who criticized it, and this effect emerged regardless of participants' level of national identification. National identification did predict their tendency to allocate more resources to their nation than a rival nation, but MS increased this bias among low-identifiers such that they no longer differed from high identifiers. In a study conducted in Turkey, a predominantly Muslim and relatively interdependent country, Kökdemir and Yeniçeri (2010) found that MS increased negative evaluations of essays that criticized the type of university (either public or private) participants were attending, and increased the desire for their country to have closer relations with ethnically similar Turkmenistan and more distant relations with the ethnically dissimilar United Kingdom and Greece.

These studies converge in showing that MS increases ingroup identification among persons from interdependent cultures, similar to the many studies documenting these effects among persons from more individualistic culture. However, other studies found subtle differences in the way this ingroup identification is exhibited. Routledge et al. (2012) found that MS increased nationalism among

Chinese students but had no such effect on American students (Study 1). However, in a follow-up study, American students who scored high on a measure of interdependence responded to MS with increased willingness to sacrifice themselves for the sake of their group (Study 3). Apparently, identification with one's ingroup is a pervasive way of defending against death concerns regardless of the individualist or interdependent nature of one's culture, but the specific way in which this is manifested depends on cultural factors.

Evidence of divergent responses to MS depending on cultural values comes from a study in which MS increased individualism among Australian college students but decreased it (or increased collectivism) among Japanese college students (Kashima, Halloran, Yuki, & Kashima, 2004). Consistent with the TMT view that high self-esteem insulates people from death concerns, these effects were found among low but not high self-esteem participants in both cultural groups. This is consistent with Harmon-Jones et al's. (1997) finding that both dispositionally and situationally induced high levels of self-esteem eliminate the effect of MS on other defensive responses; this finding also supports the TMT proposition that self-esteem reduces the impact of threats and the need to defend against them. Kashima et al. (2004) also found cultural differences in the type of death threat that produced the greatest increase in culturally consistent behavior. Whereas thoughts of one's individual death produced a greater increase in individualism than thoughts of the death of one's culture among Australians, thoughts of one's culture's death produced a greater increase in collectivism than thoughts of one's individual death among Japanese participants (Kashima et al., 2004).

Other research has compared the buffering effects of individual versus collective self-esteem in individualist and interdependent cultures. Du et al. (2013) investigated the relationship between different types of self-esteem and self-reported death anxiety in Austrian and Chinese students. Somewhat surprisingly, they found that personal but not collective self-esteem was associated with lower death anxiety among both Austrian and Chinese samples, and that both self-competence and self-liking predicted lower levels of death anxiety for Austrians but only self-liking did so for Chinese. However, a follow-up study showed that relational self-esteem, involving one's assessments of one's relationships with others, was associated with lower death anxiety among Chinese participants. Whereas pride in one's group (collective self-esteem) did not predict lower death anxiety among Chinese people, pride in one's relationships did. Follow-up studies by Du et al. (2013) showed that whereas individual self-esteem moderated the effects of MS on worldview defense for Austrians, relational self-esteem moderated the effects of MS on worldview defense for the Chinese. Interestingly, high individual self-esteem was associated with lower worldview defense among Austrians, presumably because it reduced the need to employ defenses in domains distinct from self-esteem. However, for Chinese participants, high relational self-esteem was associated with higher levels of worldview defense, presumably because this defensive reaction was related to the feelings of community upon which relational self-esteem is based (Arndt & Greenberg, 1999). The authors interpreted these findings as consistent with the greater connection between self and ingroup in interdependent cultures.

Another way this increased connection between self and others is expressed in interdependent cultures is their strong emphasis on family (Ho, 1998). Familialism refers to an orientation toward family relationships distinct from individualism and from concerns about romantic partners (Gaines et al., 1997; Gaines, Larbie, Patel, Pereira, & Sereke-Melake, 2005). To the extent that Chinese culture puts great value on the familial self, familial self-affirmation would be expected to be a particularly potent buffer against death anxiety relative to personal self-affirmation. Thus, Cai, Sedikides, and Jiang (2013) compared the effects of familial self-affirmation with that of individual self-affirmation on Chinese college students responses to MS. Whereas participants in a low self-affirmation condition responded to MS with the same increased disapproval of the Chinese birth-control policy found in other studies (Zhou, Liu, Chen, & Yu, 2008), those in the familial self-affirmation condition responded to MS with a more favorable attitude toward the birth-control policy. This suggests that familial self-affirmation may be an effective source of protection against death anxiety in interdependent cultures.

Culture, Religion, and the Meaning of Death

According to TMT, a major purpose of cultural worldviews is to provide a pathway toward literal and symbolic immortality. This raises the question of whether belief in literal immortality reduces the need for other types of death-denying defensiveness, such as the pursuit of symbolic immortality in the form of self-esteem and faith in one's worldview. Jonas and Fischer (2006) found that affirming one's religious beliefs led to low levels of DTA and worldview defense among intrinsically religious people (for whom religion permeates all aspects of their lives.) In a related vein, Dechesne et al. (2003) found that bogus scientific reports concluding that near death experiences are evidence for the existence of an after-life eliminated the increase in self-esteem and worldview defense that MS otherwise produced among Dutch and American students. These studies suggest that thoughts that affirm one's faith in the existence of an afterlife can sometimes reduce the need for other forms of death denial. But many other studies have demonstrated that MS increases diverse forms of death-denying defenses, even among highly devout people with strong faith in an afterlife. It may be that thoughts of such faith provide sufficient terror management for a while after they occur, but not enough to eliminate the need for ongoing maintenance of one's anxiety buffer once these thoughts have left consciousness.

Another important question centers on the impact of cultural beliefs that construe death as something other than the end of life (Rindfleisch & Burroughs,

2004). For example, Hinduism regards mortal life as only one of many stages in a cycle of birth and death. Confucian, Taoist, and Buddhist thought also construes death as a transition and an integral part of life (Tang, Wu, & Yan, 2002). Cross-cultural studies demonstrate that Malaysian students have lower death anxiety than Australian students as indicated by their scores on the Templar's Death Anxiety Scale (Schumaker, Barraclough, & Vagg, 1988). However, the many studies documenting MS effects in Asian populations show death remains an important existential concern despite these different ways their cultures construe death.

In a study designed to asses this type of cultural difference, Fernandez, Castano, and Singh (2010) found robust MS effects on worldview defense among Hindu Indians living in villages surrounding Varanasi, the famous holy city in which approximately 250 public cremations take place daily. This provides yet further evidence for the cross-cultural robustness of MS effects. However, workers in the Varanasi crematoria were unaffected by the MS inductions typically used in TMT studies. They did, however, show higher levels of worldview defense than other participants in the study in the absence of MS. Fernandez et al. (2010) interpreted this as evidence that chronic exposure to death from working at the crematoria produces a state of chronic death awareness and defensiveness in them.

Other studies suggest that the unique way of construing death in the Eastern philosophical context may influence the way at least some Asians respond to thoughts of death. Park and Choi (2002) found that Korean college students reminded of their own death praised socially desirable behaviors more favorably than did those who had not thought about their own death. However, this pattern was eliminated by exposure to Taoist ideas. When they read statements reflecting Taoist beliefs about life and death that underscore the transitional aspect of life, MS did not increase derogation of those who violated cultural norms compared to those in the control condition. In a similar vein, Yen (2012) found Chinese participants who were explicitly primed with Eastern cultural icons responded to MS by displaying greater belief in fatalism than Chinese participants primed with Western icons. For Westerners, however, MS did not affect the belief in fatalism. In other research in Taiwan, Yen and Cheng (2010) found MS did not increase pro-Taiwanese bias or increase belief in reincarnation, but it did increase the tendency to resign oneself to fate.

Recent studies conducted in South Korea revealed that although MS increases derogation of a person who criticizes Korea among non-Buddhists, this effect does not occur among Buddhists (Park & Pyszczynski, 2015); indeed, longer Buddhist meditation practice was associated with less derogation of the person critical of Korean culture. MS also increased self-criticism among non-Buddhists (consistent with Korean norms of humility and self-scrutiny), but had no effect on either lay Buddhists or Buddhist monks. We also found the effect of MS on derogation of a person who criticized Koreans was eliminated among Korean non-Buddhists after a 30-minute Zen meditation training exercise (Park & Pyszczynski, 2015).

Cross-cultural studies have documented that East Asians are more likely than Westerners to show dialectical emotional styles (Bagozzi, Wong, & Yi, 1999). Compared to Western culture, Eastern culture emphasizes the mutual coexistence and interdependence of life and death. Given the Eastern notion of yin and yang, rooted in Eastern Taoist philosophy, positive and negative elements are not thought of as mutually exclusive (e.g., Peng & Nisbett, 1999), leading East Asians to more comfortably accept psychological contradiction (Heine & Lehman, 1997). Chinese people with dialectical self-esteem conceive of themselves as both good and bad simultaneously (Spencer-Rogers, Peng, Wang, & Hou, 2004), whereas Euro-Americans are more likely to reconcile inconsistencies between their good and bad features (Lewin, 1951). Thus, the tendency to perceive the world as holistic, changing, and contradictory may lead East Asians to respond to death in a more dialectic manner.

Ma-Kellams & Blascovich (2012) investigated how East–West differences in cognitive style affect thoughts about enjoying one's life in responses to mortality salience. They found that for East Asians, thinking about death is linked to thinking about one's life. When primed with their own mortality, East Asians showed greater accessibility of life-related thoughts. In contrast, European Americans showed greater death-thought accessibility after an MS prime and no change in life-thought accessibility (Study 1). Later studies showed that after being reminded of one's mortality, East Asians expressed greater interest in enjoying daily life activities (Studies 2 and 5). The finding that both European Americans and Asian Americans primed with holism expressed greater life enjoyment after thinking about their own death, compared to those primed with linear thinking, provide further evidence that these tendencies are rooted in holistic thinking.

Multiculturalism

It's important to realize that today's world is an increasingly multicultural one in which people are exposed to a diverse range of cultural worldviews, with varying beliefs. Additionally, values and new ideas are being generated at an ever-increasing pace. People abstract their own unique worldviews from the vast array of ideas and teachings to which they are exposed over the course of their lives, and it is these individualized worldviews that are psychologically active in providing protection against anxiety. Although cultural psychologists focus on distinct types of cultural worldviews, it is widely recognized that people live in a world of diverse and blended cultural influences, with each person internalizing a diverse array of beliefs and values, some of which may be antithetical to other ones they embrace. Indeed, optimal distinctiveness theory (Brewer, 1991) views individualism and interdependence as aspects of self possessed by all people, with individuals and cultures varying in what they see as the optimal mix of the two tendencies.

Research shows these worldview elements vary in terms of their momentary accessibility and that people orient toward more accessible elements when in need of enhanced protection against existential fears (Jonas et al., 2008). This was demonstrated in a study of multicultural Aboriginal Australians who identify as both Aborigine and Australian. When reminded of death, these people shifted toward a more collectivist identity if their Aboriginal identity was primed but toward a more individualist identity if their Australian identity was primed (Halloran & Kashima, 2004).

Concluding Thoughts

The research reviewed in this chapter supports the TMT claim that death is a universal human problem that leads people from all cultures to seek meaning in life, value in themselves, and close interpersonal relationships. Although there is a remarkable degree of consistency in the findings of TMT research across diverse cultures, there is also evidence that culture exerts a profound influence on how people cope with death. Clearly, there is much more to be learned about cultural differences in how people deal with the universal human problem of mortality. We suspect the next generation of research on these issues will yield important insights into both the universal and culturally specific aspects of how human beings cope with this very basic existential problem that will provide clues as to how people the world over might better cope with their mortality and make the best out of their lives.

References

Abdollahi, A. (2006, July). *Terror management in Iran.* Presented at meeting of the International Society for Political Psychology, Barcelona, Spain.

Arndt, J., Cook, A., & Routledge, C. (2004). The blueprint of terror management: Understanding the cognitive architecture of psychological defense against the awareness of death. In J. Greenberg, S. L. Koole & T. Pyszczynski (Eds.), *Handbook of experimental existential psychology* (pp. 35–53). New York: Guilford.

Arndt, J., & Greenberg, J. (1999). The effects of a self-esteem boost and mortality salience on responses to boost relevant and irrelevant worldview threats. *Personality and Social Psychological Bulletin, 25,* 1331–1341. doi:10.1177/0146167299259001

Bagozzi, R. P., Wong, N., & Yi, Y. (1999). The role of culture and gender in the relationship between positive and negative affect. *Cognition and Emotion, 13*(6), 641–672. doi:10.1080/026999399379023

Bowlby, J. (1970). Disruption of affectional bonds and its effects on behavior. *Journal of Contemporary Psychotherapy, 2*(2), 75–86. doi:10.1007/BF02118173

Brewer, M. B. (1991). The Social Self: On being the same and different at the same time. *Personality and Social Psychology Bulletin, 17,* 475–482. doi:10.1177/0146167291175001

Burke, B. L., Martens, A., & Faucher, E. H. (2010). Two decades of terror management theory: A meta-analysis of mortality salience research. *Personality and Social Psychology Review, 14*(2), 155–195. doi:10.1177/1088868309352321

Cai, H., Sedikides, C., & Jiang, L. (2013). Familial self as a potent source of affirmation: Evidence from China. *Social Psychological and Personality Science, 4*(5), 529–537. doi:10.1177/1948550612469039

Carver, C. S., & Scheier, M. P. (1981). *Attention and self-regulation: A control-theory approach to human behavior.* New York: Springer-Verlag. doi:10.1007/978–1–4612–5887–2

Carver, C. S., & Scheier, M. F. (2000). On the structure of behavioral self-regulation. In M. Boekaerts, P. R. Pintrich, M. Zeidner, M. Boekaerts, P. R. Pintrich & M. Zeidner (Eds.), *Handbook of self-regulation* (pp. 41–84). San Diego, CA: Academic Press. doi:10.1016/B978–012109890–2/50032–9

Chopik, W. J., & Edelstein, R. S. (2014). Death of a salesman: Webpage-based manipulations of mortality salience. *Computers on Human Behavior, 31,* 94–99. doi:10.1016/j.chb.2013.10.022

Dechesne, M., Pyszczynski, T., Arndt, J., Ransom, S., Sheldon, K. M., van Knippenberg, A., & Janssen, J. (2003). Literal and symbolic immortality: The effect of evidence of literal immortality on self- esteem striving in response to mortality salience. *Journal of Personality and Social Psychology, 84,* 722–737. doi:10.1037/0022–3514.84.4.722

De Gray, A. D. N. J. (2005). Like it or not, life-extension research extends beyond bio-gerontology. *EMBO Reports, 6*(11), 1000–1000. doi:10.1038/sj.embor.7400565

Du, H., Jonas, E., Klackl, J., Agroskin, D., Hui, E. P., & Ma, L. (2013). Cultural influences on terror management: Independent and interdependent self-esteem as anxiety buffers. *Journal of Experimental Social Psychology, 49*(6), 1002–1011. doi:10.1016/j.jesp.2013.06.007

Fernandez, S., Castano, E., & Singh, I. (2010). Managing death in the burning grounds of Varanasi, India: A terror management investigation. *Journal of Cross-Cultural Psychology, 41*(2), 182–194. doi:10.1177/0022022109354376

Florian, V., & Mikulincer, M. (1997). Fear of Death and The Judgment of Social Transgressions: A multidimensional test of terror management theory. *Journal of Personality and Social Psychology, 73,* 369–380. doi:10.1037/0022–3514.73.2.369

Fritsche, I., Jonas, E., Fischer, P., Koranyi, N., Berger, N., & Fleischmann, B. (2007). Mortality salience and the desire for offspring. *Journal of Experimental Social Psychology, 43,* 753–762. doi:10.1016/j.jesp.2006.10.003

Gaines, S. O., Jr., Larbie, J., Patel, S., Pereira, L., & Sereke-Melake, Z. (2005). Cultural values among African-descended persons in the United Kingdom: Comparisons with European-descended and Asian-descended persons. *Journal of Black Psychology, 31,* 130–151. doi:10.1177/0095798405274720

Gaines, S. O., Marelich, W. D., Bledsoe, K. L., Steers, W. N., Henderson, M. C., Granrose, C. S., et al. (1997). Links between race/ethnicity and cultural values as mediated by race/ethnic identity and moderated by gender. *Journal of Personality and Social Psychology, 72,* 1460–1476. doi:10.1037/0022–3514.72.6.1460

Geertz, C. (1975). On the nature of anthropological understanding. *American Scientist, 63,* 47–53. http://www.jstor.org/stable/27845269

Greenberg, J., Kosloff, S., Solomon, S., Cohen, F., & Landau, M. J. (2010). Toward understanding the fame game: The effect of mortality salience on the appeal of fame. *Self and Identity, 9,* 1–18. doi:10.1080/15298860802391546

Greenberg, J., Pyszczynski, T., Solomon, S., Rosenblatt, A., Veeder, M., Kirkland, S., & Lyon, D. (1990). Evidence for terror management theory II: The effects of mortality salience reactions to those who threaten or bolster the cultural worldview. *Journal of Personality and Social Psychology, 58,* 308–318. doi:10.1037/0022–3514.58.2.308

Greenberg, J., Pyszczynski, T., Solomon, S., Simon, L., & Breus, M. (1994). The role of consciousness and accessibility of death-related thoughts in mortality salience effects. *Journal of Personality and Social Psychology, 67*, 627–637. doi:10.1037/0022-3514.67.4.627

Greenberg, J., Vail, K., & Pyszczynski, T. (2014). Terror management theory and research: How the desire for death transcendence drives our strivings for meaning and significance. *Advances in Motivation Science, 1*, 85–134. doi:10.1016/bs.adms.2014.08.003

Halloran, M., & Kashima, E. (2004). Social identity and worldview validation: The effects of ingroup identity primes and mortality salience on value endorsement. *Personality and Social Psychology Bulletin, 30*, 915–925. doi:10.1177/0146167204264080

Harmon-Jones, E., Simon, L., Greenberg, J., Pyszczynski, T., Solomon, S., & McGregor, H. (1997). Terror management theory and self-esteem: Evidence that increased self-esteem reduces mortality salience effects. *Journal of Personality and Social Psychology, 72*, 24–36. doi:10.1037/0022–3514.72.1.24

Hayes, J., Schimel, J., Arndt, J., & Faucher, E. H. (2010). A theoretical and empirical review of the death-thought accessibility concept in terror management research. *Psychological Bulletin, 136*(5), 699–739. doi:10.1037/a0020524

Heine, S. J., Harihara, M., & Niiya, Y. (2002). Terror management in Japan. *Asian Journal of Social Psychology, 5*, 187–196. doi:10.1111/1467–839x.00103

Heine, S. J., & Lehman, D. R. (1997). Culture, dissonance, and self-affirmation. *Personality and Social Psychology Bulletin, 23*, 389–400. doi:10.1177/0146167297234005

Heine, S. J., Lehman, D. R., Markus, H. R., & Kitayama, S. (1999). Is there a universal need for positive self-regard? *Psychological Review, 106*, 766–794. doi:10.1037/0033-295x.106.4.766

Ho, D. Y. F. (1998). Interpersonal relationships and relationship dominance: An analysis based on methodological relationalism. *Asian Journal of Social Psychology, 1*, 1–16. doi:10.1111/1467–839x.00002

Hui, C. H., Chan, S. W. Y., Lau, E. Y. Y., Cheung, S. F., & Mok, D. S. Y. (2014). The role of religion in moderating the impact of life events on material life goals: Some evidence in support of terror management theory. *Mental Health, Religion, & Culture, 17*, 52–61. doi:10.1080/13674676.2012.745494

Ipsos. (2011). *Supreme being, the afterlife, and evolution.* http://www.ipsos-na.com/download/pr.aspx?id=10670

Jonas, E., & Fischer, P. (2006). Terror management and religion: Evidence that intrinsic religiousness mitigates worldview defense following mortality salience. *Journal of Personality and Social Psychology, 91*(3), 553–567. doi:10.1037/0022–3514.91.3.553

Jonas, E., Martens, A., Niesta, D., Fritsche, I., Sullivan, D., & Greenberg, J. (2008). Focus theory of normative conduct and terror management theory: The interactive impact of mortality salience and norm salience on social judgment. *Journal of Personality and Social Psychology, 95*, 1239–1251. doi:10.1037/a0013593

Kashima, E. S., Halloran, M., Yuki, M., & Kashima, Y. (2004). The effects of personal and collective mortality salience on individualism: Comparing Australians and Japanese with higher and lower self-esteem. *Journal of Experimental Social Psychology, 40*, 384–392. doi:10.1016/j.jesp.2003.07.007

Kasser, T., & Sheldon, K. M. (2000). Of wealth and death: Materialism, mortality salience, and consumption behavior. *Psychological Science, 11*, 348–351. doi:10.1111/1467-9280.00269

Kesebir, P., & Chiu, C. -Y. (2008, February). *The stuff that immortality is made of: Existential functions of fame.* Poster session presented at the annual meeting of Society for Personality and Social Psychology, Albuquerque, NM.

Kesebir, P., & Pyszczynski, T. (March 2, 2011). The role of death in life: Existential aspects of human motivation. In R. Ryan (Ed.), *The Oxford handbook of motivation* (pp. 43–64). New York: Oxford University Press. doi:10.1093/oxfordhb/9780195399820.013.0004

Kökdemir, D., & Yeniçeri, Z. (2010). Terror management in a predominantly Muslim country: The effects of mortality salience on university identity and on preference for the development of international relations. *European Psychologist, 15,* 165–174. doi:10.1027/1016–9040/a000012

Kurzweil, R. (2001). *The law of accelerating return.* http://www.kurzweilai.net/articles/art0134.html.

Lewin, K. (1951). *Field theory in social science.* New York: Harper.

Ma-Kellams, C., & Blascovich, J. (2011). Culturally divergent responses to mortality salience. *Psychological Science, 22,* 1019–1024. doi:10.1177/0956797611413935

Ma-Kellams, C., & Blascovich, J. (2012). Enjoying life in the face of death: East–West differences in responses to mortality salience. *Journal of Personality and Social Psychology, 103*(5), 773–786. doi:10.1037/a0029366

Markus, H., & Kitayama, S. (1991). Culture and the self: Implications for cognition, emotion, and motivation. *Psychological Review, 98,* 224–253. doi:10.1037/0033-295x.98.2.224

Martin, L. L., & van den Bos, K. (2014). Beyond Terror: Towards a paradigm shift in the study of threat and culture. *European Review of Social Psychology, 25*(1), 32–70. doi:10.1080/10463283.2014.923144

Norenzayan, A., & Hansen, I. G. (2006). Belief in supernatural agents in the face of death. *Personality and Social Psychology Bulletin, 32,* 174–187. doi:10.1177/0146167205280251

Norenzayan, A., Shariff, A. F., Gervais, W. M., Willard, A. K., McNamara, R. A., Slingerland, E., & Henrich, J. (2014). The cultural evolution of prosocial religions. *Behavioral and Brain Sciences,* 1–86. doi:10.1017/S0140525X14001356

Osarchuk, M., & Tatz, S. J. (1973). Effect of induced fear of death on belief in afterlife. *Journal of Personality and Social Psychology, 27,* 256–260. doi:10.1037/h0034769

Park, J., & Choi, I. (2002). Does imaging one's own death make an individual a good citizen? *Korean Journal of Social and Personality Psychology, 16*(1), 75–89. (in Korean)

Park, Y., & Pyszczynski, T. (2015). *The effects of meditation and mortality salience on ingoup bias, self-compassion, and compassion-toward-other.* Manuscript in preparation.

Peng, K., & Nisbett, R. E. (1999). Culture, dialectics, and reasoning about contradiction. *American Psychologist, 54*(9), 741–754. doi:10.1037/0003–066x.54.9.741

Pyszczynski, T., Greenberg, J., Solomon, S., Arndt, J., & Schimel, J. (2004). Why do people need self-esteem? A theoretical and empirical review. *Psychological Bulletin, 130*(3), 435–468. doi:10.1037/0033–2909.130.3.435

Pyszczynski, T., Solomon, S., & Greenberg, J. (2015). Thirty years of terror management theory: From genesis to revelation. *Advances in Experimental Social Psychology, 52,* 1–70. doi:10.1016/bs.aesp.2015.03.001

Rindfleisch, A., & Burroughs, J. E. (2004). Terrifying thoughts, terrible materialism? Contemplations on a terror management account of materialism and consumer behavior. *Journal of Consumer Psychology, 14*(3), 219–224. doi:10.1207/s15327663jcp1403_4

Routledge, C., Juhl, J., Vess, M., Cathey, C., & Liao, J. (2012). Who uses groups to transcend the limits of the individual self? Exploring the effects of interdependent self-construal and mortality salience on investment in social groups. *Social Psychological and Personality Science, 4*(4), 483–491. doi:10.1177/1948550612459770

Schimel, J., Simon, L., Greenberg, J., Pyszczynski, T., Solomon, S., Waxmonsky, J., & Arndt, J. (1999). Stereotypes and terror management: Evidence that mortality salience enhances stereotypic thinking and preferences. *Journal of Personality and Social Psychology*, 77(5), 905–926. doi:10.1037/0022–3514.77.5.905

Schoenrade, P. A. (1989). When I die . . . : Belief in afterlife as a response to mortality. *Personality and Social Psychology Bulletin*, 15, 91–100. doi:10.1177/0146167289151009

Schumaker, J. F., Barraclough, R. A., & Vagg, L. M. (1988). Death anxiety in Malaysian and Australian university students. *The Journal of Social Psychology*, 128, 41–47. doi:10.1080/00224545.1988.9711682

Sedikides, C., Gaertner, L., & Toguchi, Y. (2003). Pancultural self-enhancement. *Journal of Personality and Social Psychology*, 84, 60–79. doi:10.1037/0022–3514.84.1.60

Shaver, P. R., & Mikulincer, M. (2002). Attachment-related psychodynamics. *Attachment & Human Development*, 4(2), 133–161. doi:10.1080/14616730210154171

Solomon, S., Greenberg, J., & Pyszczynski, T. (1991). A terror management theory of social behavior: The psychological functions of self-esteem and cultural worldviews. *Advances in Experimental Social Psychology*, 24, 93–159. doi:10.1016/s0065-2601(08)60328-7

Spencer-Rodgers, J., Peng, K., Wang, L., & Hou, Y. (2004). Dialectical self-esteem and East-West differences in psychological well-being. *Personality and Social Psychology Bulletin*, 30(11), 1416–1432.

Tam, K. P., Chiu, C. Y., & Lau, I. Y. (2007). Terror management among Chinese: Worldview defence and intergroup bias in resource allocation. *Asian Journal of Social Psychology*, 10, 93–102. doi:10.1111/j.1467–839x.2007.00216.x

Tang, C., Wu, A., & Yan, E. (2002). Psychosocial correlates of death anxiety among Chinese college students. *Death Studies*, 26, 491–499. doi:10.1080/074811802760139012

Triandis, H. C. (1989). The self and social behavior in differing cultural contexts. *Psychological Review*, 96, 506–520. doi:10.1037/0033–295x.96.3.506

Vicary, A. M. (2011). Mortality salience and namesaking: Does thinking about death make people want to name their children after themselves? *Journal of Research in Personality*, 45, 138–141. doi:10.1016/j.jrp.2010.11.016

Wakimoto, R. (2006). Mortality salience effects on modesty and relative self-effacement. *Asian Journal of Social Psychology*, 9, 176–183. doi:10.1111/j.1467-839x.2006.00194.x

Wakimoto, R. (2009). Effects of mortality salience on self-effacing attribution and anticipation for supportive attribution by close friends. *Japanese Journal of Experimental Social Psychology*, 49, 58–71. doi:10.2130/jjesp.49.58

Wakimoto, R. (2011). Reconstruction of the subjective temporal distance of past interpersonal experiences after mortality salience. *Personality and Social Psychology Bulletin*, 37(5), 687–700. doi:10.1177/0146167211400422

Watanabe, T., & Karasawa, K. (2012). Self-ingroup overlap in the face of mortality salience. *Japanese Journal of Experimental Social Psychology*, 52(1), 25–34. doi:10.2130/jjesp.52.25

Wisman, A., & Goldenberg, J. L. (2005). From the grave to the cradle: Evidence that mortality salience engenders a desire for offspring. *Journal of Personality and Social Psychology*, 89, 46–61. doi:10.1037/0022–3514.89.1.46

Wright, R. (2009). *The evolution of God*. New York: Little, Brown.

Yen, C. L. (2012). It is our destiny to die: The effects of mortality salience and culture-priming on fatalism and karma belief. *International Journal of Psychology*, 48(5), 818–828. doi:10.1080/00207594.2012.678363

Yen, C. L., & Cheng, C. P. (2010). Terror management among Taiwanese: Worldview defence or resigning to fate? *Asian Journal of Social Psychology*, 13, 185–194. doi:10.1111/j.1467–839x.2010.01328.x

Zaleskiewicz, T., Gasiorowska, A., Kesebir, P., Luszczynska, A., & Pyszczynski, T. (2013). Money and the fear of death: The symbolic power of money as an existential anxiety buffer. *Journal of Economic Psychology, 36*, 55–67. doi:10.1016/j.joep.2013.02.008

Zhou, X., Lei, Q., Marley, S. C., & Chen, J. (2009). Existential function of babies: Babies as a buffer of death-related anxiety. *Asian Journal of Social Psychology, 12*, 40–46. doi:10.1111/j.1467–839x.2008.01268.x

Zhou, X., Liu, J., Chen, C., & Yu, Z. (2008). Do children transcend death? An examination of the terror management function of offspring. *Scandinavian Journal of Psychology, 49*, 413–418. doi:10.1111/j.1467–9450.2008.00665.x

CONTRIBUTORS

Jamie Arndt received his B.A. from Skidmore College and his Ph.D. from the University of Arizona in 1999. He is currently a Professor in the Department of Psychological Sciences at the University of Missouri. He has authored or coauthored over 100 scholarly works pertaining to the self, existential motivation, psychological defense, and health decision-making, among other topics. Over the last 10 years his applications of social and existential motivation to health-related behavior, including collaborative work with Dr. Goldenberg on the terror management health model, have been funded by the National Cancer Institute (NCI) and reflect his increasing interest in moving basic social psychological ideas to translational health domains. Dr. Arndt has been recognized with a number of awards and is also a member of an NCI sponsored working group (Cognitive, Affective, and Social Processes in Health; CASPHR) as well as a founding member of the Social Personality and Health Network.

Theodore A. Avtgis (Ph.D., Kent State University, 1999) is a Professor and Chair, Department of Communication Studies, Ashland University, and Adjunct Associate Professor in the Department of Surgery, West Virginia School of Medicine. Dr. Avtgis has authored over 60 peer-reviewed articles and book chapters, and eight books on organizational communication, medical communication, aggressive communication, and communication theory. He has published in journals including *Management Communication Quarterly, Communication Education,* and *Critical Care.* He has served as Editor-in Chief of *Communication Research Reports.* He has also received honors including being named Centennial Scholar, Research Fellow, and Teaching Fellow of the Eastern Communication Association. He is also cofounder of Medical Communication Specialists.

Nicholas D. Bowman (Ph.D., Michigan State University, 2010) is an Associate Professor of Communication Studies at West Virginia University. His research topics and areas of expertise include the psychological impact of communication technology, including social media and video games. Some of his recent publications on these topics can be found in *Computers in Human Behavior, Journal of Media Psychology, Media Psychology,* and *New Media and Society.*

Patrick Boyd received a B.A. in Psychology from the University of Southern California in 2007 and a M.A. in Social Psychology from San Francisco State University in 2012. He began pursuing his Ph.D. at the University of South Florida in 2013. His research generally focuses on terror management theory, and within this paradigm he has explored how self-worth that is contingent upon being healthful can globally predict behaviors in a variety of health contexts.

Brian Burke is a clinical psychologist whose principal academic interests include motivational interviewing, college teaching, and terror management theory. Dr. Burke has published several meta-analyses of studies evaluating the efficacy of motivational interviewing. Motivational interviewing is an emerging treatment for substance abuse and other problem behaviors that combines the humanistic elements of client-centered therapy (Carl Rogers) with more active strategies (e.g., cognitive-behavior therapy) designed to facilitate human change. Further, Dr. Burke has a degree in college teaching and regularly attends teaching conferences, twice winning the Doug Bernstein Poster Award for innovative teaching ideas, and winning the New Faculty Teaching Award at Fort Lewis College in 2005 along with the FLC Achievement Award in 2012–2013. Finally, Dr. Burke has published several meta-analyses of terror management theory (TMT), including one focused on TMT and politics. Dr. Burke originally hails from Montreal, Canada, and received his Ph.D. from the University of Arizona in 2003. He has been a licensed psychologist in the State of Colorado since November 2004.

Grant C. Corser is an Assistant Professor of Psychology at Southern Utah University (SUU). He earned his Ph.D. in Personality and Social Psychology from the University of Mississippi. His research interests include applied personality and social psychological theories that focus specifically on motivation, emotion, and decision making. Most recently, he has been researching personality variables that affect workplace environment. Dr. Corser is a tenured associate professor at Southern Utah University and has a genuine passion for teaching undergraduate students. He currently serves as the Director of the SUU Center of Excellence for Teaching and Learning. He is active in campus and community service, and on multiple occasions served as a sports consultant for the SUU Women's Gymnastics team, and assistant football coach for the local high school. He is the proud father of three—two very active boys (Eliot, 11 and Emmitt, 8) and a brilliant daughter (Allie Jane, 2)—and is married to Jodi Mecham, who is a lecturer in the English Department at Southern Utah University.

Kyle Cranney is a graduate student at Southern Utah University in the Department of Communication. He is currently engaged in research on heteronormativity in Western culture. He completed a Bachelor of Art degree in Psychology at Southern Utah University in the spring of 2012. Kyle currently resides in St. George, Utah.

Alex Darrell is a graduate student in social psychology at the University of Colorado at Colorado Springs. He received his B.A. in Psychology from Skidmore College. His research is focused on terror management theory, political psychology, and attitudes toward science.

Jamie Goldenberg earned her PhD from the George Washington University in 1997 and is currently Professor of Psychology at The University of South Florida (USF). Her area of specialization is social psychology with a focus on terror management theory and the application of the theory to health behavior and women's health in particular. She also studies the objectification of women. She is the developer of the terror management health model along with co-author Dr. Arndt. Their collaborative research has been funded for 10 years by the National Cancer Institute and has resulted in dozens of publications, including a manuscript in Psychological Review depicting the model. Dr. Goldenberg is a collaborator member of the Moffitt Cancer Center, is on the editorial board of Journal of Personality and Social Psychology, and in 2012, she won Researcher of the Year from the Center for Women in Leadership and Philanthropy at USF.

Jennifer D. Green holds a Ph.D. in Media and Communication from Texas Tech University (2014). She is an assistant professor of strategic communication at Georgia College and State University, where she teaches a variety of courses in advertising and public relations, as well as mass communication theory, research, and media effects. Her research interests combine her passion and enthusiasm for media and psychology to include media engagement and multitasking behavior, and advertising effects.

Miliaikeala Heen received her M.A. from the University of Nevada, Las Vegas, in Criminal Justice. Currently, she is a Ph.D. student in the Environmental and Public Affairs Department at UNLV. She has worked on several research studies alongside Dr. Joel Lieberman that focus on the application of terror management concepts, cognitive persuasion models, and expert testimony manipulations within the context of jury decision-making.

Spee Kosloff is an Assistant Professor of psychology at California State University, Fresno. He received his Ph.D. in 2010 from the University of Arizona. He studies how existential motives influence attitudes and beliefs, and associations between personality and conformity.

Alexander L. Lancaster (Ph.D., West Virginia University, 2015) is an Assistant Professor in the Department of Communication at Weber State University. His current research topics include police–citizen communication, television coviewing, and workplace supervisor–subordinate friendships. His areas of scholarly interest are persuasive communication and media communication. His most recent publication can be found in *Communication Research Reports.*

Mark J. Landau is an Associate Professor at the University of Kansas. He received his Ph.D. in 2007 from the University of Arizona. He studies how existential motives influence social perceptions and behavior, and how people use conceptual metaphors to construct meaning.

Corey Jay Liberman (Ph.D., Rutgers University, 2008) is an Assistant Professor in the Department of Communication Arts at Marymount Manhattan College. His research focuses on the link among social networks, attitudes, and behaviors, as well as communication of upward dissent within organizations. He is a co-author of *Organizational Communication: Strategies of Success* (2nd ed.) and has had his scholarship published in book chapters and presented at conference proceedings.

Joel D. Lieberman is a Professor and Chair of the Criminal Justice Department at the University of Nevada, Las Vegas. He received his Ph.D. in Psychology from the University of Arizona in 1997. His work focuses on the application of social psychological theories to criminal justice issues, particularly in a jury decision-making context. This has led to numerous published articles and book chapters involving the identification of psychological factors related to jury instruction comprehension, inadmissible evidence, persuasive techniques in the courtroom, defendant characteristics, and juror comprehension of expert testimony. He has published a book titled *Scientific Jury Selection,* as well as a two-volume book titled *Psychology in the Courtroom.* In addition, his work in the area of intergroup conflict has explored topics such as hate crimes, physical aggression, and prejudice. His recent research has explored public attitudes toward unmanned aerial systems (i.e., aerial drones). Lieberman is also the Director of the Forensic Testimony Laboratory, which is a member of the Forensic and Crime Scene Investigation Consortium.

Matthew S. McGlone (Ph.D., Princeton University) is an Associate Professor in the Department of Communication Studies at the University of Texas at Austin. His primary research interest is the role of language in persuasion and social influence. He has published numerous articles on this topic and others in top journals in cognitive science, communication, psychology, and discourse studies, and has received federal grants for his research from the National Science

Foundation, Institute of Education Sciences, and National Institutes of Health. He served on the editorial board of *Psychological Science* and is currently on the boards of *Discourse Processes* and *Journal of Language and Social Psychology*. He recently edited a book on deceptive communication with Mark L. Knapp (*The Interplay of Truth and Deception*, 2012, Routledge).

Patrick F. Merle (Ph.D., Texas Tech University), a former international reporter who covered September 11, previously investigated the relationship between terror management and civic engagement (*Journal of Media Psychology*). Most of his works stand at the crossroads of several dominant research interests, namely, political communication, news processing, and cross-national evaluations.

Nicholas A. Merola (Ph.D., University of Texas–Austin) is a member of the Design and User Experience research team in the Behavioral Analytics Division of Facebook, Inc. He was previously a Postdoctoral Fellow in the Social Media Laboratory and Department of Communication Studies at Northwestern University. His primary research interests are online impression formation and relationship maintenance, message production and processing, and deception strategies.

Hilary Monson earned her Bachelor's in Psychology and minor in Communication from Southern Utah University, and is currently working on her Master of Public Administration. Her present research interests entail social psychology and persuasion. Her most recent research included intrinsic and extrinsic motivation in academic success. Hilary is the adviser for Southern Utah University Resident Hall Association for On-Campus Housing and works in the Michael O. Leavitt Center for Politics and Public Service.

Young Chin Park is a graduate student in Social Psychology at the University of Colorado at Colorado Springs, where she also received her B.A. in Psychology. Her research is focused on terror management theory, long-term effects of collective trauma, cultural influences on behavior, mindfulness, and meditation.

Stacey A. Passalacqua is an Assistant Professor in the Department of Communication at the University of Texas at San Antonio. She earned her Ph.D. in Interpersonal and Health Communication with a Ph.D. minor in Psychology from the University of Arizona, Tucson.

Tom Pyszczynski received his Ph.D. in Social Psychology under the supervision of Jack Brehm from the University of Kansas in 1980. Along with Jeff Greenberg and Sheldon Solomon, he developed terror management theory in the mid 1980s and has been working on refining and testing the theory since then, along with applying it to diverse aspects of human behavior. Pyszczynski, Greenberg, and Sheldon recently published a book using these ideas to explore the many ways the problem of death affects life, *The Worm at the Core: The Role of Death in Life*. They also wrote *In the Wake of 9/11: The Psychology of Terror, The Handbook of Experimental Existential Psychology,* and *Hanging on and Letting Go: Understanding the Onset, Progression, and Remission of Depression.* Pyszczynski is currently distinguished professor of psychology at the University of Colorado, Colorado Springs.

Dariela Rodriguez (Ph.D., University of Oklahoma, 2012) is an Assistant Professor of Communication, and Coordinator of Sport Communication at Ashland University in Ashland, Ohio. Dr. Rodriguez's expertise is in interpersonal communication with a specialization in sport communication. She has published journal articles in publications such as *Communication Education, Qualitative Health Research,* and *Communication Research Reports.* Her current research includes work in concussions in sport and leadership preferences of millennial generation athletes.

Amber L. Schow (nee Marabella) received her Master of Professional Com-munication from Southern Utah University (SUU) in 2015. She has completed numerous research projects in interpersonal and strategic Communication, often specializing in millennial-generation and pop culture topics. She currently teaches at SUU and resides in Cedar City, Utah, with her husband, Erich.

Shane M. Semmler (Ph.D., University of Oklahoma, 2010) studies political communication, narrative persuasion, and character involvement in the Department of Communication Studies at the University of South Dakota where he is an Associate Professor and Director of the university's speech and debate team. Shane's recent research investigates the influence of soliloquy in Netflix's *House of Cards* (2013–present) on character identification, resistance to narrative persuasion, and political attitudes.

Michael J. Sherratt has a Bachelor's Degree in Psychology with a minor in Communication from Southern Utah University (SUU). While at SUU, he took a class that was taught by Dr. Lindsey A. Harvell, where he developed a strong interest in terror management theory and its implications with helping soldiers with psychological challenges developed from combat. During his studies, he emphasized on psychological trauma, suicide, military, and the male gender. He is currently a Readjustment Counseling Technician for the Veterans Affairs in the process of applying to graduate programs to become a mental health therapist. Michael has been a combat soldier in the field artillery for the Utah National Guard for 21 years with multiple awards such as the 2013 Outstanding Non-commissioned Officer of the Battalion and the 1994 Utah Army National Guard Soldier of the Year. His deployments include security for the 2002 Olympics and a deployment to Iraq. He is married to Beverly Ann Parry, who is a fourth grade teacher, and the father of three: an Iraq veteran (Dustin, 23) and two wonderful daughters (Brionna, 23 and McKelle, 11).

Melissa Spina received her B.A. in Psychology from California State University, Fresno, in 2013 and began pursuing her Ph.D. at the University of Missouri, Columbia, in 2013. Her research examines motivational theories generally, with an emphasis in terror management theory, and applies these theories to such areas as health decision-making, prosociality, and environmentally friendly behaviors.

Tyler F. Stillman received a B.S. in Psychology from the University of Utah and a Ph.D. in Social Psychology from Florida State University. He studied under the mentorship of Roy F. Baumeister. Tyler currently teaches the psychology side of business for Southern Utah University's School of Business. He is married to Debra Stillman and has four loud and wonderful children.

INDEX